Advanced Perl Programming

Other Perl resources from O'Reilly

Related titles

Learning Perl

Perl 6 and Parrot Essentials

Perl Best Practices

Perl Cookbook™

Perl Debugger Pocket
   Reference

Perl in a Nutshell

Perl Testing: A Developer's
   Notebook™

Practical mod_perl

Programming Perl

**Perl Books
Resource Center**

perl.oreilly.com is a complete catalog of O'Reilly's books on Perl and related technologies, including sample chapters and code examples.

Perl.com is the central web site for the Perl community. It is the perfect starting place for finding out everything there is to know about Perl.

Conferences

O'Reilly brings diverse innovators together to nurture the ideas that spark revolutionary industries. We specialize in documenting the latest tools and systems, translating the innovator's knowledge into useful skills for those in the trenches. Visit *conferences.oreilly.com* for our upcoming events.

Safari Bookshelf (*safari.oreilly.com*) is the premier online reference library for programmers and IT professionals. Conduct searches across more than 1,000 books. Subscribers can zero in on answers to time-critical questions in a matter of seconds. Read the books on your Bookshelf from cover to cover or simply flip to the page you need. Try it today.

SECOND EDITION

Advanced Perl Programming

Simon Cozens

O'REILLY®

Beijing · Cambridge · Farnham · Köln · Paris · Sebastopol · Taipei · Tokyo

Advanced Perl Programming, Second Edition
by Simon Cozens

Copyright © 2005, 1997 O'Reilly Media, Inc. All rights reserved.
Printed in the United States of America.

Published by O'Reilly Media, Inc., 1005 Gravenstein Highway North, Sebastopol, CA 95472.

O'Reilly books may be purchased for educational, business, or sales promotional use. Online editions are also available for most titles (*safari.oreilly.com*). For more information, contact our corporate/institutional sales department: (800) 998-9938 or *corporate@oreilly.com*.

Editor:	Allison Randal
Production Editor:	Darren Kelly
Cover Designer:	Edie Freedman
Interior Designer:	David Futato
Production Services:	nSight, Inc.

Printing History:

August 1997:	First Edition.
June 2005:	Second Edition.

Nutshell Handbook, the Nutshell Handbook logo, and the O'Reilly logo are registered trademarks of O'Reilly Media, Inc. *Advanced Perl Programming*, the image of a black leopard, and related trade dress are trademarks of O'Reilly Media, Inc.

Many of the designations used by manufacturers and sellers to distinguish their products are claimed as trademarks. Where those designations appear in this book, and O'Reilly Media, Inc. was aware of a trademark claim, the designations have been printed in caps or initial caps.

While every precaution has been taken in the preparation of this book, the publisher and author assume no responsibility for errors or omissions, or for damages resulting from the use of the information contained herein.

RepKover. This book uses RepKover,™ a durable and flexible lay-flat binding.

ISBN: 0-596-00456-7
[M]

Table of Contents

Preface

It was all Nathan Torkington's fault. Our Antipodean programmer, editor, and O'Reilly conference supremo friend asked me to update the original *Advanced Perl Programming* way back in 2002.

The Perl world had changed drastically in the five years since the publication of the first edition, and it continues to change. Particularly, we've seen a shift away from techniques and toward resources—from doing things yourself with Perl to using what other people have done with Perl. In essence, advanced Perl programming has become more a matter of knowing where to find what you need on the CPAN,* rather than a matter of knowing what to do.

Perl changed in other ways, too: the announcement of Perl 6 in 2000 ironically caused a renewed interest in Perl 5, with people stretching Perl in new and interesting directions to implement some of the ideas and blue-skies thinking about Perl 6. Contrary to what we all thought back then, far from killing off Perl 5, Perl 6's development has made it stronger and ensured it will be around longer.

So it was in this context that it made sense to update *Advanced Perl Programming* to reflect the changes in Perl and in the CPAN. We also wanted the new edition to be more in the spirit of Perl—to focus on how to achieve practical tasks with a minimum of fuss. This is why we put together chapters on parsing techniques, on dealing with natural language documents, on testing your code, and so on.

But this book is just a beginning; however tempting it was to try to get down everything I ever wanted to say about Perl, it just wasn't possible. First, because Perl usage covers such a wide spread—on the CPAN, there are ready-made modules for folding DNA sequences, paying bills online, checking the weather, and playing poker. And more are being added every day, faster than any author can keep up. Second, as we've mentioned, because Perl is changing. I don't know what the next big advance

---

* The *Comprehensive Perl Archive Network* (*http://www.cpan.org*) is the primary resource for user-contributed Perl code.

in Perl will be; I can only take you through some of the more important techniques and resources available at the moment.

Hopefully, though, at the end of this book you'll have a good idea of how to use what's available, how you can save yourself time and effort by using Perl and the Perl resources available to get your job done, and how you can be ready to use and integrate whatever developments come down the line.

In the words of Larry Wall, may you do good magic with Perl!

Audience

If you've read *Learning Perl* and *Programming Perl* and wonder where to go from there, this book is for you. It'll help you climb to the next level of Perl wisdom. If you've been programming in Perl for years, you'll still find numerous practical tools and techniques to help you solve your everyday problems.

Contents

Chapter 1, *Advanced Techniques*, introduces a few common tricks advanced Perl programmers use with examples from popular Perl modules.

Chapter 2, *Parsing Techniques*, covers parsing irregular or unstructured data with `Parse::RecDescent` and `Parse::Yapp`, plus parsing HTML and XML.

Chapter 3, *Templating Tools*, details some of the most common tools for templating and when to use them, including formats, `Text::Template`, `HTML::Template`, `HTML::Mason`, and the Template Toolkit.

Chapter 4, *Objects, Databases, and Applications*, explains various ways to efficiently store and retrieve complex data using objects—a concept commonly called object-relational mapping.

Chapter 5, *Natural Language Tools*, shows some of the ways Perl can manipulate natural language data: inflections, conversions, parsing, extraction, and Bayesian analysis.

Chapter 6, *Perl and Unicode*, reviews some of the problems and solutions to make the most of Perl's Unicode support.

Chap ter 7, *POE*, looks at the popular Perl event-based environment for task scheduling, multitasking, and non-blocking I/O code.

Chapter 8, *Testing*, covers the essentials of testing your code.

Chapter 9, *Inline Extensions*, talks about how to extend Perl by writing code in other languages, using the `Inline::*` modules.

Chapter 10, *Fun with Perl*, closes on a lighter note with a few recreational (and educational) uses of Perl.

Conventions Used in This Book

The following typographical conventions are used in this book:

Plain text
> Indicates menu titles, menu options, menu buttons, and keyboard accelerators (such as Alt and Ctrl).

Italic
> Indicates new terms, URLs, email addresses, filenames, file extensions, pathnames, directories, and Unix utilities.

Constant width
> Indicates commands, options, switches, variables, attributes, keys, functions, classes, namespaces, methods, modules, parameters, values, XML tags, HTML tags, the contents of files, or the output from commands.

Constant width bold
> Shows commands or other text that should be typed literally by the user.

Constant width italic
> Shows text that should be replaced with user-supplied values.

 This icon signifies a tip, suggestion, or general note.

 This icon indicates a warning or caution.

Using Code Examples

This book is here to help you get your job done. In general, you may use the code in this book in your programs and documentation. You do not need to contact us for permission unless you're reproducing a significant portion of the code. For example, writing a program that uses several chunks of code from this book does not require permission. Selling or distributing a CD-ROM of examples from O'Reilly books does require permission. Answering a question by citing this book and quoting example code does not require permission. Incorporating a significant amount of example code from this book into your product's documentation does require permission.

We appreciate, but do not require, attribution. An attribution usually includes the title, author, publisher, and ISBN. For example: "*Advanced Perl Programming*, Second Edition by Simon Cozens. Copyright 2005 O'Reilly Media, Inc. 0-596-00456-7."

If you feel your use of code examples falls outside fair use or the permission given above, feel free to contact us at *permissions@oreilly.com*.

We'd Like to Hear from You

Please address comments and questions concerning this book to the publisher:

> O'Reilly Media
> 1005 Gravenstein Highway North
> Sebastopol, CA 95472
> (800) 998-9938 (in the United States or Canada)
> (707) 829-0515 (international or local)
> (707) 829-0104 (fax)

We have a web page for this book, where we list errata, examples, and any additional information. You can access this page at:

> *http://www.oreilly.com/catalog/advperl2/*

To comment or ask technical questions about this book, send email to:

> *bookquestions@oreilly.com*

For more information about our books, conferences, Resource Centers, and the O'Reilly Network, see our web site at:

> *http://www.oreilly.com*

Safari® Enabled

When you see a Safari Enabled icon on the cover of your favorite technology book, that means the book is available online through the O'Reilly Network Safari Bookshelf.

Safari offers a solution that's better than e-books. It's a virtual library that lets you easily search thousands of top tech books, cut and paste code samples, download chapters, and find quick answers when you need the most accurate, current information. Try it for free at *http://safari.oreilly.com*.

Acknowledgments

I've already blamed Nat Torkington for commissioning this book; I should thank him as well. As much as writing a book can be fun, this one has been. It has certainly been helped by my editors, beginning with Nat and Tatiana Apandi, and ending with the hugely talented Allison Randal, who has almost single-handedly corrected code, collated comments, and converted my rambling thoughts into something publishable. The production team at O'Reilly deserves a special mention, if only because of the torture I put them through in having a chapter on Unicode.

Allison also rounded up a great crew of highly knowledgeable reviewers: my thanks to Tony Bowden, Philippe Bruhat, Sean Burke, Piers Cawley, Nicholas Clark, James Duncan, Rafael Garcia-Suarez, Thomas Klausner, Tom McTighe, Curtis Poe, chromatic, and Andy Wardley.

And finally, there are a few people I'd like to thank personally: thanks to Heather Lang, Graeme Everist, and Juliet Humphrey for putting up with me last year, and to Jill Ford and the rest of her group at All Nations Christian College who have to put up with me now. Tony Bowden taught me more about good Perl programming than either of us would probably admit, and Simon Ponsonby taught me more about everything else than he realises. Thanks to Al and Jamie for being there, and to Malcolm and Caroline Macdonald and Noriko and Akio Kawamura for launching me on the current exciting stage of my life.

CHAPTER 1
Advanced Techniques

Once you have read the Camel Book (*Programming Perl*), or any other good Perl tutorial, you know almost all of the language. There are no secret keywords, no other magic sigils that turn on Perl's advanced mode and reveal hidden features. In one sense, this book is not going to tell you anything new about the Perl language.

What can I tell you, then? I used to be a student of music. Music is very simple. There are 12 possible notes in the scale of Western music, although some of the most wonderful melodies in the world only use, at most, eight of them. There are around four different durations of a note used in common melodies. There isn't a massive musical vocabulary to choose from. And music has been around a good deal longer than Perl. I used to wonder whether or not all the possible decent melodies would soon be figured out. Sometimes I listen to the Top 10 and think I was probably right back then.

But of course it's a bit more complicated than that. New music is still being produced. Knowing all the notes does not tell you the best way to put them together. I've said that there are no secret switches to turn on advanced features in Perl, and this means that everyone starts on a level playing field, in just the same way that Johann Sebastian Bach and a little kid playing with a xylophone have precisely the same raw materials to work with. The key to producing advanced Perl—or advanced music—depends on two things: knowledge of techniques and experience of what works and what doesn't.

The aim of this book is to give you some of each of these things. Of course, no book can impart experience. Experience is something that must be, well, *experienced*. However, a book like this can show you some existing solutions from experienced Perl programmers and how to use them to solve the problems you may be facing.

On the other hand, a book can certainly teach techniques, and in this chapter we're going to look at the three major classes of advanced programming techniques in Perl. First, we'll look at introspection: programs looking at programs, figuring out how they work, and changing them. For Perl this involves manipulating the symbol table—especially at runtime, playing with the behavior of built-in functions and using AUTOLOAD to introduce new subroutines and control behavior of subroutine dispatch dynamically. We'll also briefly look at bytecode introspection, which is the ability to inspect some of the properties of the Perl bytecode tree to determine properties of the program.

The second idea we'll look at is the class model. Writing object-oriented programs and modules is sometimes regarded as advanced Perl, but I would categorize it as intermediate. As this is an advanced book, we're going to learn how to subvert Perl's object-oriented model to suit our goals.

Finally, there's the technique of what I call *unexpected code*—code that runs in places you might not expect it to. This means running code in place of operators in the case of overloading, some advanced uses of tying, and controlling when code runs using named blocks and eval.

These three areas, together with the special case of Perl XS programming—which we'll look at in Chapter 9 on Inline—delineate the fundamental techniques from which all advanced uses of Perl are made up.

Introspection

First, though, introspection. These introspection techniques appear time and time again in advanced modules throughout the book. As such, they can be regarded as the most fundamental of the advanced techniques—everything else will build on these ideas.

Preparatory Work: Fun with Globs

Globs are one of the most misunderstood parts of the Perl language, but at the same time, one of the most fundamental. This is a shame, because a glob is a relatively simple concept.

When you access any global variable in Perl—that is, any variable that has not been declared with my—the *perl* interpreter looks up the variable name in the *symbol table*. For now, we'll consider the symbol table to be a mapping between a variable's name and some storage for its value, as in Figure 1-1.

Note that we say that the symbol table maps to *storage* for the value. Introductory programming texts should tell you that a variable is essentially a box in which you can get and set a value. Once we've looked up $a, we know where the box is, and we can get and set the values directly. In Perl terms, the symbol table maps to a reference to $a.

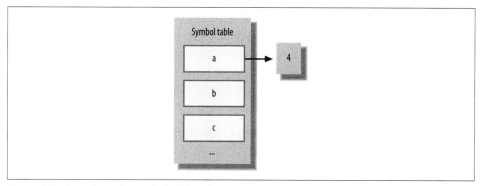

Figure 1-1. Consulting the symbol table, take 1

You may have noticed that a symbol table is something that maps names to storage, which sounds a lot like a Perl hash. In fact, you'd be ahead of the game, since the Perl symbol table is indeed implemented using an ordinary Perl hash. You may also have noticed, however, that there are several things called *a* in Perl, including $a, @a, %a, &a, the filehandle a, and the directory handle a.

This is where the glob comes in. The symbol table maps a name like a to a glob, which is a structure holding references to all the variables called a, as in Figure 1-2.

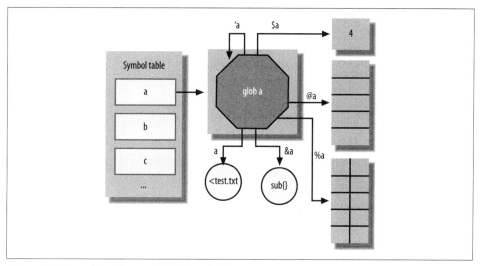

Figure 1-2. Consulting the symbol table, take 2

As you can see, variable look-up is done in two stages: first, finding the appropriate glob in the symbol table; second, finding the appropriate part of the glob. This gives us a reference, and assigning it to a variable or getting its value is done through this reference.

Aliasing

This disconnect between the name look-up and the reference look-up enables us to alias two names together. First, we get hold of their globs using the *name syntax, and then simply assign one glob to another, as in Figure 1-3.

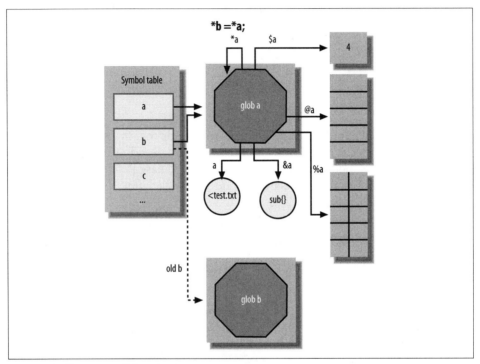

Figure 1-3. Aliasing via glob assignment

We've assigned b's symbol table entry to point to a's glob. Now any time we look up a variable like %b, the first stage look-up takes us from the symbol table to a's glob, and returns us a reference to %a.

The most common application of this general idea is in the Exporter module. If I have a module like so:

```
package Some::Module;
use base 'Exporter';
our @EXPORT = qw( useful );

sub useful { 42 }
```

then Exporter is responsible for getting the useful subroutine from the Some::Module package to the caller's package. We could mock our own exporter using glob assignments, like this:

```
package Some::Module;
sub useful { 42 }
```

```
sub import {
    no strict 'refs';
    *{caller().'::useful"} = *useful;
}
```

Remember that import is called when a module is used. We get the name of the calling package using caller and construct the name of the glob we're going to replace—for instance, main::useful. We use a symbolic reference to turn the glob's name, which is a string, into the glob itself. This is just the same as the symbolic reference in this familiar but unpleasant piece of code:

```
$answer = 42;
$variable = "answer";

print ${$variable};
```

If we were using the recommended strict pragma, our program would die immediately—and with good reason, since symbolic references should only be used by people who know what they're doing. We use no strict 'refs'; to tell Perl that we're planning on doing good magic with symbolic references.

 Many advanced uses of Perl need to do some of the things that strict prevents the uninitiated from doing. As an initiated Perl user, you will occasionally have to turn strictures off. This isn't something to take lightly, but don't be afraid of it; strict is a useful servant, but a bad master, and should be treated as such.

Now that we have the *main::useful glob, we can assign it to point to the *useful glob in the current Some::Module package. Now all references to useful() in the main package will resolve to &Some::Module::useful.

That is a good first approximation of an exporter, but we need to know more.

Accessing parts of a glob

With our naive import routine above, we aliased main::useful by assigning one glob to another. However, this has some unfortunate side effects:

```
use Some::Module;
our $useful = "Some handy string";

print $Some::Module::useful;
```

Since we've aliased two entire globs together, any changes to *any* of the variables in the useful glob will be reflected in the other package. If Some::Module has a more substantial routine that uses its own $useful, then all hell will break loose.

All we want to do is to put a subroutine into the &useful element of the *main::useful glob. If we were exporting a scalar or an array, we could assign a copy of its value to the glob by saying:

```
${caller( )."::useful"} = $useful;
@{caller( )."::useful"} = @useful;
```

However, if we try to say:

```
&{caller( )."::useful"} = &useful;
```

then everything goes wrong. The &useful on the right calls the useful subroutine and returns the value 42, and the rest of the line wants to call a currently non-existant subroutine and assign its return value the number 42. This isn't going to work.

Thankfully, Perl provides us with a way around this. We don't have to assign the entire glob at once. We just assign a reference to the glob, and Perl works out what type of reference it is and stores it in the appropriate part, as in Figure 1-4.

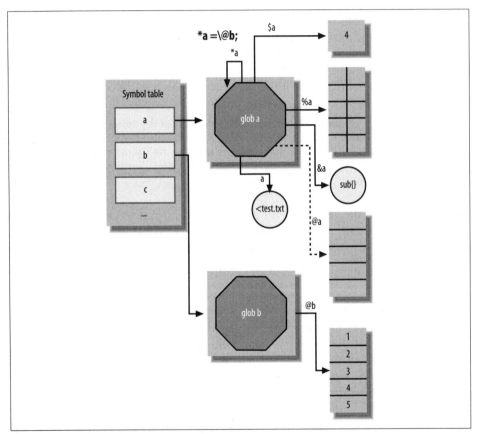

Figure 1-4. Assigning to a glob's array part

Notice that this is not the same as @a=@b; it is real aliasing. Any changes to @b will be seen in @a, and vice versa:

```
@b = (1,2,3,4);
*a = \@b;
```

```
    push @b, 5;
    print @a; # 12345

    # However:
    $a = "Bye"
    $b = "Hello there!";
    print $a; # Bye
```

Although the @a array is aliased by having its reference connected to the reference used to locate the @b array, the rest of the *a glob is untouched; changes in $b do not affect $a.

You can write to all parts of a glob, just by providing the appropriate references:

```
    *a = \"Hello";
    *a = [ 1, 2, 3 ];
    *a = { red => "rouge", blue => "bleu" };

    print $a;        # Hello
    print $a[1];     # 2
    print $a{"red"}; # rouge
```

The three assignments may look like they are replacing each other, but each writes to a different part of the glob depending on the appropriate reference type. If the assigned value is a reference to a constant, then the variable's value is unchangeable.

```
    *a = \1234;
    $a = 10; # Modification of a read-only value attempted
```

Now we come to a solution to our exporter problem; we want to alias &main::useful and &Some::Module::useful, but no other parts of the useful glob. We do this by assigning a reference to &Some::Module::useful to *main::useful:

```
    sub useful { 42 }
    sub import {
        no strict 'refs';
        *{caller()."::useful"} = \&useful;
    }
```

This is similar to how the Exporter module works; the heart of Exporter is this segment of code in Exporter::Heavy::heavy_export:

```
    foreach $sym (@imports) {
        # shortcut for the common case of no type character
        (*{"${callpkg}::$sym"} = \&{"${pkg}::$sym"}, next)
            unless $sym =~ s/^(\W)//;

        $type = $1;
        *{"${callpkg}::$sym"} =
            $type eq '&' ? \&{"${pkg}::$sym"} :
            $type eq '$' ? \${"${pkg}::$sym"} :
            $type eq '@' ? \@{"${pkg}::$sym"} :
            $type eq '%' ? \%{"${pkg}::$sym"} :
            $type eq '*' ? *{"${pkg}::$sym"} :
            do { require Carp; Carp::croak("Can't export symbol:$type$sym") };
    }
```

This has a list of imports, which have either come from the use Some::Module '...'; declaration or from Some::Module's default @EXPORT list. These imports may have type sigils in front of them, or they may not; if they do not, such as when you say use Carp 'croak';, then they refer to subroutines.

In our original case, we had set @EXPORT to ("useful"). First, Exporter checks for a type sigil and removes it:

```
(*{"${callpkg}::$sym"} = \&{"${pkg}::$sym"}, next)
    unless $sym =~ s/^(\W)//;
```

Because $sym is "useful"—with no type sigil—the rest of the statement executes with a result similar to:

```
*{"${callpkg}::$sym"} = \&{"${pkg}::$sym"};
next;
```

Plugging in the appropriate values, this is very much like our mock exporter:

```
*{$callpkg."::useful"} = \&{"Some::Module::useful"};
```

On the other hand, where there is a type sigil the exporter constructs the reference and assigns the relevant part of the glob:

```
*{"${callpkg}::$sym"} =
    $type eq '&' ? \&{"${pkg}::$sym"} :
    $type eq '$' ? \${"${pkg}::$sym"} :
    $type eq '@' ? \@{"${pkg}::$sym"} :
    $type eq '%' ? \%{"${pkg}::$sym"} :
    $type eq '*' ? *{"${pkg}::$sym"} :
    do { require Carp; Carp::croak("Can't export symbol: $type$sym") };
```

Accessing Glob Elements

The *glob = ... syntax obviously only works for assigning references to the appropriate part of the glob. If you want to access the individual references, you can treat the glob itself as a very restricted hash: *a{ARRAY} is the same as \@a, and *a{SCALAR} is the same as \$a. The other magic names you can use are HASH, IO, CODE, FORMAT, and GLOB, for the reference to the glob itself. There are also the really tricky PACKAGE and NAME elements, which tell you where the glob came from.

These days, accessing globs by hash keys is really only useful for retrieving the IO element. However, we'll see an example later of how it can be used to work with glob references rather than globs directly.

Creating subroutines with glob assignment

One common use of the aliasing technique in advanced Perl is the assignment of anonymous subroutine references, and especially closures, to a glob. For instance, there's a module called Data::BT::PhoneBill that retrieves data from British Telecom's online phone bill service. The module takes comma-separated lines of information about a call and turns them into objects. An older version of the module split the line into an array and blessed the array as an object, providing a bunch of read-only accessors for data about a call:

```perl
package Data::BT::PhoneBill::_Call;
sub new {
  my ($class, @data) = @_;
  bless \@data, $class;
}

sub installation { shift->[0] }
sub line         { shift->[1] }
...
```

Closures

A closure is a code block that captures the environment where it's defined—specifically, any lexical variables the block uses that were defined in an outer scope. The following example delimits a lexical scope, defines a lexical variable $seq within the scope, then defines a subroutine sequence that uses the lexical variable.

```perl
{
    my $seq = 3;
    sub sequence { $seq += 3 }
}

print $seq; # out of scope

print sequence; # prints 6
print sequence; # prints 9
```

Printing $seq after the block doesn't work, because the lexical variable is out of scope (it'll give you an error under use strict. However, the sequence subroutine can still access the variable to increment and return its value, because the closure { $seq += 3 } captured the lexical variable $seq.

See *perlfaq7* and *perlref* for more details on closures.

Of course, the inevitable happened: BT added a new column at the beginning, and all of the accessors had to shift down:

```perl
sub type         { shift->[0] }
sub installation { shift->[1] }
sub line         { shift->[2] }
```

Clearly this wasn't as easy to maintain as it should be. The first step was to rewrite the constructor to use a hash instead of an array as the basis for the object:

```perl
our @fields = qw(type installation line chargecard _date time
                 destination _number _duration rebate _cost);
```

```
sub new {
    my ($class, @data) = @_;
    bless { map { $fields[$_] => $data[$_] } 0..$#fields } => $class;
}
```

This code maps type to the first element of @data, installation to the second, and so on. Now we have to rewrite all the accessors:

```
sub type         { shift->{type} }
sub installation { shift->{installation} }
sub line         { shift->{line} }
```

This is an improvement, but if BT adds another column called friends_and_family_ discount, then I have to type friends_and_family_discount three times: once in the @fields array, once in the name of the subroutine, and once in the name of the hash element.

It's a cardinal law of programming that you should never have to write the same thing more than once. It doesn't take much to automatically construct all the accessors from the @fields array:

```
for my $f (@fields) {
    no strict 'refs';
    *$f = sub { shift->{$f} };
}
```

This creates a new subroutine in the glob for each of the fields in the array—equivalent to *type = sub { shift->{type} }. Because we're using a closure on $f, each accessor "remembers" which field it's the accessor for, even though the $f variable is out of scope once the loop is complete.

Creating a new subroutine by assigning a closure to a glob is a particularly common trick in advanced Perl usage.

AUTOLOAD

There is, of course, a simpler way to achieve the accessor trick. Instead of defining each accessor individually, we can define a single routine that executes on any call to an undefined subroutine. In Perl, this takes the form of the AUTOLOAD subroutine—an ordinary subroutine with the magic name AUTOLOAD:

```
sub AUTOLOAD {
    print "I don't know what you want me to do!\n";
}

yow();
```

Instead of dying with Undefined subroutine &yow called, Perl tries the AUTOLOAD subroutine and calls that instead.

To make this useful in the Data::BT::PhoneBill case, we need to know which subroutine was actually called. Thankfully, Perl makes this information available to us through the $AUTOLOAD variable:

```
sub AUTOLOAD {
    my $self = shift;
    if ($AUTOLOAD =~ /.*::(.*)/) { $self->{$1} }
```

The middle line here is a common trick for turning a fully qualified variable name into a locally qualified name. A call to $call->type will set $AUTOLOAD to Data::BT::PhoneBill::_Call::type. Since we want everything after the last ::, we use a regular expression to extract the relevant part. This can then be used as the name of a hash element.

We may want to help Perl out a little and create the subroutine on the fly so it doesn't need to use AUTOLOAD the next time type is called. We can do this by assigning a closure to a glob as before:

```
sub AUTOLOAD {
if ($AUTOLOAD =~ /.*::(.*)/) {
    my $element = $1;
    *$AUTOLOAD = sub { shift->{$element} };
    goto &$AUTOLOAD;
}
```

This time, we write into the symbol table, constructing a new subroutine where Perl expected to find our accessor in the first place. By using a closure on $element, we ensure that each accessor points to the right hash element. Finally, once the new subroutine is set up, we can use goto &subname to try again, calling the newly created Data::BT::PhoneBill::_Call::type method with the same parameters as before. The next time the same subroutine is called, it will be found in the symbol table—since we've just created it—and we won't go through AUTOLOAD again.

goto LABEL and goto &subname are two completely different operations, unfortunately with the same name. The first is generally discouraged, but the second has no such stigma attached to it. It is identical to subname(@_) but with one important difference: the current stack frame is obliterated and replaced with the new subroutine. If we had used $AUTOLOAD->(@_) in our example, and someone had told a debugger to set a breakpoint inside Data::BT::PhoneBill::_Call::type, they would see this backtrace:

. = Data::BT::PhoneBill::_Call::type ...

. = Data::BT::PhoneBill::_Call::AUTOLOAD ...

. = main::process_call

In other words, we've exposed the plumbing, if only for the first call to type. If we use goto &$AUTOLOAD, however, the AUTOLOAD stack frame is obliterated and replaced directly by the type frame:

. = Data::BT::PhoneBill::_Call::type ...

. = main::process_call

It's also conceivable that, because there is no third stack frame or call-return linkage to handle, the goto technique is marginally more efficient.

There are two things that every user of AUTOLOAD needs to know. The first is DESTROY. If your AUTOLOAD subroutine does anything magical, you need to make sure that it checks to see if it's being called in place of an object's DESTROY clean-up method. One common idiom to do this is return if $1 eq "DESTROY". Another is to define an empty DESTROY method in the class: sub DESTROY { }.

The second important thing about AUTOLOAD is that you can neither decline nor chain AUTOLOADs. If an AUTOLOAD subroutine has been called, then the missing subroutine has been deemed to be dealt with. If you want to rethrow the undefined-subroutine error, you must do so manually. For instance, let's limit our Data::BT::PhoneBill::_ Call::AUTOLOAD method to only deal with real elements of the hash, and not any random rubbish or typo that comes our way:

```
use Carp qw(croak);
...
sub AUTOLOAD {
    my $self = shift;
    if ($AUTOLOAD =~ /.*::(.*)/ and exists $self->{$1}) {
        return $self->{$1}
    }
    croak "Undefined subroutine &$AUTOLOAD called"; }
```

CORE and CORE::GLOBAL

Two of the most misunderstood pieces of Perl arcana are the CORE and CORE::GLOBAL packages. These two packages have to do with the replacement of built-in functions. You can override a built-in by importing the new function into the caller's namespace, but it is not as simple as defining a new function.

For instance, to override the glob function in the current package with one using regular expression syntax, we either have to write a module or use the subs pragma to declare that we will be using our own version of the glob typeglob:

```
use subs qw(glob);

sub glob {
    my $pattern = shift;
    local *DIR;
    opendir DIR, "." or die $!;
    return grep /$pattern/, readdir DIR;
}
```

This replaces Perl's built-in glob function for the duration of the package:

```
print "$_\n" for glob("^c.*\\.xml");

ch01.xml
ch02.xml
...
```

However, since the <*.*> syntax for the glob operator is internally resolved to a call to glob, we could just as well say:

```
print "$_\n" for <^c.*\\.xml>;
```

Neither of these would work without the use subs line, which prepares the Perl parser for seeing a private version of the glob function.

If you're writing a module that provides this functionality, all is well and good. Just put the name of the built-in function in @EXPORT, and the Exporter will do the rest.

Where do CORE:: and CORE::GLOBAL:: come in, then? First, if we're in a package that has an overriden glob and we need to get at Perl's core glob, we can use CORE::glob( ) to do so:

```
@files = <ch.*xml>;      # New regexp glob
@files = CORE::glob("ch*xml"); # Old shell-style glob
```

CORE:: always refers to the built-in functions. I say "refers to" as a useful fiction—CORE:: merely qualifies to the Perl parser which glob you mean. Perl's built-in functions don't really live in the symbol table; they're not subroutines, and you can't take references to them. There can be a package called CORE, and you can happily say things like $CORE::a = 1. But CORE:: followed by a function name is special.

Because of this, we can rewrite our regexp-glob function like so:

```
package Regexp::Glob;
use base 'Exporter';
our @EXPORT = qw(glob);

sub glob {
    my $pattern = shift;
    return grep /$pattern/, CORE::glob("*");
}
1;
```

There's a slight problem with this. Importing a subroutine into a package only affects the package in question. Any other packages in the program will still call the built-in glob:

```
use Regexp::Glob;
@files = glob("ch.*xml");       # New regexp glob

package Elsewhere;
@files = glob("ch.*xml");       # Old shell-style glob
```

Our other magic package, CORE::GLOBAL::, takes care of this problem. By writing a subroutine reference into CORE::GLOBAL::glob, we can replace the glob function throughout the whole program:

```
package Regexp::Glob;

*CORE::GLOBAL::glob = sub {
    my $pattern = shift;
    local *DIR;
```

```
    opendir DIR, "." or die $!;
    return grep /$pattern/, readdir DIR;
};


1;
```

Now it doesn't matter if we change packages—the glob operator and its <> alias will be our modified version.

So there you have it: CORE:: is a pseudo-package used only to unambiguously refer to the built-in version of a function. CORE::GLOBAL:: is a real package in which you can put replacements for the built-in version of a function across all namespaces.

Case Study: Hook::LexWrap

Hook::LexWrap is a module that allows you to add wrappers around subroutines— that is, to add code to execute before or after a wrapped routine. For instance, here's a very simple use of LexWrap for debugging purposes:

```
wrap 'my_routine',
    pre => sub { print "About to run my_routine with arguments @_" },
    post => sub { print "Done with my_routine"; }
```

The main selling point of Hook::LexWrap is summarized in the module's documentation:

> Unlike other modules that provide this capacity (e.g. Hook::PreAndPost and Hook:: WrapSub), Hook::LexWrap implements wrappers in such a way that the standard "caller" function works correctly within the wrapped subroutine.

It's easy enough to fool caller if you only have pre-hooks; you replace the subroutine in question with an intermediate routine that does the moral equivalent of:

```
sub my_routine {
    call_pre_hook();
    goto &Real::my_routine;
}
```

As we saw above, the goto &subname form obliterates my_routine's stack frame, so it looks to the outside world as though my_routine has been controlled directly.

But with post-hooks it's a bit more difficult; you can't use the goto & trick. After the subroutine is called, you want to go on to do something else, but you've obliterated the subroutine that was going to call the post-hook.

So how does Hook::LexWrap ensure that the standard caller function works? Well, it doesn't; it actually provides its own, making sure you don't use the standard caller function at all.

Hook::LexWrap does its work in two parts. The first part assigns a closure to the subroutine's glob, replacing it with an imposter that arranges for the hooks to be called, and the second provides a custom CORE::GLOBAL::caller. Let's first look at the custom caller:

```
*CORE::GLOBAL::caller = sub {
    my ($height) = ($_[0]||0);
    my $i=1;
    my $name_cache;
    while (1) {
        my @caller = CORE::caller($i++) or return;
        $caller[3] = $name_cache if $name_cache;
        $name_cache = $caller[0] eq 'Hook::LexWrap' ? $caller[3] : '';
        next if $name_cache || $height-- != 0;
        return wantarray ? @_ ? @caller : @caller[0..2] : $caller[0];
    }
};
```

The basic idea of this is that we want to emulate caller, but if we see a call in the Hook::LexWrap namespace, then we ignore it and move on to the next stack frame. So we first work out the number of frames to back up the stack, defaulting to zero. However, since CORE::GLOBAL::caller itself counts as a stack frame, we need to start the counting internally from one.

Next, we do a slight bit of trickery. Our imposter subroutine is compiled in the Hook::LexWrap namespace, but it has the name of the original subroutine it's emulating. So if we see something in Hook::LexWrap, we store its subroutine name away in $name_cache and then skip over it, without decrementing $height. If the thing we see is not in Hook::LexWrap, but comes directly after something that is, we replace its subroutine name with the one from the cache. Finally, once $height gets down to zero, we can return the appropriate bits of the @caller array.

By doing this, we've created our own replacement caller function, which hides the existence of stack frames in the Hook::LexWrap package, but in all other ways behaves the same as the original caller. Now let's see how our imposter subroutine is built up.

Most of the wrap routine is actually just about argument checking, context propagation, and return value handling; we can slim it down to the following for our purposes:

```
sub wrap (*@) {
    my ($typeglob, %wrapper) = @_;
    $typeglob = (ref $typeglob || $typeglob =~ /::/)
        ? $typeglob
        : caller().":::$typeglob";
    my $original = ref $typeglob eq 'CODE'
                    ? $typeglob
                    : *$typeglob{CODE};
    $imposter = sub {
        $wrapper{pre}->(@_) if $wrapper{pre};
        my @return = &$original;
        $wrapper{post}->(@_) if $wrapper{post};
        return @return;
    };
    *{$typeglob} = $imposter;
}
```

To make our imposter work, we need to know two things: the code we're going to run and where it's going to live in the symbol table. We might have been either handed a typeglob (the tricky case) or the name of a subroutine as a string. If we have a string, the code looks like this:

```
$typeglob = $typeglob =~ /::/ ? $typeglob : caller().":::$typeglob";
my $original = *$typeglob{CODE};
```

The first line ensures that the now badly named $typeglob is fully qualified; if not, it's prefixed with the calling package. The second line turns the string into a subroutine reference using the glob reference syntax.

In the case where we're handed a glob like *to_wrap, we have to use some magic. The wrap subroutine has the prototype (*$); here is what the perlsub documentation has to say about * prototypes:

> A "*" allows the subroutine to accept a bareword, constant, scalar expression, type-glob, or reference to a typeglob in that slot. The value will be available to the subroutine either as a simple scalar or (in the latter two cases) as a reference to the typeglob.

So if $typeglob turns out to be a typeglob, it's converted into a glob reference, which allows us to use the same syntax to write into the code part of the glob.

The $imposter closure is simple enough—it calls the pre-hook, then the original subroutine, then the post-hook. We know where it should go in the symbol table, and so we redefine the original subroutine with our new one.

So this relatively complex module relies purely on two tricks that we have already examined: first, globally overriding a built-in function using CORE::GLOBAL::, and second, saving away a subroutine reference and then glob assigning a new subroutine that wraps around the original.

Introspection with B

There's one final category of introspection as applied to Perl programs: inspecting the underlying bytecode of the program itself.

When the *perl* interpreter is handed some code, it translates it into an internal code, similar to other bytecode-compiled languages such as Java. However, in the case of Perl, each operation is represented as the node on a tree, and the arguments to each operation are that node's children.

For instance, from the very short subroutine:

```
sub sum_input {
    my $a = <>;
    print $a + 1;
}
```

Perl produces the tree in Figure 1-5.

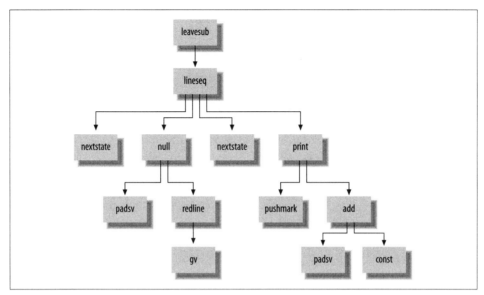

Figure 1-5. Bytecode tree

The B module provides functions that expose the nodes of this tree as objects in Perl itself. You can examine—and in some cases modify—the parsed representation of a running program.

There are several obvious applications for this. For instance, if you can serialize the data in the tree to disk, and find a way to load it up again, you can store a Perl program as bytecode. The B::Bytecode and ByteLoader modules do just this.

Those thinking that they can use this to distribute Perl code in an obfuscated binary format need to read on to our second application: you can use the tree to reconstruct the original Perl code (or something quite like it) from the bytecode, by essentially performing the compilation stage in reverse. The B::Deparse module does this, and it can tell us a lot about how Perl understands different code:

```
% perl -MO=Deparse -n -e '/^#/ || print'

LINE: while (defined($_ = <ARGV>)) {
    print $_ unless /^#/;
}
```

This shows us what's really going on when the -n flag is used, the inferred $_ in print, and the logical equivalence of X || Y and Y unless X.* (Incidentally, the O module is a driver that allows specified B::* modules to do what they want to the parsed source code.)

---

* The -MO=Deparse flag is equivalent to use O qw(Deparse);.

To understand how these modules do their work, you need to know a little about the Perl virtual machine. Like almost all VM technologies, Perl 5 is a software CPU that executes a stream of instructions. Many of these operations will involve putting values on or taking them off a stack; unlike a real CPU, which uses registers to store intermediate results, most software CPUs use a stack model.

Perl code enters the *perl* interpreter, gets translated into the syntax tree structure we saw before, and is optimized. Part of the optimization process involves determining a route through the tree by joining the ops together in a linked list. In Figure 1-6, the route is shown as a dotted line.

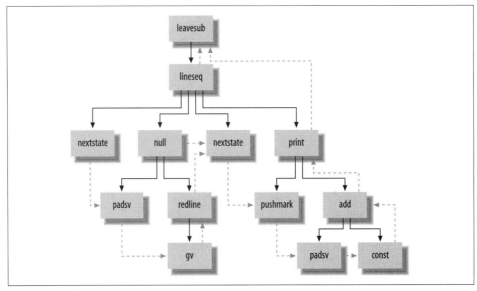

Figure 1-6. Optimized bytecode tree

Each node on the tree represents an operation to be done: we need to enter a new lexical scope (the file); set up internal data structures for a new statement, such as setting the line number for error reporting; find where $a lives and put that on the stack; find what filehandle <> refers to; read a line from that filehandle and put that on the stack; assign the top value on the stack (the result) to the next value down (the variable storage); and so on.

There are several different kinds of operators, classified by how they manipulate the stack. For instance, there are the binary operators—such as add—which take two values off the stack and return a new value. readline is a unary operator; it takes a filehandle from the stack and puts a value back on. List operators like print take a number of values off the stack, and the nullary pushmark operator is responsible for putting a special mark value on the stack to tell print where to stop.

The B module represents all these different kinds of operators as subclasses of the B::OP class, and these classes contain methods allowing us to get the next module in the execution order, the children of an operator, and so on.

Similar classes exist to represent Perl scalar, array, hash, filehandle, and other values. We can convert any reference to a B:: object using the svref_2object function:

```
use B;

my $subref = sub {
    my $a = <>;
    print $a + 1;
};

my $b = B::svref_2object($subref); # B::CV object
```

This B::CV object represents the subroutine reference that Perl can, for instance, store in the symbol table. To look at the op tree inside this object, we call the START method to get the first node in the linked list of the tree's execution order, or the ROOT method to find the root of the tree.

Depending on which op we have, there are two ways to navigate the op tree. To walk the tree in execution order, you can just follow the chain of next pointers:

```
my $op = $b->START;

do {
    print B::class($op). " : ". $op->name." (".$op->desc.")\n";
} while $op = $op->next and not $op->isa("B::NULL");
```

The class subroutine just converts between a Perl class name like B::COP and the underlying C equivalent, COP; the name method returns the human-readable name of the operation, and desc gives its description as it would appear in an error message. We need to check that the op isn't a B::NULL, because the next pointer of the final op will be a C null pointer, which B handily converts to a Perl object with no methods. This gives us a dump of the subroutine's operations like so:

```
COP : nextstate (next statement)
OP : padsv (private variable)
PADOP : gv (glob value)
UNOP : readline (<HANDLE>)
COP : nextstate (next statement)
OP : pushmark (pushmark)
OP : padsv (private variable)
SVOP : const (constant item)
BINOP : add (addition (+))
LISTOP : print (print)
UNOP : leavesub (subroutine exit)
```

As you can see, this is the natural order for the operations in the subroutine. If you want to examine the tree in top-down order, something that is useful for creating things like B::Deparse or altering the generated bytecode tree with tricks like optimizer and B::Generate, then the easiest way is to use the B::Utils module. This provides a number of handy functions, including walkoptree_simple. This allows you to set a callback and visit every op in a tree:

```
use B::Utils qw( walkoptree_simple );
...
my $op = $b->ROOT;

walkoptree_simple($op, sub{
    $cop = shift;
    print B::class($cop). " : ". $cop->name." (".$cop->desc.")\n";
});
```

Note that this time we start from the ROOT of the tree instead of the START; traversing the op tree in this order gives us the following list of operations:

```
UNOP : leavesub (subroutine exit)
LISTOP : lineseq (line sequence)
COP : nextstate (next statement)
UNOP : null (null operation)
OP : padsv (private variable)
UNOP : readline (<HANDLE>)
PADOP : gv (glob value)
COP : nextstate (next statement)
LISTOP : print (print)
...
```

Working with Perl at the op level requires a great deal of practice and knowledge of the Perl internals, but can lead to extremely useful tools like Devel::Cover, an op-level profiler and coverage analysis tool.

Messing with the Class Model

Perl's style of object orientation is often maligned, but its sheer simplicity allows the advanced Perl programmer to extend Perl's behavior in interesting—and sometimes startling—ways. Because all the details of Perl's OO model happen at runtime and in the open—using an ordinary package variable (@INC) to handle inheritance, for instance, or using the symbol tables for method dispatch—we can fiddle with almost every aspect of it.

In this section we'll see some techniques specific to playing with the class model, but we will also examine how to apply the techniques we already know to distort Perl's sense of OO.

UNIVERSAL

In almost all class-based OO languages, all objects derive from a common class, sometimes called Object. Perl doesn't quite have the same concept, but there is a single hard-wired class called UNIVERSAL, which acts as a last-resort class for method lookups. By default, UNIVERSAL provides three methods: isa, can, and VERSION.

We saw `isa` briefly in the last section; it consults a class or object's @ISA array and determines whether or not it derives from a given class:

```perl
package Coffee;
our @ISA = qw(Beverage::Hot);

sub new { return bless { temp => 80 }, shift }

package Tea;
use base 'Beverage::Hot';

package Latte;
use base 'Coffee';

package main;
my $mug = Latte->new;

Tea->isa("Beverage::Hot"); # 1
Tea->isa("Coffee"); # 0

if ($mug->isa("Beverage::Hot")) {
    warn 'Contents May Be Hot';
}
```

 isa is a handy method you can use in modules to check that you've been handed the right sort of object. However, since not everything in Perl is an object, you may find that just testing a scalar with isa is not enough to ensure that your code doesn't blow up: if you say $thing-> isa(...) on an unblessed reference, Perl will die.

The preferred "safety first" approach is to write the test this way:

```perl
my ($self, $thing) = @_;
croak "You need to give me a Beverage::Hot instance"
  unless eval { $thing->isa("Beverage::Hot"); };
```

This will work even if $thing is undef or a non-reference.

Checking isa relationships is one way to ensure that an object will respond correctly to the methods that you want to call on it, but it is not necessarily the best one. Another idea, that of *duck typing,* states that you should determine whether or not to deal with an object based on the methods it claims to respond to, rather than its inheritance. If our Tea class did not derive from Beverage::Hot, but still had temperature, milk, and sugar accessors and brew and drink methods, we could treat it as if it were a Beverage::Hot. In short, if it walks like a duck and it quacks like a duck, we can treat it like a duck.*

---

* Of course, one of the problems with duck typing is that checking that something can respond to an action does not tell us *how* it will respond. We might expect a Tree object and a Dog to both have a bark method, but that wouldn't mean that we could use them in the same way.

The universal can method allows us to check Perl objects duck-style. It's particularly useful if you have a bunch of related classes that don't all respond to the same methods. For instance, looking back at our B::OP classes, binary operators, list operators, and pattern match operators have a last accessor to retrieve the youngest child, but nullary, unary, and logical operators don't. Instead of checking whether or not we have an instance of the appropriate classes, we can write generically applicable code by checking whether the object responds to the last method:

```
$h{firstaddr} = sprintf("%#x", $ {$op->first}) if $op->can("first");
$h{lastaddr}  = sprintf("%#x", $ {$op->last})  if $op->can("last");
```

Another advantage of can is that it returns the subroutine reference for the method once it has been looked up. We'll see later how to use this to implement our own method dispatch in the same way that Perl would.

Finally, VERSION returns the value of the class's $VERSION. This is used internally by Perl when you say:

```
use Some::Module 1.2;
```

While I'm sure there's something clever you can do by providing your own VERSION method and having it do magic when Perl calls it, I can't think what it might be.

However, there is one trick you can play with UNIVERSAL: you can put your own methods in it. Suddenly, every object and every class name (and remember that in Perl a class name is just a string) responds to your new method.

One particularly creative use of this is the UNIVERSAL::require module. Perl's require keyword allows you to load up modules at runtime; however, one of its more annoying features is that it acts differently based on whether you give it a bare class name or a quoted string or scalar. That is:

```
require Some::Module;
```

will happily look up Some/Module.pm in the @INC path. However, if you say:

```
my $module = "Some::Module";
require $module;
```

Perl will look for a file called Some::Module in the current directory and probably fail. This makes it awkward to require modules by name programatically. You have to end up doing something like:

```
eval "require $module";
```

which has problems of its own. UNIVERSAL::require is a neat solution to this—it provides a require method, which does the loading for you. Now you can say:

```
$module->require;
```

Perl will treat $module as a class name and call the class method, which will fall through to UNIVERSAL::require, which loads up the module.

Similarly, the `UNIVERSAL::moniker` module provides a human-friendly name for an object's class, by lowercasing the text after the final `:::`:

```
package UNIVERSAL;

sub moniker {
    my ($self) = @_;
        my @parts = split /::/, (ref($self) || $self);
    return lc pop @parts;
}
```

This allows you to say things like:

```
for my $class (@classes) {
    print "Listing of all ".$class->plural_moniker.":\n";
    print $_->name."\n" for $class->retrieve_all;
    print "\n";
}
```

Some people disagree with putting methods into `UNIVERSAL`, but the worst that can happen is that an object now unexpectedly responds to a method it would not have before. And if it would not respond to a method before, then any call to it would have been a fatal error. At worst, you've prevented the program from breaking immediately by making it do something strange. Balancing this against the kind of hacks you can perpetrate with it, I'd say that adding things to `UNIVERSAL` is a useful technique for the armory of any advanced Perl hacker.

Dynamic Method Resolution

If you're still convinced that Perl's OO system is not the sort of thing that you want, then the time has come to write your own. Damian Conway's *Object Oriented Perl* is full of ways to construct new forms of objects and object dispatch.

We've seen the fundamental techniques for doing this; it's now just a matter of combining them. For instance, we can combine `AUTOLOAD` and `UNIVERSAL` to respond to any method in any class at all. We could use this to turn all unknown methods into accessors and mutators:

```
sub UNIVERSAL::AUTOLOAD {
    my $self = shift;
    $UNIVERSAL::AUTOLOAD =~ /.*::(.*)/;
    return if $1 eq "DESTROY";
    if (@_) {
        $self->{$1} = shift;
    }
    $self->{$1};
}
```

Or we could use it to mess about with inheritance, like `Class::Dynamic`; or make methods part of an object's payload, like `Class::Classless` or `Class::Object`. We'll see later how to implement Java-style `final` attributes to prevent methods from being overridden by derived classes.

Case Study: Singleton Methods

On the infrequent occasions when I'm not programming in Perl, I program in an interesting language called Ruby. Ruby is the creation of Japanese programmer Yukihiro Matsumoto, based on Perl and several other dynamic languages. It has a great number of ideas that have influenced the design of Perl 6, and some of them have even been implemented in Perl 5, as we'll see here and later in the chapter.

One of these ideas is the *singleton method*, a method that only applies to one particular object and not to the entire class. In Perl, the concept would look something like this:

```perl
my $a = Some::Class->new;
my $b = Some::Class->new;

$a->singleton_method( dump => sub {
  my $self = shift;
  require Data::Dumper; print STDERR Date::Dumper::Dumper($self)
});

$a->dump; # Prints a representation of the object.
$b->dump; # Can't locate method "dump"
```

$a receives a new method, but $b does not. Now that we have an idea of what we want to achieve, half the battle is over. It's obvious that in order to make this work, we're going to put a singleton_method method into UNIVERSAL. And now somehow we've got to make $a have all the methods that it currently has, but also have an additional one.

If this makes you think of subclassing, you're on the right track. We need to subclass $a (and $a only) into a new class and put the singleton method into the new class. Let's take a look at some code to do this:

```perl
package UNIVERSAL;

sub singleton_method {
    my ($object, $method, $subref) = @_;

    my $parent_class = ref $object;
    my $new_class = "_Singletons::".(0+$object);
    *{$new_class."::".$method} = $subref;

    if ($new_class ne $parent_class) {
        @{$new_class."::ISA"} = ($parent_class);
        bless $object, $new_class;
    }
}
```

First, we find what $a's original class is. This is easy, since ref tells us directly. Next we have to make up a new class—a new package name for our singleton methods to live in. This has to be specific to the object, so we use the closest thing to a unique identifier for objects that Perl has: the numeric representation of its memory address.

0+$object

We don't talk a lot about memory locations in Perl, so using something like `0+$object` to find a memory location may surprise you. However, it should be a familiar concept. If you've ever accidentally printed out an object when you expected a normal scalar, you should have seen something like `Some::Class=HASH(0x801180)`. This is Perl's way of telling you that the object is a `Some::Class` object, it's based on a hash, and it lives at that particular location in memory.

However, just like the special variable `$!`, objects have a string/integer duality. If you treat an object as an ordinary string, you get the output we have just described. However, if you treat it as a number, you just get the `0x8801180`. By saying `0+$object`, we're forcing the object to return its memory location, and since no two objects can be at the same location, we have a piece of data unique to the object.

We inject the method into the new class with glob assignment, and now we need to set up its inheritance relationship on $a's own class. Since Perl's inheritance is handled by package variables, these are open for us to fiddle with dynamically. Finally, we change $a's class by re-blessing it into the new class.

The final twist is that if this is the second time the object has had a singleton method added to it, then its class will already be in the form `_Singleton::8393088`. In this case, the new class name would be the same as the old, and we really don't want to alter @ISA, since that would set up a recursive relationship. Perl doesn't like that.

In only 11 lines of code we've extended the way Perl's OO system works with a new concept borrowed from another language. Perl's model may not be terribly advanced, but it's astonishingly flexible.

Unexpected Code

The final set of advanced techniques in this chapter covers anything where Perl code runs at a time that might not be obvious: tying, for instance, runs code when a variable is accessed or assigned to; overloading runs code when various operations are called on a value; and time shifting allows us to run code out of order or delayed until the end of scope.

Some of the most striking effects in Perl can be obtained by arranging for code to be run at unexpected moments, but this must be tempered with care. The whole point of unexpected code is that it's unexpected, and that breaks the well-known Principle of Least Surprise: programming Perl should not be surprising.

On the other hand, these are powerful techniques. Let's take a look at how to make the best use of them.

Overloading

Overloading, in a Perl context, is a way of making an object look like it isn't an object. More specifically, it's a way of making an object respond to methods when used in an operation or other context that doesn't look like a method call.

The problem with such overloading is that it can quickly get wildly out of hand. C++ overloads the left bit-shift operator, <<, on filehandles to mean *print*:

```
cout << "Hello world";
```

since it looks like the string is heading into the stream. Ruby, on the other hand, overloads the same operator on arrays to mean *push*. If we make flagrant use of overloading in Perl, we end up having to look at least twice at code like:

```
$object *= $value;
```

We look once to see it as a multiplication, once to realize it's actually a method call, and once more to work out what class $object is in at this point and hence what method has been called.

That said, for classes that more or less represent the sort of things you're overloading—numbers, strings, and so on—then overloading works fine. Now, how do we do it?

Simple operator overloading

The classic example of operator overloading is a module that represents time. Indeed, Time::Seconds, from the Time::Piece distribution does just this. Let's make some new Time::Seconds objects:

```
my $min  = Time::Seconds->new(60);
my $hour = Time::Seconds->new(3600);
```

The point of Time::Seconds is that, as well as merely representing a number of seconds, you can convert between different units of duration:

```
my $longtime = Time::Seconds->new(123456);
print $longtime->hours; # 34.2933..
print $longtime->days;  # 1.42888..
```

These objects definitely represent a number—a number of seconds. Normally, we'd have to add them together with some ugly hack like this:

```
my $new = $min->add($hour);
```

And even then it's not clear whether or not that alters the original $min. So one natural use of operator overloading would be to enable us to say $min + $hour, and get back an object representing 3,660 seconds. And that is precisely what happens:

```
my $new = $min + $hour;
print $new->seconds; # 3660
```

This is done by the following bit of code in the Time::Seconds module:

```perl
use overload '+' => \&add;
# ...
sub add {
    my ($lhs, $rhs) = _get_ovlvals(@_);
    return Time::Seconds->new($lhs + $rhs);
}

sub _get_ovlvals {
    my ($lhs, $rhs, $reverse) = @_;
    $lhs = $lhs->seconds;

    if (UNIVERSAL::isa($rhs, 'Time::Seconds')) {
        $rhs = $rhs->seconds;
    } elsif (ref($rhs)) {
        die "Can't use non Seconds object in operator overload";
    }

    if ($reverse) { return $rhs, $lhs; }
    return $lhs, $rhs;
}
```

The overload pragma is the key to it all. It tells Perl to look more carefully at operations involving objects of that class, and it registers methods for the given operators in a look-up table. When an object is involved in an overloaded operation, the operation is looked up in the table and the resulting method called. In this case, $obj + $other will call $obj->add($other, 0).

The reason Perl passes three parameters to the method is that in the case of $other + $obj, where $other is not an object that overloads +, we still expect the add method to be called on $obj. In this case, however, Perl will call $obj->add($other, 1), to signify that the arguments have been reversed.

The _get_ovlvals subroutine looks at the two arguments to an operator and tries to coerce them into numbers—other Time::Seconds objects are turned into numbers by having the seconds method called on them, ordinary numbers are passed through, and any other kind of object causes a fatal error. Then the arguments are reordered to the original order.

Once we have two ordinary numbers, we can add them together and return a new Time::Seconds object based on the sum.

The other operators are based on this principle, such as <=>, which implements all of the comparison operators:

```perl
use overload '<=>' => \&compare;
sub compare {
    my ($lhs, $rhs) = _get_ovlvals(@_);
    return $lhs <=> $rhs;
}
```

Time::Seconds also overloads assignment operators += and -=:

```perl
use overload '-=' => \&subtract_from;
sub subtract_from {
```

```
        my $lhs = shift;
        my $rhs = shift;
        $rhs = $rhs->seconds if UNIVERSAL::isa($rhs, 'Time::Seconds');
        $$lhs -= $rhs;
        return $lhs;
    }
```

This allows you to say `$new += 60` to add another minute to the new duration.

Finally, to avoid having to write such subroutines for every kind of operator, `Time::Seconds` uses a feature of `overload` called *fallback*. This instructs Perl to attempt to automatically generate reasonable methods from the ones specified: for instance, the `$x++` operator will be implemented in terms of `$x += 1`, and so on. `Time::Seconds` sets `fallback` to `undef`, which means that Perl will try to use an autogenerated method but will die if it cannot find one.

```
    use overload 'fallback' => 'undef';
```

Alternate values for `fallback` include some true value, which is the most general fallback: if it cannot find an autogenerated method, it will do what it can, assuming if necessary that overloading does not exist. In other words, it will always produce some value, somehow.

If you're using overloading just to add a shortcut operator or two onto an otherwise object-based class—for example, if you wanted to emulate C++'s (rather dodgy) use of the `<<` operator to write to a filehandle:

```
    $file << "This is ugly\n";
```

then you should use the default value of `fallback`, which is false. This means that no automatic method generation will be tried, and any attempts to use the object with one of the operations you have not overloaded will cause a fatal error.

However, as well as performing arithmetic operations on `Time::Seconds` objects, there's something else you can do with them:

```
    print $new; # 3660
```

If we use the object as an ordinary string or a number, we don't get object-like behavior (the dreaded `Time::Seconds=SCALAR(0xf00)`) but instead it acts just like we should expect from something representing a number: it looks like a number. How does it do that?

Other operator overloading

As well as being able to overload the basic arithmetic and string operators, Perl allows you to overload the sorts of things that you wouldn't normally think of as operators. The two most useful of these we have just seen with `Time::Seconds`—the ability to dictate how an object is converted to a string or integer when used as such.

This is done by assigning methods to two special operator names—the `""` operator for stringification and the `0+` operator for numification:

```
use overload '0+' => \&seconds,
            '""' => \&seconds;
```

Now anytime the Time::Seconds object is used as a string or a number, the seconds method gets called, returning the number of seconds that the object contains:

```
print "One hour plus one minute is $new seconds\n";
# One hour plus one minute is 3660 seconds.
```

These are the most common methods to make an overloaded object look and behave like the thing it's meant to represent. There are a few other methods you can play with for more obscure effects.

For instance, you can overload the way that an object is dereferenced in various ways, allowing a scalar reference to pretend that it's a list reference or vice versa. There are few sensible reasons to do this—the curious Object::MultiType overloads the @{}, %{}, &{}, and *{} operators to allow a single object to pretend to be an array, hash, subroutine, or glob, depending on how it's used.

Non-operator overloading

One little-known extension of the overload mechanism is hidden away in the documentation for overload:

> For some application Perl parser [sic] mangles constants too much. It is possible to hook into this process via overload::constant() and overload::remove_constant() functions.
>
> These functions take a hash as an argument. The recognized keys of this hash are

integer	to overload integer constants,
float	to overload floating point constants,
binary	to overload octal and hexadecimal constants,
q	to overload "q"-quoted strings, constant pieces of "qq"- and "qx"-quoted strings and here-documents,
qr	to overload constant pieces of regular expressions.

That is to say, you can cause the Perl parser to run a subroutine of your choice every time it comes across some kind of constant. Naturally, this is again something that should be used with care but can be used to surprising effect.

The subroutines supplied to overload::constant pass three parameters: the first is the raw form as the parser saw it, the second is the default interpretation, and the third is a mnemonic for the context in which the constant occurs. For instance, given "camel\nalpaca\npanther", the first parameter would be camel\nalpaca\npanther, whereas the second would be:

```
camel
alpaca
panther
```

As this is a double-quoted (qq) string, the third parameter would be qq.

For instance, the high-precision math libraries `Math::BigInt` and `Math::BigFloat` provide the ability to automatically create high-precision numbers, by overloading the constant operation.

```
% perl -MMath::BigFloat=:constant -le 'print ref (12345678901234567890\
    >1234567890)'
Math::BigFloat
```

This allows the libraries to get at all the numbers in a program, providing high-precision math without the explicit creation of overloaded `Math::BigFloat` objects. The code that does it is stunningly simple:

```
sub import {
    my $self = shift;
    # ...
    overload::constant float => sub { $self->new(shift); };
}
```

When the parser sees a floating point number (one too large to be stored as an integer) it passes the raw string as the first parameter of the subroutine reference. This is equivalent to calling:

```
Math::BigFloat->new("12345678901234567890123456789012345678901234567890")
```

at compile time.

The `Math::Big*` libraries can get away with this because they are relatively well behaved; that is, a Perl program should not notice any difference if all the numbers are suddenly overloaded `Math::BigInt` objects.

On the other hand, here's a slightly more crazy use of overloading…

I've already mentioned Ruby as being another favorite language of mine. One of the draws about Ruby is that absolutely everything is an object:

```
% irb
irb(main):001:0> 2
=> 2
irb(main):002:0> 2.class
=> Fixnum
irb(main):003:0> 2.class.class
=> Class
irb(main):004:0> 2.class.class.class
=> Class
irb(main):005:0> 2.methods
=> ["<=", "to_f", "abs", "-", "upto", "succ", "|", "/", "type",
"times", "%", "-@", "&", "~", "<", "**", "zero?", "^", "<=>", "to_s",
"step", "[  ]", ">", "=  =", "modulo", "next", "id2name",
"size", "<<",
"*", "downto", ">>", ">=", "divmod", "+", "floor", "to_int", "to_i",
"chr", "truncate", "round", "ceil", "integer?", "prec_f", "prec_i",
"prec", "coerce", "nonzero?", "+@", "remainder", "eql?",
"=  =  =",
"clone", "between?", "is_a?", "equal?", "singleton_methods", "freeze",
```

```
"instance_of?", "send", "methods", "tainted?", "id",
"instance_variables", "extend", "dup", "protected_methods", "=~",
"frozen?", "kind_of?", "respond_to?", "class", "nil?",
"instance_eval", "public_methods", "_ _send_ _", "untaint", "_ _
id_ _",
"inspect", "display", "taint", "method", "private_methods", "hash",
"to_a"]
```

I like that you can call methods on a 2. I like that you can define your own methods to call on a 2. Of course, you can't do that in Perl; 2 is not an object.

But we can fake it. *Ruby.pm* was a proof-of-concept module I started work on to demonstrate that you *can* do this sort of thing in Perl. Here's what it looks like:

```
use Ruby;
print 2->class; # "FixInt"
print "Hello World"->class->class # "Class"
print 2->class->to_s->class # "String"
print 2->class->to_s->length # "6"
print ((2+2)->class) # "FixInt"

# Or even:
print 2.class.to_s.class # "String"
```

How can this possibly work? Obviously, the only thing that we can call methods on are objects, so constants like 2 and Hello World need to return objects. This tells us we need to be overloading these constants to return objects. We can do that easily enough:

```
package Ruby;
sub import {
overload::constant(integer => sub { return Fixnum->new(shift) },
                   q       => sub { return String->new(shift) },
                   qq      => sub { return String->new(shift) });
}
```

We can make these objects blessed scalar references:

```
package Fixnum;
sub new { return bless \$_[1], $_[0] }

package String;
sub new { return bless \$_[1], $_[0] }
```

This allows us to fill the classes up with methods that can be called on the constants. That's a good start. The problem is that our constants now behave like objects, instead of like the strings and numbers they represent. We want "Hello World" to look like and act like "Hello World" instead of like "String=SCALAR(0x80ba0c)".

To get around this, we need to overload again—we've overloaded the constants to become objects, and now we need to overload those objects to look like constants again. Let's look at the string class first. The first thing we need to overload is obviously stringification; when the object is used as a string, it needs to display its string value to Perl, which we do by dereferencing the reference.

```
use overload '""' => sub { ${$_[0]} };
```

This will get us most of the way there; we can now print out our Strings and use them anywhere that a normal Perl string would be expected. Next, we take note of the fact that in Ruby, Strings can't be coerced into numbers. You can't simply say 2 + "10", because this is an operation between two disparate types.

To make this happen in our String class, we have to overload numification, too:

```
use Carp;
use overload "0+" => sub { croak "String can't be coerced into Fixnum"};
```

You might like the fact that Perl converts between types magically, but the reason why Ruby can't do it is because it uses the + operator for both numeric addition and string concatenation, just like Java and Python. Let's overload + to give us string concatenation:

```
use overload "+" => sub { String->new(${$_[0]} . "$_[1]") };
```

There are two things to note about this. The first is that we have to be sure that any operations that manipulate strings will themselves return String objects, or otherwise we will end up with ordinary strings that we can no longer call methods on. This is necessary in the Fixnum analogue to ensure that (2+2)->class still works. The other thing is that we must explicitly force stringification on the right-hand operand, for reasons soon to become apparent.

Turning temporarily to the numeric class, we can fill in two of the overload methods in the same sort of way:

```
use overload '""' => sub { croak "failed to convert Fixnum into String" },
             "0+" => sub { ${ $_[0] } },
```

However, methods like + have to be treated carefully. We might first try doing something like this:

```
use overload '+' => sub { ${ $_[0] } + $_[1] };
```

However, if we then try 2 + "12" then we get the bizarre result 122, and further prodding finds that this is a String. Why?

What happens is that Perl first sees Fixnum + String and calls the overloaded method we've just created. Inside this method, it converts the Fixnum object to its integer value and now has integer + String.

The integer is not overloaded, but the String object is. If Perl can see an overloaded operation, it will try and call it, reordering the operation as String + integer. Since String has an overloaded + method, too, that gets called, creating a new string, which catenates the String and the integer. Oops.

Ideally, we would find a way of converting the right-hand side of the + operation on a Fixnum to an honest-to-goodness number. Unfortunately, while Perl has an explicit stringification operator, "", which we used to avoid this problem in the String case, there isn't an explicit numification operator; overload uses 0+ as a convenient mnemonic for numification, but this is merely describing the operation in terms of the + operator, which can be overloaded. So to fix up our + method, we have to get a little technical:

```perl
use overload '+' => \&sum;

sub sum {
    my ($left, $right) = @_;
    my $rval;
    if (my $numify = overload::Method($right, "0+")) {
        $rval = $right->$numify;
    } else {
        $rval = $right;
    }
    Fixnum->new($$left + $rval);
}
```

To explicitly numify the right-hand side, we ask overload if that value has an overloaded numification. If it does, Method will return the method, and we can call it and explicitly numify the value into $rval. Once we've got two plain old numbers, we add them together and return a new number out of the two.

Next, we add overload fallback => 1; to each class, to provide do-what-I-mean (DWIM) methods for the operators that we don't define. This is what you want to do for any case where you want an object to completely emulate a standard built-in type, rather than just add one or two overloaded methods onto something that's essentially an object.

Finally, as a little flourish, we want to make the last line of our example work:

```perl
print 2.class.to_s.class # "String"
```

One of the reasons Ruby's concatenation operator is + is to free up . for the preferred use in most OO languages: method calls. This isn't very easy to do in Perl, but we can fake it enough for a rigged demo. Obviously we're going to need to overload the concatenation operator. The key to working out how to make it work is to realize what those things like class are in a Perl context: they're bare words, or just ordinary strings. Hence if we see a concatenation between one of our Ruby objects and an ordinary string, we should call the method whose name is in the string:

```perl
use overload "." => sub { my ($obj,$meth)=@_; $obj->$meth };
```

And presto, we have Ruby-like objects and Ruby-like method calls. The method call magic isn't perfect—we'll see later how it can be improved—but the Ruby-like objects can now respond to any methods we want to put into their classes. It's not hard to build up a full class hierarchy just like Ruby's own.

Time Shifting

The final fundamental advanced technique we want to look at is that of postponing or reordering the execution of Perl code. For instance, we might want to wait until all modules have been loaded before manipulating the symbol table, we might want to construct some code and run it immediately with eval, or we might want to run code at the end of a scope.

There are Perl keywords for all of these concepts, and judicious use of them can be effective in achieving a wide variety of effects.

Doing things now with eval/BEGIN

The basic interface to time-shifting is through a series of named blocks. These are like special subroutines that Perl stores in a queue and runs at strategic points during the lifetime of a program.

A BEGIN block is executed as soon as Perl compiles the code:

```
print "I come second!\n";
BEGIN { print "I come first!\n"; }
```

The second line appears first because Perl does not ordinarily run code as it sees it; it waits until it has compiled a program and all of its dependencies into the sort of op tree we saw in our section on B, and then runs it all. However, BEGIN forces Perl to run the code as soon as the individual block has been compiled—before the official runtime.

In fact, the use directive to load a module can be thought of as:

```
BEGIN { require Module::Name; Module::Name->import(@stuff); }
```

because it causes the module's code to be loaded up and its import method to be run immediately.

One use of the immediate execution nature of the BEGIN block is in the AnyDBM_File module. This module tries to find an appropriate DBM module to inherit from, meaning that so long as one of the five supported DBM modules is available, any code using DBMs ought to work.

Unfortunately, some DBM implementations are more reliable than others, or optimized for different types of application, so you might want to specify a preferred search order that is different from the default. But when? As AnyDBM_File loads, it sets up its @ISA array and requires the DBM modules.

The trick is to use BEGIN; if AnyDBM_File sees that someone else has put an @ISA array into its namespace, it won't overwrite it with its default one. So we say:

```
BEGIN { @AnyDBM_File::ISA = qw(DB_File GDBM_File NDBM_File); }
use AnyDBM::File;
```

This wouldn't work without the BEGIN, since the statement would then only be executed at runtime; way after the use had set up AnyDBM_File.

As well as a BEGIN, there's also an END block, which stores up code to run right at the end of the program, and, in fact, there are a series of other special blocks as well, as shown in Figure 1-7.

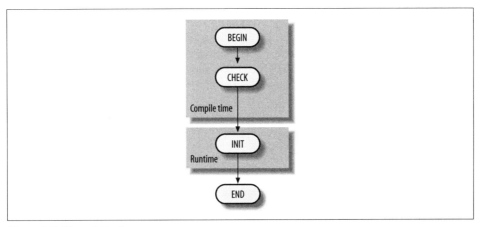

Figure 1-7. Named blocks

The CHECK blocks and the INIT blocks are pretty much indistinguishable, running just before and just after execution begins. The only difference is that executing *perl* with the -c switch (compilation checks) will run CHECK blocks but not INIT blocks. (This also means that if you load a module at runtime, its CHECK and INIT blocks won't be run, because the transition between the global compilation phase and the global runtime execution has already passed.) Let's take a look at what we can do with a CHECK block.

Doing things later with CHECK

Earlier, we talked about messing with inheritance relationships and stealing ideas from other languages. Let's now implement a new module, which gives us the Java concept of *final* methods. A final method is one that cannot be overriden by inheritance:

```
package Beverage::Hot;
sub serve :final { # I have exclusive rights to defining this method!
    my ($self, $who) = @_;
```

```
        if ($who->waitress) { $who->waitress->serve($self, $who); }
        else               { $who->take($self); }
    }

    package Tea;
    use base 'Beverage::Hot';

    sub serve { # Compile-time error.
    }
```

We'll do this by allowing a user to specify a :final attribute on a method. This attribute will mark a method for later checking. Once compile time has finished, we'll check out all the classes that derive from the marked class, and die with an error if the derived class implements the final method.

Attributes

The idea of attributes came in Perl 5.005, with the attrs module. This was part of threading support and allowed you to mark a subroutine as being a method or being locked for threading—that is, it only allows one thread to access the subroutine or the method's invocant at once. In 5.6.0, the syntax was changed to the now-familiar sub name :attr, and it also allowed user-defined attributes.

Perhaps the easiest way to get into attribute programming for anything tricky is to use Damian Conway's Attribute::Handlers module: this allows you to define subroutines to be called when an attribute is seen.

The first thing we want to do is take a note of those classes and methods marked final. We need to switch to the UNIVERSAL class, so that our attribute is visible everywhere. We'll also use a hash, %marked, to group the marked methods by package:

```
    package UNIVERSAL;
    use Attribute::Handlers;
    sub final :ATTR {
        my ($pack, $ref) = @_;
        push @{$marked{$pack}}, *{$ref}{NAME};
    }
```

The Attribute::Handlers package arranges for our handler to be called with various parameters, of which we are only interested in the first two—the package that has the marked subroutine in it and the glob reference for the subroutine itself—because we can get the subroutine's name from that. (NAME is one of the magic names we can use to access a glob's slot—it returns the name of the symbol table entry. *{Tea::serve}{NAME} would return serve.)

Now we've got our list of marked methods. We need to find a way to interrupt Perl just before it runs the script but after all the modules that we plan to use have been compiled and all the inheritence relationships set up, so that we can check nobody has been naughty and overriden a finalized method.

The CHECK keyword gives us a way to do this. It registers a block of code to be called after compilation has been finished but before execution begins.[*]

To enable us to test the module, it turns out we want to have our CHECK block call another function. This is because we can then run the checker twice, once without an offending method and once with:

```
CHECK { Attribute::Final->check }
```

What will our checking method do, though? It needs to visit all the classes that derive from those classes we have in our %marked hash, and to do that, it has to know all the packages in the system. So first we'll write a little function to recursively walk over the symbol table, collecting names of packages it sees.

The symbol table is just a hash, and we can find glob names by looking at the keys of the hash. To make matters even easier, package names are just hash keys that end in ::. So our collector function looks like this:

```perl
sub fill_packages {
    no strict 'refs';
    my $root = shift;
    my @subs = grep s/::$//, keys %{$root."::"};
    push @all_packages, $root;
    for (@subs) {
        next if $root eq "main" and $_ eq "main"; # Loop
        fill_packages($root."::".$_);
    }
}
```

The next line avoids the potential trap of looping forever, because the main:: package contains an entry to itself. Now we can start looking at the check function. It only has to deal with those packages that have some kind of inheritance relationship, so if a package does not have an @ISA, then we can discard it:

```perl
sub check {
    no strict 'refs';
    fill_packages("main") unless @all_packages;
    for my $derived_pack (@all_packages) {
        next unless @{$derived_pack."::ISA"};
        ...
    }
}
```

Next, we have a list of marked packages that contain final methods. We want to look specifically at circumstances where a derived package derives from a marked package:

---

[*] Incidentally, the O compiler module we mentioned earlier works by means of CHECK blocks—after all the code has been compiled, O has the selected compiler backend visit the opcode tree and spit out whatever it wants to do, then exits before the code is run.

```
    for my $derived_pack (@all_packages) {
        next unless @{$derived_pack."::ISA"};
        for my $marked_pack (keys %marked) {
            next unless $derived_pack->isa($marked_pack);
            ...
```

At this point, we know we have a suspect package. It has the right kind of inheritance relationship, but does it override the finalized method?

```
        for my $meth (@{$marked{$marked_pack}}) {
            my $glob_ref = \*{$derived_pack."::".$meth};
            if (*{$glob_ref}{CODE}) {
```

If the code slot is populated, then we have indeed found a naughty method. At this point, all that's left to do is report where it came from. We can do that with the B technique: by turning the glob into a B::GV object, we gain access to the otherwise unreachable FILE and LINE methods, which tell us where the glob entry was constructed.

```
            my $name = $marked_pack."::".$meth;
            my $b = B::svref_2object($glob_ref);
            die "Cannot override final method $name at ".
                $b->FILE. ", line ".$b->LINE."\n";
```

And that is the essence of working with CHECK blocks: they allow us to do things with the symbol table once everything is in place, once all the modules have been loaded, and once the inheritance relationships and other factors have been set up. If you ever feel you need to do something in a module but you don't want to do it quite yet, putting it in a CHECK block might just be the right technique.

Doing things at the end with DESTROY

We've referred to the special DESTROY method, which is called when an object goes out of scope. Generally this is used for writing out state to disk, breaking circular references, and other finalization tasks. However, you can use DESTROY to arrange for things to be done at the end of a scope:

```
sub do_later (&) { bless shift, "Do::Later" }
sub Do::Later::DESTROY { $_[0]->() };

{
    my $later = do_later { print "End of block!\n"; };
    ...
}
```

So long as $later sticks around, the code doesn't get called. When it goes out of scope, gets undefined, or the final reference to it goes away, then the code block is called. Hook::LexWrap, one of the modules we looked at earlier in the chapter, actually uses a similar trick to turn off the wrapping of a subroutine at the end of a lexical scope:

```
my $unwrap;
$imposter = sub {
    if ($unwrap) { goto &$original }
```

```
         ...
      }
      ...
      return bless sub { $unwrap=1 }, 'Hook::LexWrap::Cleanup';
```

While you keep hold of the return value from wrap, the imposter calls the wrapping code. However, once that value goes out of scope, the closure sets $unwrap to a true value, and from then on the imposter simply jumps to the original routine.

Case study: Acme::Dot

One example that puts it all together—messing about with the symbol table, shifting the timing of code execution, and overloading—is my own Acme::Dot module.

If you're not familiar with CPAN's Acme::* hierarchy, we'll cover it in more detail in Chapter 10, but for now you should know it's for modules that are not entirely serious. Acme::Dot is far from serious, but it demonstrates a lot of serious advanced techniques.

The idea of Acme::Dot was to abstract the $variable.method overloaded . operator from *Ruby.pm* and allow third-party modules to use it. It also goes a little further, allowing $variable.method(@arguments) to work. And, of course, it does so without using source filters or any other non-Perl hackery; that would be cheating—or at least inelegant.

So, how do we make this work? We know the main trick, from *Ruby.pm*, of over-loading concatentation on an object. However, there are two niggles. The first is that previously, where $foo.class was a variable "concatenated" with a literal string, $foo.method(@args) is going to be parsed as a subroutine call. That's fine, for the time being; we'll assume that there isn't going to be a subroutine called method kicking around anywhere for now, and later we'll fix up the case where there is one. We *want* Perl to call the undefined subroutine method, because if an undefined subroutine gets called, we can catch it with AUTOLOAD and subvert it.

In what way do we need to subvert it? In the *Ruby.pm* case, we simply turned the right-hand side of the concatenation (class in $var.class) and used that as a method name. In this case, we need to not only know the method name, but the method's parameters, as well. So, our AUTOLOAD routine has to return a data structure that holds the method name and the parameter. A hash is a natural way of doing this, although an array would do just as well:

```
sub AUTOLOAD {
    $AUTOLOAD =~ /.*::(.*)/;
    return if $1 eq "DESTROY";
    return { data => \@_, name => $1 }
}
```

As usual, we take care to avoid clobbering DESTROY. Now that we have the arguments and the name, we can write our overload subroutine to fire the correct method call on concatenation. On the left will be the object, and on the right will be the result of our AUTOLOAD routine—the data structure that tells us which method to fire and with what parameters.

```perl
use overload "." => sub {
    my ($obj, $stuff) = @_;
    @_ = ($obj, @{$stuff->{data}});
    goto &{$obj->can($stuff->{name})};
}, fallback => 1;
```

Just as in Ruby, we use the goto trick to avoid upsetting anything that relies on caller.* Now we have the easy part done.

I say this is the easy part because we know how to do this for one package. So far we've glossed over the fact that the methods and the overload routine are going to live in one class, and the AUTOLOAD subroutine has to be present wherever the $var.method method calls are going to be made. To make matters worse, our Acme::Dot module is going to be neither of these packages. We're going to see something like this:

```perl
package My::Class;
use Acme::Dot;
use base 'Class::Accessor';
__PACKAGE__->mk_accessors(qw/name age/);

package End::User;
use My::Class;

my $x = new My::Class;
$x.name("Winnie-the-Pooh");
```

It's the OO class that needs to use Acme::Dot directly, and it will have the overload routine. We can take care of this easily by making Acme::Dot's import method set up the overloading in its caller:

```perl
my ($call_pack);

sub import {
    no strict 'refs';
    $call_pack = (caller())[0];
    eval <<EOT
  package $call_pack;
use overload "." => sub {
    my (\$obj, \$stuff) = \@_;
    \@_ = (\$obj, \@{\$stuff->{data}});
    goto \&{\$obj->can(\$stuff->{name})};
}, fallback => 1;

EOT
    ;
}
```

<hr>

* Although, to be honest, I don't believe there really is (or ought to be) anything that relies on the behavior of caller—at least, nothing that isn't doing advanced things itself.

However, there's the third package, the End::User package, which actually never sees Acme::Dot at all. It just uses My::Class and expects to get the dot-operator functionality as part of that class. Meanwhile, our poor Acme::Dot class has to somehow find out which class is the end user and install an AUTOLOAD routine into it.

Thankfully, we know that the end-user class will call My::Class->import, so we can use glob assignment to make My::Class::import convey some information back to Acme::Dot. We can modify Acme::Dot's import routine a little:

```
my ($call_pack, $end_user);

sub import {
    no strict 'refs';
    $call_pack = (caller())[0];
    *{$call_pack."::import"} = sub { $end_user = (caller())[0]; };
    eval <<EOT
 package $call_pack;
use overload "." => sub {
    my (\$obj, \$stuff) = \@_;
    \@_ = (\$obj, \@{\$stuff->{data}});
    goto \&{\$obj->can(\$stuff->{name})};
}, fallback => 1;

EOT
    ;
}
```

As you can see, we've now glob assigned My::Class's import routine and made it save away the name of the package that used *it*: the end-user class.

And now, since everything is set up, we are at the point where we can inject the AUTOLOAD into the end user's class. We use a CHECK block to time-shift this to the end of compilation:

```
CHECK {
    # At this point, everything is ready, and $end_user contains
    # the calling package's calling package.
    no strict;
    if ($end_user) {
        *{$end_user."::AUTOLOAD"} = sub {
            $AUTOLOAD =~ /.*::(.*)/;
            return if $1 eq "DESTROY";
            return { data => \@_, name => $1 }
        }
    }
}
```

And that is essentially how Acme::Dot operates. It isn't perfect; if there's a subroutine in the end-user package with the same name as a method on the object, AUTOLOAD won't be called, and we will run into problems. It's possible to work around that, by moving all the subroutines to another package, dispatching everything via AUTOLOAD and using B to work out whether we're in the context of a concatenation operator, but…hey, it's only an Acme::* module. And I hope it's made its point already.

Conclusion

We've now looked at many of the advanced techniques used in pure Perl modules, most of them involving how to manipulate the way Perl operates. We've divided those roughly into sections on messing with the symbol table, messing with the class model, and making code run where code might not be expected.

In a sense, everything else in this book will be built on the techniques that we've seen here. However, Perl is a pragmatic language, and instead of looking in the abstract at techniques that might be useful, we're going to see how these tricks are already being used in real-life code—in CPAN modules—and how they can make your programming life easier.

## CHAPTER 2

Parsing Techniques

One thing Perl is particularly good at is throwing data around. There are two types of data in the world: regular, structured data and everything else. The good news is that regular data—colon delimited, tab delimited, and fixed-width files—is really easy to parse with Perl. We won't deal with that here. The bad news is that regular, structured data is the minority.

If the data isn't regular, then we need more advanced techniques to parse it. There are two major types of parser for this kind of less predictable data. The first is a *bottom-up* parser. Let's say we have an HTML page. We can split the data up into meaningful chunks or *tokens*—tags and the data between tags, for instance—and then reconstruct what each token means. See Figure 2-1. This approach is called bottom-up parsing because it starts with the data and works toward a parse.

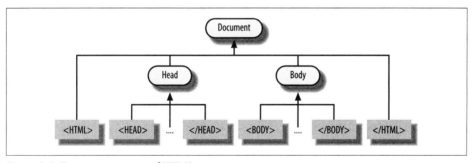

Figure 2-1. Bottom-up parsing of HTML

The other major type of parser is a *top-down* parser. This starts with some ideas of what an HTML file ought to look like: it has an <html> tag at the start and an </html> at the end, with some stuff in the middle. The parser can find that pattern in the document and then look to see what the stuff in the middle is likely to be. See Figure 2-2. This is called a top-down parse because it starts with all the possible parses and works down until it matches the actual contents of the document.

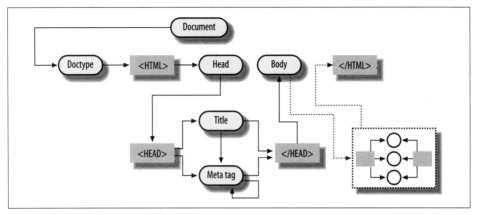

Figure 2-2. Top-down parsing of HTML

Parse::RecDescent Grammars

Damian Conway's Parse::RecDescent module is the most widely used parser genera-
tor for Perl. While most traditional parser generators, such as yacc, produce bottom-
up parsers, Parse::RecDescent creates top-down parsers. Indeed, as its name implies,
it produces a recursive descent parser. One of the benefits of top-down parsing is
that you don't usually have to split the data into tokens before parsing, which makes
it easier and more intuitive to use.

Simple Parsing with Parse::RecDescent

I'm a compulsive player of the Japanese game of Go.* We generally use a file format
called Smart Game Format (*http://www.red-bean.com/sgf/*) for exchanging information about Go games. Here's an example of an SGF file:

```
(;GM[1]FF[4]CA[UTF-8]AP[CGoban:2]ST[2]
RU[Japanese]SZ[19]HA[5]KM[5.50]TM[ ]
PW[Simon Cozens]PB[Keiko Aihara]AB[dd][pd][jj][dp][pp]
;W[df];B[fd];W[cn]
    (;B[dl])
    (;B[fp]CR[fp]C[This is the usual response.])
    (;B[co]CR[co]C[This way is stronger still.]
     ;W[dn];B[fp])
)
```

This little game consists of three moves, followed by three different variations for
what happens next, as shown in Figure 2-3. The file describes a tree structure of variations, with parenthesised sections being variations and subvariations.

---

* The American Go Association provides an introduction to Go by Karl Baker called *The Way to Go* (*http://*
www.usgo.org/usa/waytogo/W2Go8x11.pdf).

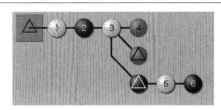

Figure 2-3. Tree of moves

Each variation contains several nodes separated by semicolons, and each node has several parameters. This sort of description of the format is ideal for constructing a top-down parser.

The first thing we'll do is create something that merely works out whether some text is a valid SGF file by checking whether it parses. Let's look at the structure carefully again from the top and, as we go, translate it into a grammar suitable for Parse::RecDescent.

Let's call the whole thing a *game tree*, since as we've seen, it turns out to be a tree-like structure. A game tree consists of an open parenthesis, and a sequence of nodes. We can then have zero, one, or many variations—these are also stored as game trees—and finally there's a close parenthesis:

```
GameTree : "(" Sequence GameTree(s?) ")"
```

Read this as "You can make a GameTree if you see (, a Sequence, …". We've defined the top level of our grammar. Now we need to define the next layer down, a sequence of nodes. This isn't difficult; a sequence contains one or more nodes:

```
Sequence: Node(s)
```

A node starts with a semicolon and continues with a list of properties. A property is a property identifier followed by a list of values. For example, the RU[Japanese] property—with the property identifier RU—specifies that we're using Japanese rules in this game.

```
Node: ";" Property(s)
Property: PropIdent PropValue(s)
```

We've covered most of the high-level structure of the file; we have to start really defining things now. For instance, we need to be able to say that a property identifier is a bunch of capitalized letters. If we were trying to do the parsing by hand, now would be the time to start thinking about using regular expressions. Thankfully, Parse::RecDescent allows us to do just that:

```
PropIdent : /[A-Z]+/
```

Next come our property values: these are surrounded by square brackets and contain any amount of text; however, the text itself may contain square brackets. We can mess about with the grammar to make this work, or we can just use the Text:: Balanced module.

Text::Balanced

Text::Balanced is another module that should be in your toolbox if you have to deal with any kind of structured data. It's a companion module to Parse::RecDescent, which takes care of extracting "balanced" text sequences. For instance, given a string:

```
(lambda (x) (append x '(hacker))) ((lambda (x) (append '(just another) x))
'(LISP))
```

the expression ($first, $rest) = extract_bracketed($jalh, "()") will return (lambda (x) (append x '(hacker))) in $first, and the rest of the string in $rest.

Text::Balanced also contains routines for extracting quoted strings while allowing backslash escapes, Perl quotelike strings (qq|xyz| and the like), XML-tagged text, and much more.

The Text::Balanced way of extracting a square-bracketed expression is:

```
extract_bracketed($text, '[]');
```

and Parse::RecDescent allows us to plug that directly into the grammar:

```
PropValue : { extract_bracketed($text, '[]') }
```

Parse::RecDescent automatically fills the magic variable $text with the input to the parser.

We've now reached the bottom of the structure, which completes our grammar. Let's look again at the rules we've defined:

```
my $grammar = q{
    GameTree  : "(" Sequence GameTree(s?) ")"
    Sequence  : Node(s)
    Node      : ";" Property(s)
    Property  : PropIdent PropValue(s)
    PropIdent : /[A-Z]+/
    PropValue: { extract_bracketed($text, '[]') }
}
```

Now that we have the grammar wrapped up in a Perl string, we can feed it to Parse::RecDescent:

```
my $sgf_parser = Parse::RecDescent->new($grammar);
```

This returns an object with methods for each of our rules: we can call $sgf_parser->GameTree to begin parsing a whole file, and this method will in turn call $sgf_parser->Sequence, which will call $sgf_parser->Node and so on. So let's give it a valid SGF file—encoding the famous Shusaku opening—and see what it makes of it:

```
use strict;
use Parse::RecDescent;
```

```
my $grammar = q{
    GameTree  : "(" Sequence GameTree(s?) ")"
    Sequence  : Node(s)
    Node      : ";" Property(s)
    Property  : PropIdent PropValue(s)
    PropIdent : /[A-Z]+/
    PropValue: { extract_bracketed($text, '[]') }
};
my $sgf_parser = Parse::RecDescent->new($grammar);

undef $/; my $sgf = <DATA>;
print $sgf_parser->GameTree($sgf);

__DATA__
(;GM[1]FF[4]AP[CGoban:2]ST[2]RU[Japanese]
PW[Honinbo Shuwa]PB[Yasuda Shusaku]
WR[7d]BR[5d]
;B[qd];W[dc];B[pq];W[oc];B[cp];W[qo]
;B[pe]C[This is the famous "Shusaku opening".])
```

When we run this, we may be surprised to find out that it prints nothing but a single parenthesis:

```
)
```

because we haven't defined what we want to *do* with the parsed data yet. This is only fair enough; Parse::RecDescent is offering us the last token it saw, which was a close parenthesis. If, on the other hand, we give it a broken SGF file:

```
(;GM[1]FF[4]AP[CGoban:2]ST[2]RU[Japanese]
PW[Honinbo Shuwa]PB[Yasuda Shusaku]
WR[7d]BR[5d]
;B[qd];W[dc];B[pq];W[oc];B[cp];W[qo]
;B[pe]C[This)
```

then we get no output at all—it could not be parsed.

Let's briefly run over how we constructed that grammar, then we'll see how we can turn the parser into something more useful.

Types of match

So far we've seen several different ways to match portions of a data stream:

- Plain quoted text, such as the semicolon at the start of a node
- Regular expressions, as used to get the property name
- Subrules, to reference other parts of the grammar
- Code blocks, to use ordinary Perl expressions to extract text

We also used several types of repetition directive, as shown in Table 2-1.

Table 2-1. Types of repetition directive

Directive	Meaning
(s)	Tells Parse::RecDescent that we want to find one or more of the given subrules
(s?)	To mean 0 or more
(?)	To mean 1 or 0
(5)	To match precisely 5 times
(5..)	To match 5 or more
(..5)	To match 0 to 5
(5..10)	To match between 5 and 10 times

These repetition specifiers can only be applied to subrule-type matches.

Actions

What we've constructed so far is strictly called a *recognizer*. We can tell whether or not some input conforms to the given structure. Now we need to tell Parse::RecDescent what to do with the data once it's been recognized, and we do this with *actions*.

At its simplest, an action is a block of Perl code that sits at the end of a grammar rule. For instance, we could say:

```
Node       : ";" Property(s) { print "I saw a node!\n" }
```

When this runs with the input from the previous section "Simple Parsing with Parse:: RecDescent," we see the output:

```
I saw a node!
I saw a node!
I saw a node!
I saw a node!
I saw a node!
I saw a node!
I saw a node!
I saw a node!
)
```

This is quite reassuring, as there are actually eight nodes in our example SGF file.

We can also get at the results of each match, using the @item array:

```
Property   : PropIdent PropValue(s)
                    { print "I saw a property of type $item[1]!\n" }
```

Notice that this array is essentially one-based: the data matched by PropIdent is element one, not element zero. Anyway, this now gives:

```
I saw a property of type GM!
I saw a property of type FF!
I saw a property of type AP!
```

```
I saw a property of type ST!
I saw a property of type RU!
I saw a property of type PW!
I saw a property of type PB!
I saw a property of type WR!
I saw a property of type BR!
I saw a node!
I saw a property of type B!
...
```

As we saw with the curious case of the) returned by our recognizer, by default
Parse::RecDescent sets the value of a match equal to the last token matched. This
works just fine for simple rules like PropIdent, but for complex rules such as
GameTree, it falls down pretty flat. Not to worry! There's one final piece of the puz-
zle: you can set the magic variable $return to be the output that you want each rule
to return.

For instance, let's concentrate on the Property rule. We'd like this to return some
kind of data structure that represents the property: its type and its value. So, we say
something like this:

```
Property   : PropIdent PropValue(s)
               { $return = { type => $item[1], value => $item[2] } }
```

Now, there's nothing forcing us to start by parsing an entire GameTree. Remember
that Parse::RecDescent's new method returns an object with a method for each rule?
We can just parse a single Property:

```
my $prop = $sgf_parser->Property("RU[Japanese]");
print "I am a property of type $prop->{type}, ";
print "with values $prop->{value}";
```

And Perl tells us:

```
I am a property of type RU, with values ARRAY(0x2209d4)
```

Because we specified that the PropValue may be repeated, Parse::RecDescent has
helpfully put all its values into an array reference for us. Well, that's great, but to be
honest, the majority of properties in real SGF files only have one value each, so we
can make the output a bit friendlier by replacing the array reference $items[2] by its
first element if it only has the one element.

```
Property   : PropIdent PropValue(s)
               { $return = { type => $item[1], value => @{$item[2]}==1 ?
                 $item[2][0] : $item[2] } }
```

This time we have something a little easier to deal with:

```
I am a property of type RU, with values [Japanese]
```

Oops! We forgot that extract_bracketed keeps the square brackets around the extracted text. So let's look again at the PropValue rule:

```
PropValue : { extract_bracketed($text, '[]') }
```

This is a code block match—a block of Perl code that determines whether or not something matches—but it looks just like the actions that we've been adding. So how does Parse::RecDescent know whether something's a code block match or an action?

Well, there's a dirty little secret here—code block matches and actions are precisely the same thing. When Parse::RecDescent sees a block of Perl code as it's working its way though a rule, it immediately executes it. If it returns true, then we consider that to be a successful match. So, as a general principle, it's important that your actions return a true value, or otherwise they'll make the match fail.

So, we can strip off the brackets inside the PropValue rule, only when the call to extract_bracketed was successful:

```
PropValue : { my $value = extract_bracketed($text, '[]');
              ($return) = $value =~ /^\[(.*)\]/ if $value; }
```

And this will now do what we expected. One final change to the GameTree rule:

```
GameTree  : "(" Sequence GameTree(s?) ")"
                { $return = { mainline => $item[2], variations => $item[3] } }
```

so that Parse::RecDescent returns a handy data structure representing any valid SGF file:[*]

```
$VAR1 = {
          'variations' => [],
          'mainline' => [
                          [
                            {
                              'value' => '1',
                              'type' => 'GM'
                            },
                            {
                              'value' => '4',
                              'type' => 'FF'
                            },
                            {
                              'value' => 'CGoban:2',
                              'type' => 'AP'
                            },
                            {
                              'value' => '2',
                              'type' => 'ST'
                            },
    ...
```

---

[*] In fact, my module Games::Go::SGF does something similar to this.

For reference, the final program looks like this:

```
use strict;
use Parse::RecDescent;
my $grammar = q{
    GameTree  : "(" Sequence GameTree(s?) ")"
                { $return = { mainline => $item[2], variations => $item[3] } }
    Sequence  : Node(s)
    Node      : ";" Property(s)
    Property  : PropIdent PropValue(s)
                { $return = { type => $item[1], value => @{$item[2]}==1 ?
                $item[2][0] : $item[2] } }
    PropIdent : /[A-Z]+/
    PropValue : { my $value = extract_bracketed($text, '[]');
       ($return) = ($value =~ /^\[(.*)\]/) if $value; }
};
my $sgf_parser = Parse::RecDescent->new($grammar);

undef $/; my $sgf = <DATA>;
use Data::Dumper;

my $tree = $sgf_parser->GameTree($sgf);
print Dumper($tree);
```

Debugging

It's all very well to be presented with a completed grammar like that, but what about debugging? Well, I'll be honest and admit that I did make a few mistakes when I wrote the preceding example. First time through, I got too clever with extract_bracketed in PropValue, so it looked like this:

```
PropValue : { my ($value) = extract_bracketed($text, '[]');
   ($return) = ($value =~ /^\[(.*)\]/) }
```

You see, extract_bracketed is context sensitive. In scalar context it modifies its input, stripping out the bracketed section that it found, but in list context it leaves the original input alone returning two values: what matched and what remained. In my list-context version, $text wasn't being changed, and the output looked something like this:

```
$VAR1 = undef;
```

Oops. How do you debug something like that? Thankfully, Parse::RecDescent has a very capable built-in tracing system, which spits out masses of debugging output. You can turn this on with the global variable $RD_TRACE, or from the command line using the -s flag to Perl, like this:

```
% perl -s test.pl -RD_TRACE
```

The output is in two parts. The first is how Parse::RecDescent understood the grammar:

```
Parse::RecDescent: Treating "GameTree :" as a rule declaration
Parse::RecDescent: Treating ""("" as an interpolated literal terminal
Parse::RecDescent: Treating "Sequence" as a subrule match
```

This is nearly always correct, so we don't need to worry about that. The next part comes when Parse::RecDescent is attempting to process some text. It tells us which rule it's processing, what it's doing, and what input it has:

```
| GameTree |Trying rule: [GameTree]          |
| GameTree |                                 |"(;GM[1]FF[4]AP[CGoban:2]ST[2
|          |                                 |]RU[Japanese]\nPW[Honinbo
|          |                                 |Shuwa]PB[Yasuda
|          |                                 |Shusaku]\nWR[7d]BR[5d]\n;B[qd
|          |                                 |];W[dc];B[pq];W[oc];B[cp];W[q
|          |                                 |o]\n;B[pe]C[This is the
|          |                                 |famous "Shusaku
|          |                                 |Opening".])\n"
| GameTree |Trying production: ['(' Sequence |
|          |GameTree ')']                    |
| GameTree |Trying terminal: ['(']           |
| GameTree |>>Matched terminal<< (return value: |
|          |[(])                             |
```

This tells us that it's in the middle of trying to match a GameTree, and that in doing so, it has to try to match '(' Sequence GameTree ')'. So, it looks for the first thing, a *terminal symbol,* (, and it finds one.

When you're trying to work out why something didn't match, it's sometimes easier to work from the bottom up, because Parse::RecDescent will give up soon after failing the test that's broken. About three-quarters of the way through the trace, we find the following:

```
|   Node   |>>Matched repeated subrule:      |
|          |[Property]<< (1 times)           |
```

This is a problem, because we know the first node has more than one property. So we look up a bit more, and we see:

```
| Property |Trying action                    |
| Property |>>Matched action<< (return value: |
|          |[HASH(0x20b324)])                |
| Property |>>Matched production: [PropIdent |
|          |PropValue]<<                     |
| Property |>>Matched rule<< (return value:  |
|          |[HASH(0x20b324)])                |
| Property |(consumed: [GM])                 |
```

Aha! It thinks that it's matched a valid property, but all that it's consumed is "GM"—it hasn't sucked up the "[1]" at all.

This should tell us that there's something wrong with the way the grammar is parsing the property value and, moreover, that it's matching without sucking up any text. That's precisely what the bug was.

More Difficult Parsing

Of course, this isn't all you can do with Parse::RecDescent; the module has a sophisticated system of directives, options, and magic variables to help you get around any parsing problem.

Commit, reject, and error

One of the problems with recursive descent grammars is that they can be terribly slow; there are a huge number of possible matches in any decent-sized grammar, and Parse::RecDescent has to try absolutely all of them. It certainly ends up trying a lot of parses that can't possibly make sense.

To ameliorate this problem, Parse::RecDescent has a series of directives that can help us prune the tree of possibilities. All directives have the same format: a keyword in angle brackets. For instance, the directive <commit> specifies that there's no turning back from what we've just seen. Suppose we have the following rules for method calling in an OO programming language:

```
Method:
        Variable '.' Methodname '(' Arguments ')'
        | Variable '.' Property
        | ClassIdentifier '.' Methodname '(' Arguments ')'
        | ClassIdentifier '.' Property
```

Now, if we have some text $obj.frob(gargle gargle howl) we know that it's *supposed* to be a method call of the first type. If something goes wrong parsing the arguments, then there's no point coming back and seeing if it's a property call on an object, or whether it's some kind of class method.

In fact, as soon as we've seen Variable . Methodname (then there's no turning back; we can be sure that this is supposed to be a method call on an object, with arguments. At this point, we can *commit* to this parse. The same goes for class methods, and we can optimize our grammar like so:

```
Method:
        Variable '.' Methodname '(' <commit> Arguments ')'
        | Variable '.' Property
        | ClassIdentifier '.' Methodname '(' <commit> Arguments ')'
        | ClassIdentifier '.' Property
```

The effect of a commit is to cause the whole production to fail if the current subrule fails; if Arguments doesn't parse or we don't see a closing bracket, then the Method rule fails, without checking the other options. This massively cuts down the number of possibilities that Parse::RecDescent has to try.

 One oft-encountered gotcha is that directives take a place in the @item array; to refer to Arguments in the first rule, you need to specify $item[6], not $item[5].

Unfortunately, there are times when we want this pruning behavior, but we also want to try the other options. The typical example of this is an if-then-else-end sequence. Let's try and write a grammar for this sort of sequence:

```
Conditional:
        "if" Cond "then" Block "end"
        | "if" Cond "then" Block "else" Block "end"
```

As soon as we see the if, we know we're parsing a conditional. So, we can say:

```
Conditional:
        "if" <commit> Cond "then" Block "end"
        | "if" <commit> Cond "then" Block "else" Block "end"
```

Unfortunately, this will never parse an else block properly. We'll commit to the first option and parse the conditional, the then, and the block, but instead of seeing end as we expect, we see else. This fails, and since we're committed, the whole rule fails.

So, while we want to commit to an if statement, we want the ability to change our minds later, reversing the commitment when there's a valid option. The directive to do this is called uncommit, and so our final grammar looks like this:

```
Conditional:
        "if" <commit> Cond "then" Block <uncommit> "end"
        | "if" <commit> Cond "then" Block "else" Block "end"
```

The opposite of commit, however, is called reject, and that states that we can't even go down this road at all. One usage of this would be to restrict a rule to a subset of its possibilities. Suppose we've got the rule control_modifier, which matches if, unless, while, and until statement modifiers. If there's a time when we want to match just the conditionals, you could say:

```
conditional_modifier:
        "while" <reject>
        | "until" <reject>
        | control_modifier
```

Of course, this is horribly lazy—we should just have defined `control_modifier` as a superset of `conditional_modifier`, not the other way around. Worse, it's inefficient, since when we get to `control_modifier`, we have to check for `while` and `until` again.

So what is `<reject>` actually useful for, then? The most useful application of it is using a rule purely for its side effects without being interested in whether it matches. For instance, you might want to use a rule to set up some global variable that will affect the parsing later:

```
conditional_modifier:  { $::in_modifier = 1 }  <reject>
    | "if" expr
        { ... $::in_modifier = 0; }
    | "unless" expr
        { ... $::in_modifier = 0; }
```

Now `expr` can take note of the `$::in_modifier` variable and alter its parsing behavior accordingly.

Similarly, if you get overwhelmed by debugging the grammar with `RD_TRACE`, you can insert simple debugging statements followed by a reject directive:

```
conditional_modifier:
    { warn "I'm trying to parse a conditional modifier!" }  <reject>
    | "if" expr
    | "unless" expr
```

Another way of trimming the grammar, similar to `<commit>`, is to report an error when something impossible happens. Just like `<commit>`, the idea is to fail as quickly as possible, hence saving on backtracking. The predictably named `<error>` directive helps us to do this:

```
subroutine: "sub" sub_declaration

block: <perl_codeblock>

sub_name: /[a-zA-Z_]\w+/

sub_declaration : block
                | sub_name block
                | <error>
```

`<perl_codeblock>` is a directive that extracts one block in curly braces.

Now if we say `sub 01234 { }`, we get:

```
ERROR (line 1): Invalid sub declaration: Was expecting block, or sub
                name
```

The `<error>` directive automatically derives a sensible and useful error message from the grammar. If you don't want that, write your own error message:

```
subroutine: "sub" sub_declaration
```

```
block: <perl_codeblock>

sub_name: /[a-zA-Z_]\w+/

sub_declaration : block
               | sub_name block
               | <error: Bad subroutine definition>
```

If you're using `<commit>` and `<error>` together, you can use the variant `<error?>` form to provide a useful error message for failed committed matches:

```
Method:
        Variable '.' Methodname '(' <commit> Arguments ')'
        | Variable '.' Property
        | ClassIdentifier '.' Methodname '(' <commit> Arguments ')'
        | ClassIdentifier '.' Property
        | <error?>
```

This won't produce an error message unless we're in a committed state, but it will wail if something goes wrong with argument processing:

```
ERROR (line 1): Invalid Method: Was expecting Arguments but found "foo
                bar)" instead
```

Creative use of `<commit>` and `<error>` can greatly speed up a highly complex grammar.

Syntactic whitespace

In the examples we've seen so far, whitespace hasn't been significant: Parse::RecDescent happily skipped over spaces, tabs, and newlines alike. Unfortunately, whitespace is significant for some data formats. In particular, there are some data formats in which, for instance, newlines mark the end of a particular *rule*.

Headers in a mail message are one such format: a newline marks the end of a header, unless there's a continuation line following. A continuation line is marked by yet more significant whitespace: a space at the beginning of the line. There's also a significant newline between the header and the body.

What we need to do is to tell Parse::RecDescent what whitespace it can skip over and what is significant. The variable used to tell Parse::RecDescent of this is $Parse::RecDescent::skip.

The normal setting is to skip over any whitespace: /\s*/. However, in this case, it can't skip over anything!

```
$Parse::RecDescent::skip = '';
```

If we say this, we now have to specify newlines and possible spaces explicitly in our grammar.

```
message : header "\n" body
header : header_line(s)
```

```
header_line : field ":" value "\n" continuation
            | field ":" value "\n"
field: /\w+/
value: /.*/;
continuation : " " /.*/ "\n" continuation(?)
body : body_line(s?)
body_line : /.*/ "\n"
```

We'll see more applications of significant whitespace in our example grammars.

Automating the process

What we've seen so far is great, but we're still doing a lot of work ourselves. This isn't particularly lazy, and laziness, as you know, is a key virtue of a Perl programmer. So let's let the module do some of the work.

The first thing we can do is set a default action; the magic variable $::RD_AUTOACTION can be set to a string that will be evaled and used as the action for any rule that doesn't have one. If we set a sufficiently general autoaction, we can let Parse::RecDescent get on with parsing the input while we massage the data structure when it's done.

In fact, the sufficiently general autoaction turns out to be this:

```
$::RD_AUTOACTION = '[@item]';
```

This sticks everything that gets parsed into an array reference and builds up a list-of-lists representing the parse tree. Of course, this will give us every single item in the input whether we want it or not, but the point is that we're going to post-process it. If we use autoactions in our Shusaku example, we get something a little like this:

```
$VAR1 = [
          'GameTree',
          '(',
          [
            'Sequence',
            [
              [
                'Node',
                ';',
                [
                  [
                    'Property',
                    [
                      'PropIdent',
                      'GM'
                    ],
                    [
                      '1'
                    ]
                  ],
...
```

Another interesting autoaction idea is to bless what got parsed into a class representing the rule. The autoaction looks like this:

```
$::RD_AUTOACTION = 'bless [@item[1..$#item]], "SGFParser::$item[0]";';
```

You'll then end up with an `SGFParser::GameTree` object. It's then a trivial matter to add the appropriate methods to get a bunch of `SGFParser::Sequence` objects, explore the `SGFParser::Nodes`, and so on.

Of course, we could be lazier still. The `<autotree>` directive, placed at the top of a grammar, will generate a parse tree and bless nodes into appropriately named classes. Here's our grammar now:

```
my $grammar = q{
    <autotree>

    GameTree  : "(" Sequence GameTree(s?) ")"
    Sequence  : Node(s)
    Node      : ";" Property(s)
    Property  : PropIdent PropValue(s)
    PropIdent : /[A-Z]+/
    PropValue : { my $value = extract_bracketed($text, '[]');
      ($return) = ($value =~ /^\[(.*)\]/) if $value; }
};
```

Each object is a hash looking something like this:

```
$tree= {
    __RULE__  => "GameTree",
    __STRING1__ => "(",
    Sequence => Sequence=HASH(0x23feb8),
    GameTree => ARRAY(0x24fcd4),
    __STRING2__ => ")"
};
```

There's obviously a trade-off here between laziness in specifying actions and control over the data structure you get back, so autoactions and autotrees need to be used carefully.

On the other hand, the final piece of laziness is extremely useful when developing a grammar. Let's suppose we're still working out how to specify an SGF property for our grammar, but we want to make sure everything else works first. So, we write a test grammar like this:

```
my $grammar = q{
    GameTree  : "(" Sequence GameTree(s?) ")"
    Sequence  : Node(s)
    Node      : ";" Property(s)
    Property  : "foo"
};
```

And now we can test our parser with dummy pseudo-SGF files:

```
(;foo;foo;foo(;foo;foo foo))
```

and so on. When we're happy that this does what we want, we can work on developing the property specification properly. If you're constructing a very complex grammar, you might want to do this sort of thing for quite a few rules. This is where autostubbing comes in.

All we need do is set `$::RD_AUTOSTUB`, and `Parse::RecDescent` will allow us to replace undefined rules by their names. That's to say:

```
$::RD_AUTOSTUB = 1;
my $grammar = q{
    GameTree  : "(" Sequence GameTree(s?) ")"
    Sequence  : Node(s)
    Node      : ";" Property(s)
};
```

will enable us to match:

```
(;Property;Property;Property(Property;Property;Property Property))
```

When we're done, simply remove the `$::RD_AUTOSTUB` line, and `Parse::RecDescent` will go back to warning us about undefined rules!

And much more...

There are many more obscure features of `Parse::RecDescent` that you'll probably never use but may be useful in some particularly troublesome situation.

For instance, `Parse::RecDescent` populates not just the `@item` array but also a wide variety of local variables to help with the parsing. Perhaps the most useful of these is the `%item` hash. Suppose we've got a rule:

```
structure: type "{" definition(s) "}" name modifier(s?) ";"
```

That's not so bad—if we want to get at the value of the modifiers, we just say `$item[6]`. But suppose we add a rule in the future; are we going to remember to update all the offsets and turn it into `$item[7]`? What if we add a directive? Are we going to remember that this also changes the offsets?

`%item` stops us worrying about this; we can just refer to `$item{modifier}` and we'll get the right thing. Of course, if we have a rule with two `modifiers` in it, this method won't work so well—`Parse::RecDescent` only records the value of the second `modifier` in the hash.

We've already met the `$return` variable, which stores the return code; there's also `$text`, which stores the remaining text being parsed. This allows us to modify the incoming text stream. The standard example of this is an `#include`-style facility:

```
include: "#include" filespec { $text = main::include_file($item[2]) . $text; }
```

Notice that, since `Parse::RecDescent`'s runtime is in its own little package, we must explicitly state where to find `include_file`.

Another useful feature is the ability to have rules that are called when the parser starts up—these start-up rules are placed outside any rule, like so:

```
{ my ($fish, $fowl) = (0, 0); print "Checking for fishes and fowls\n"; }

list: item(s)
    {
        print "Found $fish fish and $fowl fowl\n";
    }

item:  "fish"
            { $fish++; }
    | "fowl"
            { $fowl++; }
    | <error: "Neither fish nor fowl">
```

There are a wealth of other features: scoring of ambiguous rules, parsing of blocks and Perl-like structures, explicit specification of operator precedence, passing parameters between rules, and so on. However, the basic features of `Parse::RecDescent` as we've described them will be able to help you solve a huge number of parsing challenges.

Some Examples

To finish off our survey of `Parse::RecDescent`, here are a few full examples of parsing real-life data. We've seen a bunch of techniques for creating parsers with `Parse::RecDescent`, but how do we actually go about creating real-life parsers? The following two examples show data formats that I recently needed to parse, and how I went about it.

Parsing iCalendar data

Apple's iCal application for calendaring and scheduling events speaks a standard data format called iCalendar (RFC 2445), *www.ietf.org/rfc/rfc2445.txt*. This is a fairly simple line-based protocol that looks a little like this:

```
BEGIN:VCALENDAR
CALSCALE:GREGORIAN
X-WR-TIMEZONE;VALUE=TEXT:Europe/London
METHOD:PUBLISH
PRODID:-//Apple Computer\, Inc//iCal 1.0//EN
X-WR-CALNAME;VALUE=TEXT:Home
VERSION:2.0
BEGIN:VEVENT
SEQUENCE:5
DTSTART;TZID=Europe/London:20020923T193000
DTSTAMP:20020913T204302Z
SUMMARY:Bert Jansch at the Camden Jazz Cafe
UID:543A3F74-D09B-11D6-8A6E-000393D74DB6
STATUS:CONFIRMED
DTEND;TZID=Europe/London:20020923T223000
```

```
END:VEVENT
...
END:VCALENDAR
```

I needed to get some simple information out of these calendar files. `Net::ICal` is an extensive set of modules to read and write iCalendar data—and generally the tool of choice for such tasks—but for my limited needs it made sense to extract the information with a quick grammar.

As you can see, the format is essentially colon-separated key-value lines, with options denoted by `;NAME=OPTION` before the value. Normally we'd parse it with the techniques in the first section of this chapter, but because there's a bit more structure—the calendar is split up into events, and each event has a set of data associated with it—a more structured approach is needed.

We'll start off with a simple approximation:

```
calendarfile: calendar(s)
calendar: "BEGIN:VCALENDAR\n" line(s) "END:VCALENDAR\n"
line: /\w+/ option(s?) ":" /.*/ "\n"
option: ";" /\w+/ "=" /[^;:]+/
```

Because newlines are significant, we need to remember to set the `$Parse::RecDescent::skip` variable to `'[ \t]+'`.

Now, this simple approximation looks good, but it has a bit of a problem. Given a simple calendar:

```
BEGIN:VCALENDAR
NAME:Test
END:VCALENDAR
```

the parser will fail. Why? Because the `line(s)` subrule consumes *both* the `NAME` line and the `END` line. `Parse::RecDescent` grammars don't backtrack in the same way as regular expressions and won't give up the `END` line for another reparse. This is where we need to use `<reject>`. This is one way to do it:

```
line: "END" <reject>
    | /\w+/ option(s?) ":" /.*/ "\n"
```

but we can be a bit neater; `<reject>` allows us to specify a conditional, like so:

```
line: /\w+/ <reject: $item[1] eq "END"> option(s?) ":" /.*/ "\n"
```

Now our simple test works. Let's add some event handling to it:

```
calendarfile: calendar(s)
calendar: "BEGIN:VCALENDAR\n" line(s) "END:VCALENDAR\n"

line: event | dataline

event: "BEGIN:VEVENT\n" dataline(s) "END:VEVENT\n"
dataline: /\w+/ <reject: $item[1] eq "END"> option(s?) ":" /.*/
option: ";" /\w+/ "=" /[^;:]+/
```

There are other types of iCalendar events—VJOURNAL, VALARM, and so on; they all have more or less the same format, but inspecting the data that I needed to parse, I found that iCal didn't use these in my case. It's easy enough to make the parser completist, but I wasn't really interested in doing that at the time. Similarly, the RFC defines which individual data lines are allowed, but for this example, let's be pragmatic and accept whatever items iCal wants to throw at us.

Now it's time to try it on some real calendar data—and we find quickly that it fails. So, we bring out RD_TRACE, and we find that the last thing that matched was:

```
| dataline |Trying rule: [dataline]              |
| dataline |Trying production: [/[\w]+/          |
|          |<reject:<reject: $item[1] eq "END">> |
|          |option ':' /.*/]                     |
| dataline |Trying terminal: [/[\w]+/]           |
| dataline |>>Matched terminal<< (return value:  |
|          |[X])                                 |
| dataline |                                     |"-WR-
```

The line in question was:

```
X-WR-TIMEZONE;VALUE=TEXT:Europe/London
```

Oops! \w+ wasn't quite right for the key names. Let's try [\w-]+.

```
use Parse::RecDescent;
my $grammar = q{
calendarfile: calendar(s)
calendar: "BEGIN:VCALENDAR\n" line(s) "END:VCALENDAR\n"
line: event | dataline
event: "BEGIN:VEVENT\n" dataline(s) "END:VEVENT\n"
dataline: /[\w-]+/ <reject: $item[1] eq "END"> option(s?) ":" /.*/
option: ";" /\w+/ "=" /[^;:]+/
};

my $p = Parse::RecDescent->new($grammar);
use Data::Dumper;
open IN, "test.ics" or die $!;
undef $/;
print Dumper($p->calendarfile(<IN>));
```

And now this works...partially:

```
$VAR1 = [
            'END:VCALENDAR
    '
        ];
```

We now need some actions to sort out the output data structure.

Let's start at the bottom. We want to turn the options (the name=option pairs) into a hash, so we'll put each option into its own hash ref for the time being:

```
option: ";" /\w+/ "=" /[^;:]+/
    { $return = { $item[2] => $item[4] }; }
};
```

And when we aggregate the options into a data line, we can turn the array of hash references into a single hashref:

```
dataline: /[\w-]+/ <reject: $item[1] eq "END"> option(s?) ":" /.*/
    { my %options = map { %$_ } @{$item{3} };
      $return = {
        key => $item[1],
        value => $item[5],
        options => \%options
      }; }
```

An event is an array of data lines, but we want to turn that into one big hash reference. So we look at each one, turn the "key" element into the key, and file it into a hashref:

```
event: "BEGIN:VEVENT\n" dataline(s) "END:VEVENT\n"
    { $return = {};
      for (@{$item[2]}) {
        $return->{delete $_->{key}} = $_;
      }
    }
```

Now things get a little tricky; each line in a calendar can be a data line of information about the whole calendar, or it can be part of an event. So we need to propagate up information about what we've just parsed so we can assemble it appropriately later. event and dataline both return hash references, so we can just add another element into that hash stating what we've got:

```
line: event    { $return = { type => "event", %{$item[1]} }; }  |
      dataline { $return = { type => "data",  %{$item[1]} }; }
```

Finally, we'll end up with an array full of events or calendar-wide data, and we need to put that together into one big data structure, using the same sort of tricks we used for event. This time, however, we push events onto an array. And, just for a touch of class, we'll sort the events array by date:

```
calendarfile: calendar(s)
calendar: "BEGIN:VCALENDAR\n" line(s) "END:VCALENDAR\n"
    {   $return = {};
        my @events;
        for (@{$item[2]}) {
            my $type = delete $_->{type};
            if ($type eq "event") {
                push @events, $_;
            } else {
                $return->{delete $_->{key}} = $_;
            }
        }
        $return->{events} = [ sort {$a->{DTSTART}->{value} cmp
                                    $b->{DTSTART}->{value}} @events ];
    }
```

And now we have an iCalendar parser that will handle what I got out of iCal:

```
my $p = Parse::RecDescent->new($grammar);
use Data::Dumper;
open IN, "test.ics" or die $!;
undef $/;
my $cal = $p->calendarfile(<IN>);
for (@{$cal->[0]{events}}) {
    my $when = $_->{DTSTART}->{value};
    my $what = $_->{SUMMARY}->{value};
    $when =~ s/T.*//; # Don't care about time of day
    $when =~ s/(\d{4})(\d{2})(\d{2})/$1-$2-$3/;
    $what =~ s/\\//g;
    print "$when: $what\n";
}
```

```
2002-09-14: Leaving Drinks at the Porterhouse
2002-09-21: Star Wars
2002-09-23: Bert Jansch at the Camden Jazz Cafe
2002-09-28: .pad Party?
2002-10-03: Go Home
```

.procmailrc

When I wrote the Mail::Audit mail filtering library, I wanted to build in the ability for those using procmail to convert their configuration files over automatically. This time, instead of using Parse::RecDescent to produce a data structure, we're going to use it to create a Mail::Audit filter—more generically known as a Perl program.

As usual, we'll start with a top-down description of a procmail configuration file. Thankfully, the *procmailrc(5)* manual page is extremely clear in detailing the syntax of the file, including some sections we can basically steal almost verbatim:

> A word beginning with # and all the following characters up to a NEWLINE are ignored. This does not apply to condition lines, which cannot be commented.

> A line starting with ':' marks the beginning of a recipe. It has the following format:
> ```
>             :0 [flags] [ : [locallockfile] ]
>             <zero or more conditions (one per line)>
>             <exactly one action line>
> ```

> Conditions start with a leading '*', everything after that character is passed on to the internal egrep literally, except for leading and trailing whitespace.

From this and a little more digging in the main page, we can derive the following rules:

```
            program: thing(s)
            thing: recipe | assignment | blank
            blank : /^\s+/
            assignment: /^(.*)=(.*)/
```

```
recipe : ':0' flags(?) locallock(?) "\n" condition(s) action "\n"
       | ':0' flags(?) locallock(?) "\n" action "\n"
locallock : ':' filename(?)
filename: /[\w/-+\.]+/
flags : /[HBDAaEehbfcwWir]+/
```

(We'll strip comments when we preprocess the data.) We also need to set `$Parse::RecDescent::skip`, because *procmailrcs* are line-oriented.

Next, we'll look at the range of actions that are permissible:

!	Forwards to all the specified mail addresses
|	Starts the specified program, possibly in `$SHELL` if any of the characters `$SHELLMETAS` are spotted
{	Followed by at least one space, tab, or newline will mark the start of a nesting block

Anything else will be taken as a mailbox name (either a filename or a directory, absolute or relative to the current directory (see `MAILDIR`)). If it is a (possibly yet nonexistent) filename, the mail will be appended to it.

Hence, our action rule can be specified as:

```
action : '|' /.*/
       | '!' /.*/
       | '{' /\s+/ program '}'
       | filename
```

Notice that we have a recursive use of `program` here to reflect the recursive nature of nested rules.

All that's left is the rule that determines a condition:

Conditions start with a leading "*", everything after that character is passed on to the internal egrep literally, except for leading and trailing whitespace.

...

There are some special conditions you can use that are not straight regular expressions. To select them, the condition must start with:

!	Invert the condition.
$	Evaluate the remainder of this condition according to `sh(1)` substitution rules inside double quotes, skip leading whitespace, then reparse it.
?	Use the exitcode of the specified program.
<	Check if the total length of the mail is shorter than the specified (in decimal) number of bytes.
>	Analogous to '<'.
variablename??	Match the remainder of this condition against the value of this environment variable...
\	To quote any of the above at the start of the line.

So, we have a definition of a condition, and it looks like this:

```
condition : '*' /[*!?<>\\$]?/ /.*/ "\n"
```

Now, once again, we have a recognizer; we need to add some rules to it. As before, we're not interested in providing absolutely everything that procmail does, just a reasonable sample—most of the time, the 80% solution is just fine.

The easiest to start with is the assignment; this sets an environment variable, interpolating any variables in the right-hand side of the expression:

```
assignment: /^(.*)=(.*)/
    { my $from=$1;
      my $what;
      ($what = $2) =~ s/\$(\w+)/\$ENV{$1}/g;
      $return = "\$ENV{$from}=qq($what)"; }
```

For each recipe, we're going to set up a set of conditions, and then perform a method on a Mail::Audit object if the condition tests true. So, let's have a look at the actions again. If we have a pipe, we want to emit code that pipes the mail to the specified program; if we have a forward, we want to emit code that calls the resend method to forward the mail, and if we have a filename, we call the accept method.

```
action : '|' /.*/
            { $return = qq{\$item->pipe("$item[2]");}   ; }
        | '!' /.*/
            { $return = qq{\$item->resend('$item[2]');} ; }
```

The only slight trick is the nesting action, but this turns out to be pretty simple. Since we've parsed the action recursively, and turned it into a set of Perl statements, we can just return them in place:

```
        | '{' program '}'
            { $return = $item[2] }
        | filename
            { $return = qq{\$item->accept("$item[1]");} }
```

Conditions are tricky, so we'll hand them off to subroutines to deal with and turn into Perl code. We're not interested in all of the flags: the most important at this stage is whether or not this is an if or an elsif condition.

```
flag: /[HBDAaEehbfcwWir]+/
        { %::flags = map { $_ => 1 } split //, $item[1];
          $return = $::flags{E} ? " elsif " : "if"; }

condition : '*' /[*!?<>\\\$]?/ /.*/ "\n"
        { $return = main::parse_condition($item[2], $item[3])}
```

We're going to use the flags in the parse_condition subroutine, and hence we need to store them in a global variable so that that subroutine can see them. However, flags aren't global—they're specific to each recipe. So, at the beginning of each recipe, we need to reset the flags variable. This can be done with an action and a <reject> directive:

```
recipe : { %main::flags = (); } <reject>
```

Now, what is a recipe? As the manual page says, it's a set of conditions that are ANDed together. In Perl terms, that's an if (or elsif if the E flag is set) followed by the conditions we parsed using parse_condition:

```
recipe : ':0' flags(?) locallock(?) "\n" condition(s) action "\n"
    {
      $return = "if " unless @{$item[2]}; # If there are no flags
      $return .= "@{$item[2]} ("; # "if" or "elsif" if there are flags
      $return .= join(" and\n\t", @{$item[5]});
```

Next we perform the action; we'll call upon a subroutine to indent the Perl code returned from the action subrule for readability. Also, if the c flag is set, we continue; otherwise, we exit here.

```
$return .= ")\n{".
    main::indent($item[6] . ($main::flags{c} ? "" :"\n exit 1;\n"))
    ."}\n";
}
```

The same goes for recipes with no conditions, so we end up with a recipe rule looking like this:

```
recipe : ':0' flags(?) locallock(?) "\n" condition(s) action "\n"
    {
      $return = "if " unless @{$item[2]}; # If there are no flags
      $return .= "@{$item[2]} ("; # "if" or "elsif" if there are flags
      $return .= join(" and\n\t", @{$item[5]});
      $return .= ")\n{".
          main::indent($item[6] . ($main::flags{c} ? "" :"\n exit 1;\n"))
          ."}\n";
    }
      | ':0' flags(?) locallock(?) "\n" action "\n"
    {
      if ("@{$item[2]}" eq "else") { $return = "else " }
      $return . = "{ " .
          main::indent($item[5] . ($main::flags{c} ? "" :"\n exit 1;\n"))
          ."}\n";
    }
```

And that's essentially it! All we need is a driver that sets up the input, calls the parser, and spits out some housekeeping code around the generated program, like so:

```
my $parser = Parse::RecDescent->new($grammar) or die;
undef $/;
my $data = <ARGV>;
$data =~ s/#.*//g;
my $program = $parser->program($data);

print 'use Mail::Audit; my $item = Mail::Audit->new();', "\n";
print $program;
print "\n\$item->accept()";
```

The full program can be found in the Mail::Audit distribution and can be used to turn this (from the *procmailex(5)* manual page):

```
:0 c
* ^From.*peter
* ^Subject:.*compilers
! william@somewhere.edu

:0
* ^From.*peter
* ^Subject:.*compilers
petcompil
```

into this:

```
use Mail::Audit; my $item = Mail::Audit->new();
if ($item->header() =~ /^From.*peter/i and
        $item->$item->header() =~ /^Subject:.*compilers/i)
{       $item->resend('william@somewhere.edu');}


if ($item->header() =~ /^From.*peter/i and
        $item->header() =~ /^Subject:.*compilers/i)
{       $item->accept("petcompil");
        exit 1;
}

$item->accept()
```

Parse::Yapp

If you're more familiar with tools like yacc, you may prefer to use François Désarménien's Parse::Yapp module. This is more or less a straight port of yacc to Perl.

---

yacc

yacc, Yet Another Compiler Compiler, is a tool for C programmers to generate a parser from a grammar specification. The grammar specification is much the same as we've seen in our investigation of Parse::RecDescent, but yacc produces bottom-up parsers.

For instance, let's use Parse::Yapp to implement the calculator in Chapter 3 of *lex & yacc* (O'Reilly). This is a very simple calculator with a symbol table, so you can say things like this:

```
a = 25
b = 30
a + b
55
```

Here's their grammar:

```
%{
double vbltable[26];
%}

%union {
    double dval;
    int vblno;
}

%token <vblno> NAME
%token <dval> NUMBER
%left '-' '+'
%left '*' '/'
%nonassoc UMINUS

%type <dval> expression
%%
statement_list:    statement '\n'
    |    statement_list statement '\n'
    ;

statement:    NAME '=' expression    { vbltable[$1] = $3; }
    |    expression        { printf("= %g\n", $1); }
    ;

expression:    expression '+' expression { $$ = $1 + $3; }
    |    expression '-' expression { $$ = $1-$3; }
    |    expression '*' expression { $$ = $1 * $3; }
    |    expression '/' expression
            {    if($3 == 0.0)
                    yyerror("divide by zero");
                else
                    $$ = $1 / $3;
            }
    |    '-' expression %prec UMINUS    { $$ = -$2; }
    |    '(' expression ')'    { $$ = $2; }
    |    NUMBER
    |    NAME            { $$ = vbltable[$1]; }
    ;
%%
```

Converting the grammar is very straightforward; the only serious change we need to consider is how to implement the symbol table. We know that Perl's internal symbol tables are just hashes, so that's good enough for us. The other changes are just cosmetic, and we end up with a Parse::Yapp grammar like this:

```
%{ my %symtab; %}
%token NAME
%token NUMBER
%left '-' '+'
%left '*' '/'
%nonassoc UMINUS
```

```
%%

statement_list: statement '\n'
    | statement_list statement '\n'
    ;

statement: NAME '=' expression { $symtab{$_[1]} = $_[3]; }
    | expression {  print "= ", $_[1], "\n"; }
    ;

expression:
    expression '+' expression { $_[1] + $_[3] }
    | expression '-' expression { $_[1] - $_[3] }
    | expression '*' expression { $_[1] * $_[3] }
    | expression '/' expression
                    {   if ($_[3] == 0)
                            { $_[0]->YYError("divide by zero") }
                        else
                            { $_[1] / $_[3] }
                    }
    | '-' expression %prec UMINUS { -$_[2] }
    | '(' expression ')' { $_[2] }
    | NUMBER
    | NAME { $symtab{$_[1]} }
    ;

%%
```

As you can see, we've declared a hash %symtab to hold the values of the names. Also, notice that that Yacc variables $1, $2, etc. become real subroutine parameters in the @_ array: $_[1], $_[2], and so on.

Next we need to produce a lexer that feeds tokens to the parser. Parse::Yapp expects a subroutine to take input from the data store of the parser object. The Parse::Yapp object is passed in as the first parameter to the lexer, and so the data store ends up looking like $_[0]->YYData->{DATA}.* The lexing subroutine should modify this data store to remove the current token, and then return a two-element list.

The list should consist of the token type followed by the token data. For instance, in our calculator example, we need to tokenize 12345 as ("NUMBER", 12345). Operators, brackets, equals, and return should be returned as themselves, and names of variables need to be returned as ("NAME", "whatever"). At the end of the input, we need to return an empty string and undef: ('', undef).

Here's a reasonably simple Perl routine that does all of that:

```
sub lex {
#    print " Lexer called to handle (".$_[0]->YYData->{DATA}.")\n";
```

---

* There's nothing in Parse::Yapp that says the data has to live in {DATA}, but it's a good practice. If you have extremely complex data as input, you may want to use several different parts of $_[0]->YYData.

```
$_[0]->YYData->{DATA} =~ s/^ +//;
return ('', undef) unless length $_[0]->YYData->{DATA};

$_[0]->YYData->{DATA} =~ s/^(\d+)// and return ("NUMBER", $1);
$_[0]->YYData->{DATA} =~ s/^([\n=+\(\)\-\/*])//    and return ($1, $1);
$_[0]->YYData->{DATA} =~ s/^(\w+)//    and return ("NAME", $1);
die "Unknown token (".$_[0]->YYData->{DATA}.".\n";
}
```

Now that we have our grammar and our lexer, we need to run the grammar through the command-line utility yapp to turn it into a usable Perl module. If all is well, this should be a silent process:

```
% yapp Calc.yapp
%
```

and we should have a new file *Calc.pm* ready for use.

Parse::Lex

Our lexer in this case is pretty simple, so we could code it up in a fairly straightforward subroutine. However, for more difficult lexing operations, it might make sense to use a dedicated lexing language; Parse::Lex is to lex what Parse::Yapp is to yacc. Here's our lexer (crudely) rewritten for Parse::Lex.

```
my @lex = qw(
    NUMBER \d+
    NAME \w+
    "+" "+"
    "-" "-"
    "*" "*"
    "/" "/"
    "=" "="
    "(" "("
    ")" ")"
)
my $lexer = Parse::Lex->new(@lex);
$lexer->from(\*STDIN);

sub lex {
    my $token = $lexer->next;
    return ('', undef) if $lexer->eoi;
    return ($token->name, $token->getstring);
}
```

We can now put it all together: our parser, the lexer, and some code to drive them.

```
sub lex {
    $_[0]->YYData->{DATA} =~ s/^ +//;
    return ('', undef) unless length $_[0]->YYData->{DATA};
```

```
        $_[0]->YYData->{DATA} =~ s/^(\d+)// and return ("NUMBER", $1);
        $_[0]->YYData->{DATA} =~ s/^([\n=+\(\)\-\/*])//    and return ($1, $1);
        $_[0]->YYData->{DATA} =~ s/^(\w+)//     and return ("NAME", $1);
        die "Unknown token (".$_[0]->YYData->{DATA}.")\n";
    }

    use Calc;
    my $p = Calc->new( );
    undef $/;
    $p->YYData->{DATA} = <STDIN>;
    $p->YYParse(YYlex => \&lex);
```

This will take a stream of commands on standard input, run the calculations, and print them out, like this:

```
% perl calc

a = 2+4
b = a * 20
b + 15
^D


=135
```

For most parsing applications, this is all we need. However, in the case of a calculator, you hardly want to put all the calculations in first and get all the answers out at the end. It needs to be more interactive.

What we need to do is modify the lexer so that it can take data from standard input, using the YYData area as a buffer.

```
    sub lex {
        $_[0]->YYData->{DATA} =~ s/^ +//;
        unless (length $_[0]->YYData->{DATA}) {
            return ('', undef) if eof STDIN;
            $_[0]->YYData->{DATA} = <STDIN>;
            $_[0]->YYData->{DATA} =~ s/^ +//;
        }

        $_[0]->YYData->{DATA} =~ s/^(\d+)// and return ("NUMBER", $1);
        $_[0]->YYData->{DATA} =~ s/^([\n=+\(\)\-\/*])//    and return ($1, $1);
        $_[0]->YYData->{DATA} =~ s/^(\w+)//     and return ("NAME", $1);
        die "Unknown token (".$_[0]->YYData->{DATA}.")\n";
    }
```

This time, we check to see if the buffer's empty, and instead of giving up, we get another line from standard input. If we can't read from *that*, then we give up. Now we can intersperse results with commands, giving a much more calculator-like feel to the application.

Other Parsing Techniques

Of course, we don't want to always be writing our own parsers for most of the data we come across, as there's a good chance someone else has come across that sort of data before. The best examples are HTML and XML: there's a vast amount of code out there that deals with these file formats, and most of the hard work has been put into CPAN modules. We'll look at a few of these modules in this section.

HTML::Parser

I'll start by saying something that is anathema to a lot of advanced Perl programmers: in certain circumstances, it is acceptable to use regular expressions to extract the data you want from HTML. I've written a bunch of screen-scraping programs to automate access to various web sites and applications, and because I knew the pages were machine-generated and unlikely to change, I had no qualms about using regular expressions to get what I wanted.

In general, though, you should do things properly. The way to parse HTML properly is to use the HTML::Parser module.

HTML::Parser is incredibly flexible. It supports several methods of operation: you can use OO inheritance, you can use callbacks, you can determine what data gets sent to callbacks and when the callbacks are called, and so on. We'll only look here at the simplest way of using it: by subclassing the module.

Let's begin by examining a way to dump out the URL and link text for every hyperlink in a document. Because we're inheriting from HTML::Parser, we need to say something like this:

```
package DumpLinks;
use strict;
use base 'HTML::Parser';
```

Next, we specify what happens when we see a start tag: if it's not an <a> tag, then we ignore it. If it is, we make a note of its href attribute and remember that we're currently in an <a> tag.

```
sub start {
    my ($self, $tag, $attr) = @_;
    return unless $tag eq "a";
    $self->{_this_url} = $attr->{href};
    $self->{_in_link} = 1;
}
```

Notice that our method is called with the literal name of the current tag, plus a hash of the attributes given in the tag. It's actually called with a few more parameters, but these two are by far the most important; take a look at the HTML::Parser documentation for the rest.

Now let's add a text handler: this is called for any ordinary text that isn't a tag. This needs to store away any text it finds while we're inside a link and do nothing otherwise.

```
sub text {
    my ($self, $text) = @_;
    return unless $self->{_in_link};
    $self->{_urls}->{$self->{_this_url}} .= $text;
}
```

Note that we have to use concatenation so that the following comes out correctly:

```
<a href="http://www.perl.com/">The <code>Perl</code> home page</a>
```

The text handler will be called three times for this chunk: once for The, once for Perl, and once for home page. We want all three of these pieces of text, so we concatenate them together.

Finally, we need an end tag handler to take us out of _in_link mode, like so:

```
sub end {
    my ($self, $tag) = @_;
    $self->{_in_link} = 0 if $tag eq "a";
}
```

Let's look at our complete parser package again before we use it:

```
package DumpLinks;
use strict;
use base 'HTML::Parser';

sub start {
    my ($self, $tag, $attr) = @_;
    return unless $tag eq "a";
    $self->{_this_url} = $attr->{href};
    $self->{_in_link} = 1;
}

sub text {
    my ($self, $text) = @_;
    return unless $self->{_in_link};
    $self->{_urls}->{$self->{_this_url}} .= $text;
}

sub end {
    my ($self, $tag) = @_;
    $self->{_in_link} = 0 if $tag eq "a";
}
```

Using it couldn't be more simple: we instantiate a DumpLinks object, call its parse_file method on the HTML file of our choice, and we'll have a handy hash reference in $parser->{_urls} we can inspect.

```
Use DumpLinks;
my $parser = DumpLinks->new();
$parser->parse_file("index.html");
```

```
for (keys %{$parser->{_urls}}) {
    print qq{Link to $_ (Link text: "}. $parser->{_urls}->{$_}. qq{")\n};
}
```

Running this on the front page of this week's *www.perl.com* edition produces something like this:

```
Link to /cs/user/query/q/6?id_topic=42 (Link text: "Files")
Link to /pub/a/universal/pcb/solution.html (Link text: "Do it now.")
Link to http://www.oreillynet.com/python/ (Link text: "Python")
Link to http://training.perl.com/ (Link text: "Training")
Link to /cs/user/query/q/6?id_topic=68 (Link text: "Sound and Audio")
Link to /cs/user/query/q/6?id_topic=62 (Link text: "User Groups")
Link to http://search.cpan.org/author/DARNOLD/DBD-Chart-0.74 (Link text: "DBD-Chart-
0.74")
Link to http://www.oreilly.com/catalog/perlxml/ (Link text: "Perl & XML")
Link to http://www.oreilly.com/catalog/regex2/ (Link text: "Mastering Regular
Expressions, 2nd Edition")
Link to http://www.openp2p.com/ (Link text: "openp2p.com")
...
```

As if that wasn't easy enough, there are a few other modules you might consider when dealing with HTML text. For doing something like the above, if you don't care about the link text, HTML::LinkExtor can do the job in seconds:

```
use HTML::LinkExtor;
my $parser = HTML::LinkExtor->new();
$parser->parse_file("index.html");
for ($parser->links) {
    my ($tag, %attrs) = @$_;
    print $attrs{href},"\n";
}
```

If you're not interested in writing callbacks, another module worth looking into is HTML::TokeParser, which parses an HTML file one token at a time. Another favorite is HTML::TreeBuilder, which allows you to navigate the document's structure as a tree of Perl objects.

For more on HTML parsing with Perl modules, you should check out Sean Burke's *Perl and LWP* (O'Reilly).

XML Parsing

Of course, nowadays HTML is old hat, and everything is being written in the much more right-on XML. The principles are the same, only the module name changes: instead of using HTML::Parser, there's an XML::Parser module.

This works in the same way as HTML::Parser—you set callbacks for start tags, end tags, and the stuff in between. Of course, for 99% of the things you need to do with

XML, this method is complete overkill. Just like with so many other things in Perl, if you want the flexibility, you can have it, but if you want things to be simple, you can have that, too. Simple is good—and a good module for handling XML simply is called, simply, XML::Simple.

The job of XML::Simple is to turn some XML into a Perl data structure or vice versa. It exports two subroutines: XMLin and XMLout. Let's see how it copes with a real-life XML file. This is a description of the opcodes in Microsoft's Common Interpreted Language, as implemented by the Mono project (*http://www.mono-project.com*[*]):

```
<opdesc>
<opcode name="nop" input="Pop0" output="Push0" args="InlineNone" o1="0xFF" o2="0x00"
flow="next"/>
<opcode name="break" input="Pop0" output="Push0" args="InlineNone" o1="0xFF"
o2="0x01" flow="break"/>
<opcode name="ldarg.0" input="Pop0" output="Push1" args="InlineNone" o1="0xFF"
o2="0x02" flow="next"/>
<opcode name="ldarg.1" input="Pop0" output="Push1" args="InlineNone" o1="0xFF"
o2="0x03" flow="next"/>
...
</opdesc>
```

For instance, this tells us that the ldarg.0 operator takes no arguments from the stack, returns one value to the stack, has no arguments inline, is represented by the assembly code FF 02, and passes control flow to the next operation.

We'll use XML::Simple to read the file and Data::Dumper to take a look at the resulting data structure:

```
% perl -MData::Dumper -MXML::Simple -e
'print Dumper XMLin("/usr/local/share/mono/cil/cil-opcodes.xml")'


$VAR1 = {
          'opcode' => {
                        'stloc.2' => {
                                       'args' => 'InlineNone',
                                       'input' => 'Pop1',
                                       'o1' => '0xFF',
                                       'o2' => '0x0C',
                                       'output' => 'Push0',
                                       'flow' => 'next'
                                     },
                        'stloc.3' => {
                                       'args' => 'InlineNone',
                                       'input' => 'Pop1',
                                       'o1' => '0xFF',
                                       'o2' => '0x0D',
                                       'output' => 'Push0',
```

---

[*] If you've got Mono installed, you can probably find this file as */usr/local/share/mono/cil/cil-opcodes.xml*.

```
                                    'flow' => 'next'
                                },
                       ...
                  }
        };
```

As you can see, this is pretty much exactly what we could have hoped for. So if we want to see how the `shl` operator took its arguments, we can ask:

```
use XML::Simple;
my $opcodes = XMLin("/usr/local/share/mono/cil/cil-opcodes.xml");
my $shl = $opcodes->{opcode}->{shl};
print "shl takes its input by doing a ".$shl->{input}."\n";
print "And it returns the result by doing a ".$shl->{output}."\n";
```

The other function that `XML::Simple` exports is `XMLout`, which, as you might be able to guess, turns a Perl data structure into XML. For instance, we could introduce a new opcode:

```
$opcodes->{opcode}->{hcf} = {
                             'args' => 'InlineNone',
                             'input' => 'Pop0',
                             'o1' => '0xFF',
                             'o2' => '0xFF',
                             'output' => 'Push0',
                             'flow' => 'explode'
                            };

print XMLout($opcodes);
```

And now we'd find another item in that list of XML:

```
<opcode args="InlineNone" input="Pop0" o1="0xFF" o2="0xFF" output="Push0"
flow="explode" name="hcf" />
```

`XML::Simple` is particularly handy for dealing with configuration files—simply state that the config should be given in XML, and use `XML::Simple` to read and write it. The `XMLin` and `XMLout` functions do all the rest.

If you need to do anything more sophisticated with XML parsing, take a look at *Perl and XML*.

And Everything Else...

While we're on the subject of configuration files, there are plenty of other file formats out there that the Perl programmer will need to throw around during her programming life, and config files make up a good number of them. The rest of this chapter suggests a few other techniques for dealing with standard file formats.

First of all, I have a personal favorite, but that's only because I wrote it. `Config::Auto` parses a variety of file formats, if necessary sniffing out what the file format is likely to be. Here's the Samba configuration from a default install of Mac OS X 10.2:

```
% perl -MData::Dumper -MConfig::Auto -e 'print Dumper Config::Auto::parse("/etc/smb.
conf")'

$VAR1 = {
          'global' => {
                        'guest account' => 'unknown',
                        'client code page' => 437,
                        'encrypt passwords' => 'yes',
                        'coding system' => 'utf8'
                      },
          'homes' => {
                        'read only' => 'no',
                        'browseable' => 'no',
                        'comment' => 'User Home Directories',
                        'create mode' => '0750'
                      }
        };
```

Other modules worth looking out for are `AppConfig`, `Parse::Syslog` (which provides access to Unix system logs), `SQL::Statement`, and `Mac::PropertyList`.

Conclusion

In this chapter, we've seen many of the techniques used for parsing structured data with Perl. Whether it's a case of creating your own parsers with `Parse::RecDescent` or `Parse::Yapp`, or choosing a ready-made parsing module, Perl is perfect for throwing around data and converting it into a different format.

## CHAPTER 3

Templating Tools

A recent thread on comp.lang.perl.moderated enumerated the Perl rites of passage—the perfectly good wheels that every journeyman Perl programmer reinvents. These were found to be a templating system, a database abstraction layer, an HTML parser, a processor for command-line arguments, and a time/date handling module.

See if you recognize yourself in the following story: you need to produce a form letter of some description. You've got a certain amount of fixed content, and a certain amount that changes. So you set up a template a little like this:

```
my $template = q{
    Dear $name,

    We have received your request for a quote for $product, and have
    calculated that it can be delivered to you by $date at a cost of
    approximately $cost.

    Thank you for your interest,

    Acme Integrated Foocorp.
};
```

Then you struggle with some disgusting regular expression along the lines of s/(\$\w+)/$1/eeg, and eventually you get something that more or less does the job.

As with all projects, the specifications change two days after it goes live, so you suddenly need to extend your simple template to handle looping over arrays, conditionals, and eventually executing Perl code in the middle of the template itself. Before you realize what's happened, you've created your own templating language.

Don't worry if that's you. Nearly everyone's done it at least once. That's why there's a wide selection of modules on CPAN for templating text and HTML output, ranging from being only slightly more complex than s/(\$\w+)/$1/eeg to complete independent templating languages.

Before we start looking at these modules, though, let's consider the built-in solution—the humble Perl format.

Formats and Text::Autoformat

Formats have been in Perl since version 1.0. They're not used very much these days, but for a lot of what people want from text formatting, they're precisely the right thing.

Perl formats allow you to draw up a picture of the data you want to output, and then paint the data into the format. For instance, in a recent application, I needed to display a set of IDs, dates, email addresses, and email subjects with one line per mail. If we assume that the line is fixed at 80 columns, we may need to truncate some of those fields and pad others to wider than their natural width. In pure Perl, there are basically three ways to get this sort of formatted output. There's sprintf (or printf) and substr:

```
for (@mails) {
    printf "%5i %10s %40s %21s\n",
        $_->id,
        substr($_->received,0,10),
        substr($_->from_address,-40,40),
        substr($_->subject,0,21);
}
```

Then there's pack, which everyone forgets about (and which doesn't give as much control over truncation):

```
for (@mails) {
    print pack("A5 A10 A40 A21\n",
        $_->id, $_->received, $_->from_address, $_->subject);
}
```

And then there's the format:

```
format STDOUT =
@<<<< @<<<<<<<<< @<<<<<<<<<<<<<<<<<<<<<<<<<<<<<<<<<<<<<<<< @<<<<<<<<<<<<<<<<<<<<
$_->id $_->received $_->from_address                      $_->subject
.

for (@mails) {
    write;
}
```

Personally, I think this is much neater and more intuitive than the other two solutions—and has the bonus that it takes the formatting away from the main loop, making the code less cluttered.[*]

Formats are associated with a particular filehandle; as you can see from the example, we've determined that this format should apply to anything we write on standard output. The picture language of formats is pretty simple: fields begin with @ or ^ and

---

[*] As it happens, I didn't actually use formats in my code, because I wanted to have a variable-width instead of a fixed-width display. But for cases where a fixed-width output is acceptable, this solution is perfect.

are followed by <, |, or > characters specifying left, center, and right justified respectively. After each line of fields comes a line of expressions that fill those fields, one expression for each field. If we like, we could change the format to multiple lines of fields and expressions:

```
format STDOUT =
Id      : @<<<<
$_->id
Date    : @<<<<<<<
$_->received
From    : @<<<<<<<<<<<<<<<<<<<<<<<<<<<<<<<<<<<
$_->from_address
Subject : @<<<<<<<<<<<<<<<<<<<<<<<<<<<<<<<<<<<<<<<<<<<<<<
$_->subject

.
```

We've seen examples of the @-type field. If you're dealing with multi-line formats, you might find that you want to break up a value and show it across several lines of the format. For instance, to display the start of an email alongside metadata about it:

```
Id      : 1                          Hi Simon, Thank you for the
Date    : 10/12/02                   supply of widgets that you sent
From    : fred@funglyfoobar.com      me last week. I can assure you
Subject : Widgets                    that they have all been put ...
```

This is where the other type of field, the ^ field, comes in: you can achieve the preceding output by using a format like this:

```
format STDOUT =
Id      : @<<<<                      ^<<<<<<<<<<<<<<<<<<<<<<<<<<<<
$_->id                               $message
Date    : @<<<<<<<                   ^<<<<<<<<<<<<<<<<<<<<<<<<<<<<
$_->received                         $message
From    : @<<<<<<<<<<<<<<<<<<         ^<<<<<<<<<<<<<<<<<<<<<<<<<<<<
$_->from_address                     $message
Subject : @<<<<<<<<<<<<<<<<<<...      ^<<<<<<<<<<<<<<<<<<<<<<<<<<<...
$_->subject                          $message

.
```

Unlike the values supplied to an @ field, which can be any Perl expression, these ^ values must take an ordinary scalar. What happens is that each time the format processor sees a ^ field, it outputs as much as it can from the supplied value and then chops that much off the beginning of the value for the next iteration. The ... sign at the end of the field indicates that if the supplied value is too long, the format should truncate the value and show three dots instead. If you use ^ fields with values found in lexical variables, such as $message in the previous example, you need to declare the lexical variable *before* the format, or else it won't be able to see the variable.

Another boon of using formats is that you can set a header to be sent out at the top of each page—Perl keeps track of how many lines have been printed by a format so it knows when to send out the next page. The header for a particular filehandle is a format named with _TOP appended to the filehandle's name. The simple use of this is to give column headers to your one-line records:

```
format STDOUT_TOP =
ID    Received    From                                              Subject
===== ========== ================================================= =======
=============
.

format STDOUT =
@<<<< @<<<<<<<<< @<<<<<<<<<<<<<<<<<<<<<<<<<<<<<<<<<<<<<<< @<<<<<<<<<<<<<<<<<<<<
$_->id $_->received $_->from_address                              $_->subject
.
```

Formats are quite handy, especially as you can associate different formats with different filehandles and send data out to multiple locations in different ways. On the other hand, they have some serious shortcomings that you should bear in mind if you're thinking of using them in a bigger application.

First, they're a camping ground for obscure special variables: $% is the current format page number, $= is the number of printable lines per page, $- is the number of lines currently left on the page, $~ is the name of the current output format, $^ is the name of the current header format, and so on. I could not remember a single one of these variables and had to look them up in *perlvar*.

Formats also deal pretty badly with lexical variables, changing filehandles, variable-length lines, changing formats on the fly, and so on. But they're handy for neat little hacks.

   For complete details on Perl's built-in formats, read *perlform*.

Text::Autoformat

There's a more 21st century way to deal with formatting, however, and that's the Text::Autoformat module. This has two main purposes—it wraps text more sensitively than the usual Text::Wrap module or the Unix fmt command, and it provides a syntactically simpler but more featureful replacement for the built-in format language.

Text::Autoformat's text wrapping capabilities are only tangentially related to templating, but they're still worth mentioning here.

The idea behind autoformat is to solve the problem of wrapping structured text; it was created specifically for email messages (with special consideration for quoted text, signatures, etc.), but it's applicable to any structured textual data. For instance, given the text:

```
You have:
    * a splitting headache
    * no tea
    * your gown (being worn)
      It looks like your gown contains:
        . a thing your aunt gave you which you don't know what it is
        . a buffered analgesic
        . pocket fluff
```

fmt fails rather spectacularly:

```
You have:
    * a splitting headache * no tea * your gown
    (being worn)
      It looks like your gown contains:
        . a thing your aunt gave you which
        you don't know what it is . a buffered
        analgesic . pocket fluff
```

In this case, the autoformat subroutine does things a lot better, as it looks ahead at the structure of the text it's formatting:

```
You have:
    * a splitting headache
    * no tea
    * your gown (being worn) It looks like your
      gown contains:
        . a thing your aunt gave you which you
          don't know what it is
        . a buffered analgesic
        . pocket fluff
```

Text::Autoformat's format language is quite similar to Perl's native one, but with some simplifications. First, the distinction between filling @ fields and continuing ^ fields is made by the choice of picture character, not the prefix to the field. Hence, what was:

```
@<<<< @<<<<<<<<< @<<<<<<<<<<<<<<<<<<<<<<<<<<<<<<<<< @<<<<<<<<<<<<<<<<<<<
```

now simply becomes:

```
<<<<< <<<<<<<<<< <<<<<<<<<<<<<<<<<<<<<<<<<<<<<<<<<<< <<<<<<<<<<<<<<<<<<<<
```

For continuation formats, you now use [and], which repeat as necessary on subsequent lines:

```
Id      : <<<<<
Message :
          [[[[[[[[[[[[[[[[[[[[[[[[[[[[[[[[[[[[[[[[[[[[[[[[[[[[[[[[[[[[[[[
```

This will produce output like the following:

```
Id      :    1
Message :
          Hi Simon, Thank you for the supply of widgets that you sent me
          last week. I can assure you that they have all been put to good...
```

Unlike Perl's built-in continuation formats, however, be aware that the [and] lines repeat the entire format time and time again until the variable is completely printed out. So this, for instance, won't do what you expect:

```
Id      : <<<<<   [[[[[[[[[[[[[[[[[[[[[[[[[[[[[[[[[[[[[[[[[[[[[[[[[[[[[[[[[[[[[
```

Instead, it'll produce output something like this:

```
Id      :       1   Hi Simon, Thank you for the supply of widgets that you sent
Id      :           me last week. I can assure you that they have all been put
Id      :           to good use, and have been found, as usual to be the very...
```

with even more spectacularly bad results for formats longer than one line.

One big advantage, though, is that with Text::Autoformat, formats are just plain strings instead of cleverly compiled patterns interleaved with code. These strings are processed with the form function, which needs to be exported specifically:

```perl
use Text::Autoformat qw(form);

my $format = <<EOF;
Id      : <<<<<
Date    : <<<<<<<<
From    : <<<<<<<<<<<<<<<<<<<
Subject : <<<<<<<<<<<<<<<<<<<<<<...
EOF
my $id = 10;
my $date = "20/12/02";
my $from = "Fred Foonly";
my $subject = "Autoformatted message";
print form($format, $id, $date, $from, $subject);
```

Text::Autoformat also provides extremely flexible control over the hyphenation of form fields in a multi-line block, including the ability to plug in other hyphenation routines such as Jan Pazdziora's TeX::Hyphen, the hyphenation algorithm used in Donald Knuth's TeX package. The main disadvantage, however, is that you don't get the same control over headers and footers as you would with write.

Both Perl formats and Text::Autoformat are great for producing formatted output in the style of 1980s form-based programs, but when people think of forms these days, they're more likely to think of things like form letters. Let's move on to look at modules that are more suited to this style of templating.

Text::Template

Mark-Jason Dominus' Text::Template has established itself as the de facto standard templating system for plain text. Its templating language is very simple indeed—anything between { and } is evaluated by Perl; everything else is left alone.

It is an object-oriented module—you create a template object from a file, filehandle, or string, and then you fill it in:

```
use Text::Template;
my $template = Text::Template->new(TYPE => "FILE",
                                   SOURCE => "email.tmpl");

my $output = $template->fill_in();
```

So, let's say we've got the following template:

```
Dear {$who},
    Thank you for the {$modulename} Perl module, which has saved me
{$hours} hours of work this year. This would have left me free to play
{ int($hours*2.4) } games of go, which I would have greatly appreciated
had I not spent the time goofing off on IRC instead.

Love,
Simon
```

We set up our template object and our variables, and then we process the template:

```
use Text::Template;
my $template = Text::Template->new(TYPE => "FILE",
                                   SOURCE => "email.tmpl");

$who = "Mark";
$modulename = "Text::Template";
$hours = 15;
print $template->fill_in();
```

And the output would look like:

```
Dear Mark,
    Thank you for the Text::Template Perl module, which has saved me
15 hours of work this year. This would have left me free to play
36 games of go, which I would have greatly appreciated
had I not spent the time goofing off on IRC instead.

Love,
Simon
```

Notice that the fill-in variables—$who, $modulename, and so on—are not my variables. When you think about it, this ought to be obvious—the my variables are not in Text::Template's scope, and therefore it wouldn't be able to see them. This is a bit unpleasant: Text::Template has access to your package variables, and you have to do a bit more work if you want to avoid giving use strict a fit.

Text::Template has two solutions to this. The first is pretty simple—just move the fill-in variables into a completely different package:

```
use Text::Template;
my $template = Text::Template->new(TYPE => "FILE",
                                   SOURCE => "email.tmpl");

$Temp::who = "Mark";
$Temp::modulename = "Text::Template";
$Temp::hours = 15;
print $template->fill_in(PACKAGE => "Temp");
```

That's slightly better, but it still doesn't please people for whom global variables are pure evil. If that's you, you can get around the problem by passing in a portable symbol table—that is, a hash:

```
use Text::Template;
my $template = Text::Template->new(TYPE => "FILE",
                                   SOURCE => "email.tmpl");

print $template->fill_in(HASH => {
    who => "Mark",
    modulename => "Text::Template",
    hours => 15
});
```

Loops, Arrays, and Hashes

So much for simple templates. Because Text::Template evaluates the code in braces as honest-to-goodness Perl code, we can do a whole lot more with templates. Let's suppose we're invoicing for some design work:

```
$client = "Acme Motorhomes and Eugenics Ltd.";
%jobs =
    ("Designing the new logo" => 450.00,
     "Letterheads" => 300.00,
     "Web site redesign"     => 900.00,
     "Miscellaneous Expenses" => 33.75
    );
```

We can create a template to do the work for us—the invoicing work, that is, not the design work:

```
{my $total=0; ''}
To {$client}:

Thank you for consulting the services of Fungly Foobar Design
Associates. Here is our invoice in accordance with the work we have
carried out for you:

{
  while (my ($work, $price) = each %jobs) {
      $OUT .= $work . (" " x (50 - length $work)). sprintf("£%6.2f", $price)."\n";
      $total += $price;
  }
}

Total                                       {sprintf "£%6.2f",$total}

Payment terms 30 days.

Many thanks,
Fungly Foobar
```

What's going on here? First, we set up a private variable, $total, in the template and set it to zero. However, since we don't want a 0 appearing at the top of our template, we make sure our code snippet returns ' ' so it adds nothing to the output. This is a handy trick.

Next we want to loop over the jobs hash. Adding each price to the total is simple enough, but we also want to add a line to the template for each job. What we'd like to say is something like this:

```
{
  while (my ($work, $price) = each %jobs) {
}

{$work}                                        £{$price}

{
      $total += $price;
  }
}
```

However, Text::Template doesn't work like that: each snippet of code must be an independent, syntactically correct piece of Perl. So how do we write multiple lines to the template? This is where the magical $OUT variable comes in. If you use $OUT in your template, that's taken as the output from the code snippet. We can append to this variable each time we go through the loop, and it'll all be filled into the template at the end.

Security and Error Checking

One of the advantages of templating is that you can delegate the non-programming bits of your application—design of HTML pages, wording of form letters, and so on—to people who aren't necessarily programmers. One of the disadvantages with powerful templating systems like Text::Template is that it only takes one joker to discover { system("rm -rf /") } and one or both of you is out of a job. Clearly there needs to be a way to secure your templates against this sort of abuse.

Text::Template offers two ways to protect yourself from this kind of coworker, um, I mean abuse. The first is through Perl's ordinary tainting mechanism. In taint mode, Perl will refuse to run templates from external files. This protects you from people meddling with the template files, but only because you can't use template files at all any more; you must specify templates as strings instead.

If you can actually trust the files in the filesystem, then you'll need to tell Text::Template to untaint the file data; this is done with the UNTAINT option:

```
my $template = new Text::Template (TYPE => "FILE",
                                   UNTAINT => 1,
                                   SOURCE => $filename);
```

Now you will be able to use the template in $filename, if $filename itself has passed taint checks.

The second mechanism is much more fine-grained; the SAFE option allows you to specify a Safe compartment in which to run the code snippets:

```
my $compartment = new Safe; # Default set of operations is pretty safe
$text = $template->fill_in(SAFE => $compartment);
```

If you're really concerned about security, you'll want to do more tweaking than just using the default set of restricted operations.

What if things go wrong in other ways? You don't want your application to die if the code snippets contain invalid Perl, or throw a divide-by-zero error. While Text::Template traps eval errors by default, you may find yourself wanting more control of error handling. This is where the BROKEN option comes in.

The BROKEN option allows you to supply a subroutine reference to execute when a code snippet produces a syntax error or fails in any other way. Without BROKEN, you get a default error message inserted into your output:

```
Dear Program fragment delivered error ``syntax error at template line 1'',
```

By specifying a BROKEN subroutine, you get more control over what is inserted into the output. In many cases, the only sensible thing to do if your template is broken would be to abort processing of the template altogether. You can do this by returning undef from your BROKEN routine, and Text::Template will return as much output as it was able to build up.

Of course, you now need to be able to tell whether the template completed successfully or whether it was aborted by a BROKEN routine. The way to do this is to use the callback argument BROKEN_ARG. If you pass a BROKEN_ARG to your template constructor, it will be passed into your BROKEN callback.* This allows us to do something like this:

```
my $succeeded = 1;

$template->fill_in(BROKEN => \&broken_sub, BROKEN_ARG => \$succeeded);

if (!$suceeded) {
    die "Template failed to fill in...";
}

sub broken_sub {
    my %params = @_;
    ${$params{arg}} = 0;
    undef;
}
```

---

* Allowing a user-defined argument is a great way to make a callback extremely extensible.

As you can see, the callback is called with a hash; the argument specified by `BROKEN_ARG` is the `arg` element of the hash. In this case, that's a reference to the `$succeeded` flag; we dereference the reference and set the flag to zero, indicating an error, before returning `undef` to abort processing.

In case you feel you can make use of the broken template, `Text::Template` supplies the code snippet as the text element of the hash; I haven't been able to think of anything sensible to do with this yet. To assist with error reporting, the other entries in the hash are `line`, the line number in the template where the error occurred, and `error`, the value of `$@` indicating the error.

Text::Template Tricks

Using { and } to delimit code is fine for most uses of `Text::Template`—when you're generating form letters or emails, for instance. But what if you're generating text that makes heavy use of { and }—HTML pages including JavaScript, for example, or TEX code for typesetting?

One solution is to escape the braces that you don't want to be processed as Perl snippets with backslashes:

```
if (browser == "Opera") \{
   ...
\}
```

However, as one user pointed out, if you're generating TeX, which attaches meaning to backslashes and braces, you're entering a world of pain:

```
\\textit\{ {$title} \} \\dotfill \\textbf\{ \\${$cost} \}
```

A much nicer solution would be to specify alternate delimiters, and get rid of the backslash escaping:

```
\textit{ [[[ $title ]]] } \dotfill \textbf{ [[[ $cost ]]] }
```

Much clearer!

To do this with `Text::Template`, use the `DELIMITERS` option on either the constructor or the `fill_in` method:

```
print $template->fill_in(DELIMITERS => [ '[[[', ']]]' ]);
```

This actually runs faster than the default because it doesn't do any special backslash processing, but needless to say, you have to ensure that your delimiters do not appear in the literal text of your template.

Mark suggests a different trick if this isn't appropriate: use Perl's built-in quoting operators to escape the braces. If we have a program fragment { q{ Hello } }, this returns the string "Hello" and inserts it into the template output. So another way to get literal text without escaping the braces is simply to add more braces!

```
{ q{

  if (browser == "Opera") { ... }

} }
```

Another problem is that your fingers fall off from typing:

```
my $template = new Text::Template(...);
$template->fill_in();
```

all the time. The object-oriented style is perfect when you have a template that you need to fill in hundreds of times—a form letter, for instance—but not so great if you're just filling it in once. For these cases, Text::Template can export a subroutine, fill_in_file. This does the preparation and filling in all in one go:

```
use Text::Template qw(fill_in_file);

print fill_in_file("email.tmpl", PACKAGE => "Q", ...);
```

Note that you do have to import this function specifically.

HTML::Template

HTML formatting is slightly different from plaintext formatting—there are essentially two main schools of thought. The first, used by HTML::Template, is similar to the method we saw in Text::Template; the template is stored somewhere, and a Perl program grabs it and fills it in. The other school of thought is represented by HTML::Mason, which we'll look at next; this is inside-out—instead of running a Perl program that prints out a load of HTML, you create an HTML file that contains embedded snippets of Perl and run that.

To compare these two approaches, we're going to build the same application in HTML::Template, HTML::Mason, and Template Toolkit, an aggregator of RSS (Remote Site Summary) feeds to grab headlines from various web sites and push them onto a single page. (Similar to Amphetadesk, *http://www.disobey.com/amphetadesk/*, and O'Reilly's Meerkat, *http://www.oreillynet.com/meerkat/*.) RSS is an XML-based format for providing details of individual items on a site; it's generally used for providing a feed of stories from news sites.

Variables and Conditions

First, though, we'll take a brief look at how HTML::Template does its stuff, how to get values into it, and how to get HTML out.

As with Text::Template, templates are specified in separate files. HTML::Template's templates are ordinary HTML files, but with a few special tags. The most important of these is <TMPL_VAR>, which is replaced by the contents of a Perl variable. For instance, here's a very simple page:

```
<html>
    <head><title>Product details for <TMPL_VAR NAME=PRODUCT></title></head>
    <body>
        <h1> <TMPL_VAR NAME=PRODUCT> </h1>
        <div class="desc">
            <TMPL_VAR NAME=DESCRIPTION>
        </div>
        <p class="price">Price: $<TMPL_VAR NAME=PRICE></p>
        <hr />
        <p>Price correct as at <TMP_VAR NAME=DATE></p>
    </body>
</html>
```

When filled in with the appropriate details, this should output something like:

```
<html>
    <head><title>Product details for World's Biggest Enchilada</title></head>
    <body>
        <h1> World's Biggest Enchilada </h1>
        <div class="desc">
            Recently discovered in the Mexican rain forests....
        </div>
        <p class="price">Price: $1504.39</p>
        <hr />
        <p>Price correct as at 15:18 PST, 7 Mar 2005</p>
    </body>
</html>
```

In order to fill in those values, we write a little CGI program similar to the following one:

```
use strict;
use HTML::Template;

my $template = HTML::Template->new(filename => "catalogue.tmpl");

$template->param( PRODUCT      => "World's Biggest Enchilada" );
$template->param( DESCRIPTION => $description );
$template->param( PRICE        => 1504.39 );
$template->param( DATE         => format_date(localtime) );

print "Content-Type: text/html\n\n", $template->output;
```

Again, as with Text::Template, our driver program is very simple—load up the template, fill in the values, produce it. However, there are a few other things we can do with our templating language, and hence there are a few other tags that allow us a little more flexibility.

For instance, suppose we happen to have a picture of the world's biggest enchilada—that would be something worth putting on our web page. However, we don't have pictures for everything in the database; we want to output a pictures section only if we actually do have an image file kicking about. So, we could add something like this to our template:

```
<TMPL_IF NAME=PICTURE_URL>
<div class="photo">
```

```
      <img src="<TMP_VALUE NAME=PICTURE_URL>" />
    </div>
    </TMPL_IF>
```

This means that if `PICTURE_URL` happens to have a true value—that is, if we've given it something like a real URL—then we include the photo `<DIV>`. As these `<TMPL_...>` tags are not real HTML tags, only things processed by `HTML::Template`, it's not a problem to stick one in the middle of another HTML tag, as we have here with `<IMG SRC="...">`.

Of course, if we don't have a picture, we might want to stick another one in its place, which we can do with the `<TMPL_ELSE>` pseudotag:

```
<div class="photo">
<TMPL_IF NAME=PICTURE_URL>
    <img src="<TMP_VALUE NAME=PICTURE_URL>" />
<TMPL_ELSE>
    <img src="http://www.mysite.com/images/noimage.gif" />
</TMPL_IF>
</div>
```

Notice that although our `<TMPL_IF>` must be matched by a `</TMPL_IF>`, `<TMPL_ELSE>` is not matched.

But perhaps we're being unduly complex; all we need in this example is a default value for our `PICTURE_URL`, and we can do this directly with a `DEFAULT` attribute to `<TMPL_VALUE>`:

```
<div class="photo">
    <img src="
<TMPL_VALUE NAME=PICTURE_URL
            DEFAULT="http://www.mysite.com/images/noimage.gif">
    "/>
</div>
```

Validation

Some people worry, quite rightly, about the effect that this sort of indiscriminate SGML abuse has on checking templates for validity. (Although, sadly many more people *don't* worry about HTML validity.) Further, those who use DTD-aware validating editors might wonder how to get these pseudotags into their documents in a nice way.

`HTML::Template` has a way around this; instead of writing the tags as though they were ordinary HTML tags, you can also write them as though they were comments, like so:

```
<!-- TMPL_IF NAME=PICTURE_URL -->
<div class="photo">
    <img src="<!-- TMP_VALUE NAME=PICTURE_URL -->" />
</div>
<!-- /TMPL_IF -->
```

Loops

If we're going to get anywhere with our RSS example, we'll need to loop over a series of items—the stories in our newsreel. Thankfully, HTML::Template provides the <TMPL_LOOP> pseudotag for treating a variable as an array. For instance, the following code:

```
<ul>
<TMPL_LOOP NAME=STORIES>
    <li> From <TMPL_VAR NAME=FEED_NAME>: <TMPL_VAR NAME=STORY_NAME> </li>
</TMPL_LOOP>
</ul>
```

when provided the appropriate data structure, loops over the items in the STORIES array reference and produces output like so:

```
<ul>

    <li> From Slashdot: NASA Finds Monkeys on Mars </li>

    <li> From use.perl: Perl 6 Release Predicted for 2013 </li>

</ul>
```

The trick is that the array reference needs to contain an array of hashes, and each hash provides the appropriate variable names:

```
$template->param(STORIES => [
  { FEED_NAME => "Slashdot", STORY_NAME => "NASA Finds Monkeys on Mars" },
  { FEED_NAME => "use.perl", STORY_NAME => "Perl 6 Release Predicted for 2013" }
]);
```

RSS Aggregation

With this knowledge, putting together our RSS aggregator is pretty trivial; first, we grab all the feeds we're interested in, then sort out their stories and put them into a data structure suitable for feeding to a <TMPL_LOOP>.

We'll use LWP and XML::RSS to obtain and parse the RSS feeds. In our example, we're going to pretend that we're behind a pretty impressive web cache, so we have no problems fetching the RSS feeds repeatedly; in real life, you may want to save the XML to files with fixed names and check how old the files on disk are before fetching them from the web again.

We'll start our RSS aggregator by writing a little Perl program to grab and organize the feeds:

```
#!/usr/bin/perl

use LWP::Simple;
use XML::RSS;
my @stories;
```

```
while (<DATA>) {
    chomp;
    my $xml = get($_) or next;
    my $rss = XML::RSS->new;
    eval { $rss->parse($xml) }; next if $@;
    for my $item (@{$rss->{'items'}}) {
        push @stories, {
            FEED_NAME  => $rss->channel->{'title'},
            FEED_URL   => $rss->channel->{'link'},

            STORY_NAME => $item->{'title'},
            STORY_URL  => $item->{'link'},
            STORY_DESC => $item->{'description'},
            STORY_DATE => $item->{'dc'}->{'date'}
        }
    }
}

@stories = sort { $b->{STORY_DATE} cmp $a->{STORY_DATE} } @stories;

__DATA__
http://slashdot.org/slashdot.rss
http://use.perl.org/perl-news-short.rdf
http://www.theregister.co.uk/tonys/slashdot.rdf
http://blog.simon-cozens.org/blosxom.cgi/xml
http://www.oreillynet.com/~rael/index.rss
```

Next we need to design a template to receive this list of feeds. Now, I'm an abysmal HTML designer, which is why I like templates so much. I can create something rough that does the job and hand it to someone with imagination to do the presentation bits. So here's a rough-and-ready template:

```
<html>
    <head> <title> Today's News </title> </head>
    <body>
        <h1> News Stories Collected at <TMPL_VAR TIME> </h1>

    <TMPL_LOOP STORIES>
        <table border="1">
          <tr>
          <td>
            <h2>
              <a href="<TMPL_VAR STORY_URL>"> <TMPL_VAR STORY_NAME> </a>
            </h2>
            <p> <TMPL_VAR STORY_DESC> </p>
            <hr>
            <p> <i> From
                <a href="<TMPL_VAR FEED_URL>"> <TMPL_VAR FEED_NAME> </a>
            </i> </p>
          </td>
          </tr>
        </table>
    </TMPL_LOOP>
    </body>
</html>
```

(Notice that we're using short forms of the pseudotags: it's OK to say SOME_VARIABLE instead of NAME=SOME_VARIABLE where it's unambiguous.)

Finally, we put the finishing touches on our driver program, which merely takes the array we generated and feeds it to HTML::Template:

```perl
#!/usr/bin/perl

use LWP::Simple;
use XML::RSS;
use HTML::Template;

my @stories;

while (<DATA>) {
    chomp;
    my $xml = get($_) or next;
    my $rss = XML::RSS->new;
    eval { $rss->parse($xml) }; next if $@;
    for my $item (@{$rss->{'items'}}) {
        push @stories, {
            FEED_NAME  => $rss->channel->{'title'},
            FEED_URL   => $rss->channel->{'link'},

            STORY_NAME => $item->{'title'},
            STORY_URL  => $item->{'link'},
            STORY_DESC => $item->{'description'},
            STORY_DATE => $item->{'dc'}->{'date'}
        }
    }
}

my $template = HTML::Template->new(filename => "aggregator.tmpl");

$template->param( STORIES => [
    sort {$b->{STORY_DATE} cmp $a->{STORY_DATE} } @stories
                ] );
$template->param( TIME => scalar localtime );

delete $_->{STORY_DATE} for @stories;

print "Content-Type: text/html\n\n", $template->output;

__DATA__
http://blog.simon-cozens.org/blosxom.cgi/xml
http://slashdot.org/slashdot.rss
http://use.perl.org/perl-news-short.rdf
http://www.theregister.co.uk/~tonys/slashdot.rdf
http://www.oreillynet.com/~rael/index.rss
```

We need to delete the STORY_DATE once we've used it for ordering, as HTML::Template gets irate if we have loop variables that we don't use in our template.

Plug this into a CGI-enabled web server, and, lo and behold, we have a cheap and cheerful Amphetadesk clone.

HTML::Mason

One of the big drawbacks of HTML::Template is that it forces us, to some degree, to mix program logic and presentation, something that we sought to avoid by using templates. For instance, that last template got a little difficult to follow, with variable and HTML tags crowding up the template and obscuring what was actually going on. What we would prefer, then, is a system that allows us to further abstract out the individual elements of what we expect our templates to do, and this is where HTML::Mason comes in.

As we've mentioned, HTML::Mason is an inside-out templating system. As well as templating, it could also be described as a component abstraction system for building HTML web pages out of smaller, reusable pieces of logic. Here's a brief overview of how to use it, before we go on to implement the same RSS aggregator application.

Basic Components

In Mason, everything is a component. Here's a simple example of using components. Suppose we have three files: *test.html* in Example 3-1, *Header* in Example 3-2, and *Footer* in Example 3-3.

Example 3-1. test.html

```
<& /Header &>
<p>
  Hello World
</p>
<& /Footer &>
```

Example 3-2. Header

```
<!DOCTYPE HTML PUBLIC "-//W3C//DTD HTML 4.01 Transitional//EN">
<html>
  <head>
     <title>Some Web Application</title>
     <link rel=stylesheet type="text/css" href="nt.css">
  </head>

<body>
```

Example 3-3. Footer

```
    <hr>
    <div class="footer">
      <address>
        <a href="mailto:webmaster@yourcompany.com">webmaster@yourcompany.com</a>
```

Example 3-3. Footer (continued)

```
      </address>
    </div>
  </body>
</html>
```

HTML::Mason builds up the page by including the components specified inside <& and &> tags. When creating *test.html*, Mason first includes the *Header*component found at the document root, then the rest of the HTML, then the *Footer* component.

Components may call other components. So far, we've done nothing outside the scope of server-side includes.

Basic Dynamism

So where does the templating come in? There are three basic ways of adding templates to Mason pages. Here's the first, a simple modification to our *Footer* component.

```
      <hr>
      <div class="footer">
        <address>
          <a href="mailto:webmaster@yourcompany.com">webmaster@yourcompany.com</a>
        </address>
        Generated: <% scalar localtime %>
      </div>
    </body>
  </html>
```

If you wrap some Perl code in <% ... %> tags, the result of the Perl expression is inserted into the resulting HTML.

That's all very well for simple expressions, but what about actual Perl logic? For this, Mason has an ugly hack: a single % at the beginning of a line is interpreted as Perl code. This lets you do things like Example 3-4, to dump out the contents of a hash.

Example 3-4. Hashdump

```
<table>
  <tr>
    <th> key </th>
    <th>value</th>
  </tr>

% for (keys %hash) {
  <tr>
    <td> <% $_ %> </td>
    <td> <% $hash{$_} %> </td>
  </tr>
% }
</table>
```

Example 3-4. Hashdump (continued)

```
<%ARGS>
%hash => undef
</%ARGS>
```

There's a few things to notice in this example. First, see how we intersperse ordinary HTML with logic, using `%` ... , and evaluated Perl expressions, using `<% ... %>`. The only places `%` is special are at the start of a line and as part of the `<% ... %>` tag; the `%` of `%hash` is plain Perl.

The second thing to notice in the example is how we get the hash into the component in the first place. That's the purpose of the `<%ARGS>` section—it declares arguments to pass to the component. And how do we pass in those arguments? Here's something that might call *Hashdump*:

```
% my %foo = ( one => 1, two => 2 );

<& /Hashdump, hash => %foo &>
```

So altogether, we have an example of declaring `my` variables inside a component, passing a named parameter to another component, and having that component receive the parameter and make use of it. Mason will try to do something sensible if you pass parameters of different types than the types you've declared in the `<%ARGS>` section of the receiving component (here we passed a hash to fill in the `%hash` parameter, for instance), but life is easier if you stick to the same types.

Perl Blocks

There's a final way of adding Perl logic to your components, but it's not used much in the form we're about to describe. If you've got long Perl sections, you won't want to put a `%` at the beginning of every line. Instead, you can wrap the whole thing up in a `<%PERL>...</%PERL>` block.

However, something you will see quite often in real-life components is the `<%INIT>...</%INIT>` block. This can be placed anywhere in the component, although typically it's placed at the end to keep it away from all the HTML. No matter where it's placed, it always runs first, before anything else in the component. It's a good place to declare and initialize any variables you're going to use (by the way—Mason forces use `strict`...) and do any heavy computation that needs to happen before you do the displaying.

Another vaguely useful thing to know about is the `<%ONCE>...</%ONCE>` block, which is executed only at startup—think of it as the Mason equivalent of a Perl `BEGIN` block.

Our RSS Aggregator

We're now in a position where we can start putting together our RSS aggregator. The example in this section is taken from some code I wrote for a portal site. It's worth

---

noting that I threw it together in a matter of around two or three hours. The intention was to support logins, personalized lists of feeds, personalized ordering, and so on. Although I didn't get that far, what I had after those two or three hours is worth looking at.[*]

Let's start by thinking of what we want on the front page. I opted for a two-column design, shown in Figure 3-1, with the left column containing an invitation to log in to the portal and a list of the feeds available. As an additional flourish, the list of feeds are categorized into folders, represented by directories in the filesystem. The right column contains the logged-in user's favorite feeds, the feeds from a given folder if a folder has been clicked, or a default set of feeds in all other cases.

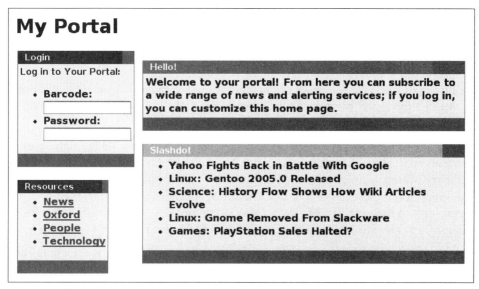

Figure 3-1. The RSS aggregator

Let's begin to build the site. First, we'll want a header and a footer to take away most of the boring parts of the HTML generation, as in Examples 3-5 and 3-6.

Example 3-5. Header

```
<!DOCTYPE HTML PUBLIC "-//W3C//DTD HTML 4.0 Transitional//EN">
<html lang="en">

<head>
<title> My Portal </title>
<link rel="stylesheet" type="text/css" href="/stylesheets/portal.css">
</head>
<body class="pagetable">
```

---

[*] Feel free, of course, to implement all these things as an exercise in HTML::Mason programming.

Example 3-5. Header (continued)

```
<img src="/images/portal-logo.gif" id="toplogo">
<h1>My Portal</h1>
```

Example 3-6. Footer

```
</body>
</html>
```

Now we're going to use a slight Mason trick: instead of wrapping every page in the header and footer manually, we use an *autohandler*, a component that is applied to all pages, as in Example 3-7.

Example 3-7. Autohandler

```
<& /header &>
<% $m->call_next %>
<& /footer &>
```

Behind the scenes, Mason pages are processed by one or more *handlers*, reminiscent of Apache mod_perl handlers. Indeed, $m in our code is the Mason request object, which is similar to the Apache request object.[*]

In the lineup of Mason handlers, first come the autohandlers, which handle every request; then come dhandlers, which handle particular URIs; and finally comes the ordinary Mason handler for the page you're trying to process. Our example shows the simplest but most common autohandler: call a header component, then pass this request on to the next handler in the Mason handler chain, and finally call a footer component. This ensures that every page has its header and footer.

Next, we'll think about what the index has to be. As we've said, we're going for a two-column design, something like Example 3-8.

Example 3-8. index.html

```
<table>

<tr>
<td valign="top">
<& /LoginBox &>
<& /Directories &>

<%INIT>
$open = ($open =~ /(\w+)/) ? $1 : '';
</%INIT>

</td>
<td width=4> </td>
```

---

[*] If you need the actual Apache request object in Mason, it's available as $r.

Example 3-8. index.html (continued)

```
<td width='100%'>

%# Am I logged in ?
% if (0) {
<& /LoggedInPane &>
%} elsif ($open) {
<& /DirectoryPane, open => $open &>
%} else {
<& /StandardPane &>
%}
</td>

</table>

<%ARGS>
$open => undef
</%ARGS>
```

As promised, the column on the left contains a login box and the directory of feeds. The right-hand side has three states: one pane for those who are logged in (which is ifdef'ed out since user control is left for future expansion), one if a particular directory has been opened, and one if the user has just come to the site's front page.[*]

What about the value of $open? Mason allows components to take arguments, either via CGI or by being passed in from other components. In this case, *index.html* is a top-level component and will receive its arguments via CGI—that is, if we request the URL *http://www.oursite.com/rss/index.html?open=News*, then $open will be set to News. The directory pane component receives its arguments from *index.html*, and so we pass it the value of $open we received.

Because $open later names a directory on the web server, we sanitize its value to avoid directory-perusal attacks such as passing in a query of open=../../... We do this in the <%INIT%> phase by replacing the parameter passed in with the first word in the string. If the parameter has no word characters, we set it to an empty string so the remainder of the code acts as if no directory was selected.

Now, our site is going to be made up of a load of boxes of various titles and different colors, so let's have a couple of helper components to draw boxes for us. We're going to allow the box to have a user-defined color, title, and optional title link. Experience has shown that the best way to do this is to create components for the start of the box and the end of the box. The start of the box, shown in Example 3-9, creates a table inside a table.

---

[*] Therefore, as it happens, all requests will go through *index.html,* and we could have put our header and footer code in there, but using an autohandler is cleaner and actually more conventional.

Example 3-9. BoxTop

```
<table bgcolor="#777777" cellspacing=0 border=0 cellpadding=0>
<tr><td rowspan=2></td>
<td valign=middle align=left bgcolor="<%$color%>">
 
<font size=-1 color="#ffffff">
<b>
<% $title_href && "<a  href=\"$title_href\">"|n %>
<%$title |n %>
<% $title_href && "</a>" |n %>
</b></font></td>
<td rowspan=2> </td></tr>
<tr><td colspan=2 bgcolor="#eeeeee" valign=top align=left width=100%>
<table cellpadding=2 width=100%><tr><td>

<%ARGS>
$title_href => undef
$title => undef

$color => "#000099"
</%ARGS>
```

One thing to notice from this is the |n directive that appears at the end of some of the interpolated Perl sections. The reason for these is to turn off Mason's default HTML entity escaping code. For instance, if we had passed in a value for $title_href, then this line:

```
<% $title_href && "</a>" %>
```

would want to output </a>. However, as Mason tries to escape HTML entities for you, this would become </a>—so we need to turn that off.

The box ending code, shown in Example 3-10, is much simpler and merely ends the two tables we opened.

Example 3-10. BoxEnd

```
</td></tr></table>

</td></tr>
<tr><td colspan=4> </td></tr>
</table>
```

As an example of these box drawing components, let's first dispatch the dummy login box for completeness, as in Example 3-11.

Example 3-11. LoginBox

```
<& BoxTop, title=>"Login" &>
<small>Log in to Your Portal:</small><br/>
<form>
<ul>
<li> Barcode: <input name="barcode">
```

Example 3-11. LoginBox (continued)

```
<li> Password: <input name="password">

</ul>

</form>
<& BoxEnd &>
```

When Mason processes that component, it produces HTML that looks like this:

```
<table bgcolor="#777777" cellspacing=0 border=0 cellpadding=0>
<tr><td rowspan=2></td>
<td valign=middle align=left bgcolor="#000099">
 
<font size=-1 color="#ffffff">
<b> Login </b></font></td>
<td rowspan=2> </td></tr>
<tr><td colspan=2 bgcolor="#eeeeee" valign=top align=left width=100%>
<table cellpadding=2 width=100%><tr><td>
<small>Log in to Your Portal:</small><br/>
<form>
<ul>
<li> Barcode: <input name="barcode">
<li> Password: <input name="password">

</ul>

</form>
</td></tr></table>

</td></tr>
<tr><td colspan=4> </td></tr>
</table>
```

Now we need to make some decisions about our site's layout. As we've mentioned, we're going to put our feeds in the filesystem, categorized by directory. We'll actually have each individual feed be a Mason component, drawing on a library component we'll call *RSSBox*. Our *Directories* component is a box containing a list of categories; clicking on a category displays all the feeds in that category. As each category is a directory, we can create the list, as in Example 3-12.

Example 3-12. Directories

```
<& /BoxTop, title=> "Resources" &>

<ul>
<%$Portal::dirs%>
</ul>
<& /BoxEnd &>

<%ONCE>
    my $root = "/var/portal/";
    for my $top (grep { -d $_ } glob("$root*")) {
```

Example 3-12. Directories (continued)

```
        $top =~ s/$root//;
        $Portal::dirs .= qq{
            <li><a href="/?open=$top">$top</a>
        } unless $top =~ /\W/;
    }
</%ONCE>
```

What's happening here is that when the server starts up, it looks at all the subdirectories of our portal directory and strips them of their root (in this instance, */var/portal/*) to turn them into a link for the purposes of our application. For instance, a directory called */var/portal/News* would turn into a link */?open=News* with the heading *News*. This link redirects back to our home page, where the open parameter causes the *DirectoryPane* to be presented and opens the feeds in the selected directory. The code skips any directories with non-word characters in the name, so it only generates links that will pass the parameter check on open.

Let's think about how that pane is implemented. We know that we open a directory and find it full of Mason component files. We want to then dynamically include each of those component files in turn, to build up our directory of feeds.

The trick to dynamically calling a component is the comp method on the Mason request object $m; this is the Perl-side version of the <& comp &> component include tag. Hence, our directory pane ends up looking like Example 3-13.

Example 3-13 . DirectoryPane

```
<%ARGS>
$open
</%ARGS>

% for (grep {-f $_} glob( "/var/portal/$open/*") ) {
% s|/var/portal/||;

<% $m->comp($_) %>
% }
```

We first receive the name of the directory we're trying to open. Next we look at each file in that directory, strip off the name of the root directory (ideally this would all be provided by a configuration file), and then call the component with that name. This means that if we have a directory called *Technology* containing the following files:

```
01-Register
02-Slashdot
03-MacNews
04-LinuxToday
05-PerlDotCom
```

then calling <& /DirectoryPane, open => "Technology" &> would have the effect of saying:

```
<& /Technology/01-Register  &>
<& /Technology/02-Slashdot  &>
<& /Technology/03-MacNews   &>
<& /Technology/04-LinuxToday &>
<& /Technology/05-PerlDotCom &>
```

The standard pane, shown in Example 3-14, appears when no directory is open. It consists of whatever feeds we choose to make default.

Example 3-14. StandardPane

```
<& /BoxTop, title=> "Hello!", color => "dd2222"&>
Welcome to your portal! From here you can subscribe to a wide range of
news and alerting services; if you log in, you can customize this home
page.
<& /BoxEnd &>

<& /Weather/01-Oxford &>
<& /Technology/02-Slashdot &>
<& /News/01-BBC &>
<& /People/03-Rael &>
...
```

So what's in the individual files? As we've mentioned, they make use of an *RSSBox* component, and they simply pass in the URL for the feed and optionally a color, a maximum number of items, and a name for the feed. They also pass in a parameter to say whether we want to display just the titles and links for each RSS item, or the description as well. For instance, */News/01-BBC* looks like this:

```
<& /RSSBox, URL =>"http://www.newsisfree.com/HPE/xml/feeds/60/60.xml",
Color =>"#dd0000" &>
```

whereas Rael Dornfest's blog looks like this:

```
<& /RSSBox, URL => "http://www.oreillynet.com/~rael/index.rss",
Color=> "#cccc00", Title => "Rael Dornfest", Full => 0 &>
```

As we'll see in a moment, the beauty of this modular system is that we can have components that do things other than fire off RSS feeds if we want.

But first, let's complete our portal by writing the *RSSBox* library that all these sources use. First, we want a ONCE block to load up the modules we need:

```
<%ONCE>
use XML::RSS;
use LWP::Simple;
</%ONCE>
```

Next we take our arguments, setting appropriate defaults:

```
<%ARGS>
$URL
$Color => "#0000aa"
$Max => 5
$Full => 1
```

```
$Title => undef
</%ARGS>
```

Before we start outputting any content, we load up the feed in question and parse it
with the XML::RSS module. We call Mason's cache_self method to have this component handle caching its output; if the same URL is accessed within 10 minutes, the
cached copy will be presented instead:

```
<%INIT>
return if $m->cache_self(key => $URL, expires_in => '10 minutes');
my $rss = new XML::RSS;
eval { $rss->parse(get($URL));};
my $title = $Title || $rss->channel('title');
</%INIT>
```

And now we are ready to go. So let's look at this altogether in Example 3-15.

Example 3-15. RSSBox

```
<%ONCE>
use XML::RSS;
use LWP::Simple;
</%ONCE>

<%ARGS>
$URL
$Color => "#0000aa"
$Max => 5
$Full => 1
$Title => undef
</%ARGS>

<%INIT>
my $rss = new XML::RSS;
eval { $rss->parse(get($URL));};
my $title = $Title || $rss->channel('title');
my $site = $rss->channel('link');
</%INIT>

<BR>
<& BoxTop, color => $Color, title => $title, title_href => $site &>

    <dl class="rss">
% my $count = 0;
% for (@{$rss->{items}}) {
    <dt class="rss">
    <a href="<% $_->{link} %>"> <% $_->{title} %> </a>
    </dt>
% if ($Full) {
    <dd> <% $_->{description} %> </dd>
% }

%    last if ++$count >= $Max;
% }
```

Example 3-15. RSSBox (continued)

```
    </dl>
<& /BoxEnd &>
```

There isn't much to it; for each item in the feed, we want to provide a link, the item's title, and, optionally, the description. We stop if we have more items than we want.

This demonstrates how powerful Mason can be; as I said, the total development time for this site was a couple of hours at most. The entire site takes considerably fewer than 200 lines of code. And, as we mentioned, we have the flexibility to include components that are not RSS. For instance, we don't actually have an RSS feed of the Oxford weather. However, there is a web page that spits out a weather report in a well-known format. This means that *Weather/01-Oxford* does not call *RSSBox* at all, but is in fact the following:

```
<%INIT>
use LWP::Simple;
my @lines = grep /Temperature|Pressure|humidity|^Sun|Rain/,
            split /\n/,
            get('http://www-atm.physics.ox.ac.uk/user/cfinlay/now.htm');
</%INIT>

<br>
<& /BoxTop, title => "Oxford Weather", color => "#dd00dd" &>

<ul>
% for (@lines) {
 <li> <% $_ %> </li>
% }
</ul>

<& /BoxEnd &>
```

And that sums up Mason—simple, extensible, and highly powerful.

 Of course, there are many other Mason tricks for you to learn—too many to cover here. Dave Rolsky and Ken Williams's fantastic book *Embedding Perl in HTML with Mason* (*http://www.masonbook.com/*) covers many of them, including more details about getting Mason up and running in your web server. Also check out the Mason home page (*http://www.masonhq.com*).

Template Toolkit

While the solutions we've seen so far have been primarily for Perl programmers—embedding Perl code in some other medium—Andy Wardley's Template Toolkit (*http://www.template-toolkit.org/*) is slightly different. It uses its own templating language to express components, loops, method calls, data structure elements, and more; it's therefore useful for teaching to designers who have no knowledge of the

Perl side of your application[*] but who need to work on the presentation. As the documentation puts it, you should think of the Template Toolkit language as a set of layout directives for displaying data, not calculating it.

Like Mason, it seamlessly handles compiling, caching, and delivering your templates. However, unlike Mason, it's designed to provide general-purpose display and formatting capabilities in a very extensible way. As an example, you can use Template Toolkit to dynamically serve up PDF documents containing graphs based on data from a database—and all this using nothing other than the standard plugins and filters and all within the Template Toolkit mini language.

But before we look at the clever stuff, let's look at the very simple uses of Template Toolkit. In the simplest cases, it behaves a lot like Text::Template. We take a template object, feed it some values, and give it a template to process:

```
use Template;
my $template = Template->new( );
my $variables = {
    who        => "Andy Wardley",
    modulename => "Template Toolkit",
    hours      => 30,
    games      => int(30*2.4)
};
$template->process("thankyou.txt", $variables);
```

This time, our template looks like the following:

```
Dear [% who %],
    Thank you for the [% modulename %] Perl module, which has saved me
[% hours %] hours of work this year. This would have left me free to play
[% games %] games of go, which I would have greatly appreciated
had I not spent the time goofing off on IRC instead.

    Love,
    Simon
```

Lo and behold, the templated text appears on standard output. Notice, however, that our variables inside the [% and %] delimiters aren't Perl variables with the usual type sign in front of them; instead, they're now Template Toolkit variables. Template Toolkit variables can be more than just simple scalars, though; complex data structures and even Perl objects are available to Template Toolkit through a simple, consistent syntax. Let's go back to our design work invoices, but with a slightly different data structure:

```
my $invoice = {
    client => "Acme Motorhomes and Eugenics Ltd.",
    jobs => [
    { cost => 450.00, description => "Designing the new logo" },
    { cost => 300.00, description => "Letterheads and complements slips" },
```

---

[*] And probably no desire to find out!

```
        { cost => 900.00, description => "Web site redesign" },
        { cost =>  33.75, description => "Miscellaneous Expenses" }
      ],
      total => 0
};

$invoice->{total} += $_->{cost} for @{$invoice->{jobs}};
```

How would we design a template to fit that data? Obviously, we're going to need to loop over the jobs in the anonymous array and extract various hash values. Here's how it's done:

```
To [% client %]:

Thank you for consulting the services of Fungly Foobar Design
Associates. Here is our invoice in accordance with the work we have
carried out for you:

[% FOREACH job = jobs %]
    [% job.description %]  : [% job.cost %]
[% END %]

Total                                   $[% total %]

Payment terms 30 days.

Many thanks,
Fungly Foobar
```

As you can see, the syntax is inspired by Perl—we can foreach over a list and use a local variable job to represent each element of the iterator. The dot operator is equivalent to Perl's ->—it dereferences array and hash reference elements and can also call methods on objects.

However, there's something slightly wrong with this example; since we can expect our descriptions to be of variable width, our costs aren't going to line up nicely at the end.* What can we do about this? This is where a nice, extensible feature of the Template Toolkit called *filters* comes in.

Filters

Template Toolkit filters are a little like Unix filters—they're little routines that take an input, transform it, and spit it back out again. And just like Unix filters, they're connected to our template output with a pipe symbol (|).

In this case, the filter we want is the oddly named format filter, which performs printf-like formatting on its input:

```
[% job.description | format("%60s") %]  : [% job.cost %]
```

---

* We completely glossed over this in the Text::Template example; did you notice?

This fixes the case where the data is being produced by our template processor—job.description is turned into a real description, and then filtered. But we can also filter whole blocks of template content. For example, if we wanted to format the output as HTML, we could apply the html_entity filter to replace entities with their HTML encoding:

```
[% FILTER html_entity %]
Payment terms: < 30 days.
[% END %]
```

This turns into: Payment terms: < 30 days.

This is another example of a Template Toolkit block; we've seen FOREACH blocks and FILTER blocks. There's also the IF/ELSIF/ELSE block:

```
[% IF delinquent %]
   Our records indicate that this is the second issuing of this
invoice. Please pay IMMEDIATELY.
[% ELSE %]
   Payment terms: <30 days.
[% END %]
```

Other interesting filters include the upper, lower, ucfirst, and lcfirst filters to change the casing of the text; uri to URI-escape any special characters; eval to treat the text to another level of template processing, and perl_eval to treat the output as Perl, eval it, and then add the output to the template. For a more complete list of filters with examples, see the Template::Manual::Filters documentation.

Plugins

While filters are an interface to simple Perl functionality—built-in functions like eval, uc, and sprintf, or simple text substitutions—plugins are used to interface to more complex functions. Typically, they're used to expose the functionality of a Perl module to the format language.

For instance, the Template::Plugin::Autoformat plugin allows one to use Text::Autoformat's autoformatting functionality. Just as with the Perl module, use the USE directive to tell the format processor to load the plugin. This then exports the autoformat subroutine and a corresponding autoformat filter:

```
[% USE autoformat(right=78) %]
```
```
                                      [% address | autoformat %]
```

This assures that the address is printed in a nice block on the right-hand side of the page.

A particularly neat plugin is the Template::Plugin::XML::Simple module, which allows you to parse an XML data file using XML::Simple and manipulate the resulting data structure from inside a template. Here we use USE to return a value:

```
[% USE document = XML.Simple("app2ed.xml") %]
```

And now we have a data structure created from the structure and text of an XML document. We can explore this data structure by entering the elements, just as we did in "XML Parsing" in Chapter 2:

```
The author of this book is
[% document.bookinfo.authorgroup.author.firstname # 'Simon'  %]
[% document.bookinfo.authorgroup.author.surname   # 'Cozens' %]
```

Actually writing a plugin module like this is surprisingly easy—and, in fact, something we're going to need to do for our RSS example. First, we create a new module called Template::Plugin::Whatever, where Whatever is what we want our plugin to be known as inside the template language. This module will load up whatever module we want to interface to. We'll also need it to inherit from Template::Plugin. Let's go ahead and write an interface to Tony Bowden's Data::BT::PhoneBill, a module for querying UK telephone bills.

```
package Template::Plugin::PhoneBill;
use base 'Template::Plugin';
use Data::BT::PhoneBill;
```

Now we want to receive a filename when the plugin is USEd and turn that into the appropriate object. Therefore we write a new method to do just that:

```
sub new {
    my ($class, $context, $filename) = @_;
    return Data::BT::PhoneBill->new($filename);
}
```

$context is an object passed by Template Toolkit to represent the context we're being evaluated in. And that's basically it—you can add error checking to make sure the filename exists and that the module can parse the phone bill properly, but the guts of a plugin are as we've shown.

Now that we've created the plugin, we can access the phone bill just like we did with the XML::Simple data structure:

```
[% USE bill = PhoneBill("mybill.txt") %]

[% WHILE call = bill.next_call %]
Call made on [% call.date %] to [% call.number %]...
[% END %]
```

An interesting thing to notice is that when we were using the XML.Simple plugin, we accessed elements of the data structure with the dot operator: document.bookinfo and so on. In that case, we were navigating hash references; the Perl code would have looked like $document->{bookinfo}->{authorgroup}->{author}.... In this example, we're using precisely the same dot operator syntax, but, instead of navigating hash references, we're calling methods: call.date would translate to $call->date. However, it all looks the same to the template writer. This abstraction of the underlying data structure is one of the big strengths of Template Toolkit.

Components and Macros

When we looked at HTML::Mason, one of the things we praised was the ability to split template functionality up into multiple components, then include those components with particular parameters. It shouldn't be a surprise that we can do precisely the same in Template Toolkit.

The mechanism through which we pull in components is the INCLUDE directive. For instance, we can specify our box drawing library in a way very similar to the HTML::Mason method, as in Example 3-16.

Example 3-16. BoxTop

```
<table bgcolor="#777777" cellspacing=0 border=0 cellpadding=0>
<tr>
  <td rowspan=2></td>
  <td valign=middle align=left bgcolor="[% color %]">
     
   <font size=-1 color="#ffffff">
   <b>
   [% IF title_href %]
      <a href="[% title_href %]"> [% title %] </a>
   [% ELSE %]
      [% title %]
   [% END %]
   </b>
   </font>
  </td>
  <td rowspan=2> </td>
</tr>
<tr>
  <td colspan=2 bgcolor="#eeeeee" valign=top align=left width=100%>
  <table cellpadding=2 width=100%>
    <tr><td>
```

And in the same way as HTML::Mason, we can use local parameters when we include these components:

```
[% INCLUDE boxtop
           title = "Login"
             ...
   %]
```

However, Template Toolkit provides another method of abstracting out common components, the MACRO directive. We can define a MACRO to expand to any Template Toolkit code; let's start by defining it to simply INCLUDE the drawing component:

```
[% MACRO boxtop INCLUDE boxtop %]
[% MACRO boxend INCLUDE boxend %]
```

With this, we can draw boxes with a little less syntax:

```
[% boxtop(title="My Box") %]
```

```
    <P> Hello, people! </P>
[% boxend %]
```

Instead of using a component file and INCLUDE, we can also associate a block of Template Toolkit directives with a macro name.

```
[% MACRO boxtop BLOCK %]
<table bgcolor="#777777" cellspacing=0 border=0 cellpadding=0>
<tr>
  ...
[% END %]

[% MACRO boxend BLOCK %]
</td></tr></table>

</td></tr>
<tr><td colspan=4> </td></tr>
</table>
[% END %]
```

Eventually, we can build up a library of useful macros and then INCLUDE that, instead of having a bunch of component files hanging around.

Let's assume we've created such a library and it contains these two box-drawing macros, and now we'll move on to putting together our RSS aggregator.

The RSS Aggregator

When it comes to writing the aggregator, we first look at the list of Template Toolkit plugins and notice with some delight that there's already a Template::Plugin::XML::RSS, which talks to XML::RSS. Unfortunately, our delight is short-lived, as we soon discover that this expects to get a filename rather than a URL or a string of XML data. We don't really want to be writing out files and then parsing them in again.

So let's create our own subclass of Template::Plugin::XML::RSS that fetches URLs and parses those instead:

```perl
package Template::Plugin::XML::RSS::URL;
use base 'Template::Plugin::XML::RSS';
use LWP::Simple;

sub new {
    my ($class, $context, $url) = @_;

    return $class->fail('No URL specified') unless $url;

    my $url_data = get($url)
      or return $class->fail("Couldn't fetch $url");

    my $rss = XML::RSS->new
      or return $class->fail('failed to create XML::RSS');

    eval { $rss->parse($url_data) } and not $@
```

```
        or return $class->fail("failed to parse $url: $@");

    return $rss;
}

1;
```

Now we can build up the equivalent of the *RSSBox* component we made in Mason:

```
[% MACRO RSSBox(url) USE rss = XML.RSS.URL(url) %]
[% box_top(title = rss.channel.title, title_href = rss.channel.link) %]

<dl class="rss">
[% FOREACH item = news.items %]
    <dt class="rss">
        <a href="[% item.link  %]"> [% item.title %] </a>
    [% IF full %]
        <dd> [% item.description %] </dd>
    [% END ]
    </dt>
[% END %]
</dl>
[% box_end %]
[% END %]
```

The important difference between this and the Mason example is that this piece of code handles everything itself—the whole process of obtaining and parsing the RSS feed is available to the template designer. There's no Perl code here to be seen at all. It's also considerably more concise and easier to read and understand. Now that we have this macro, we can produce an HTML box full of RSS stories with a simple call to it:

```
[% RSSBox("http://slashdot.org/slashdot.rss") %]
```

From here on, constructing an RSS aggregator is a simple matter of templating; all of the Perl work has been abstracted away.

AxKit

Although we include it in our list of templating systems, AxKit (*http://www.axkit.org*) is a slightly different kettle of fish from the modules we've seen so far; this is no mere templating system, it's a fully fledged XML application server for Apache. The most common use of AxKit is to transform XML to HTML on-the-fly for delivery over the web.

However, thanks to XSP (Extensible Server Pages), developed by the Apache Cocoon project, AxKit can be used as an extraordinarily extensible templating system. The basic idea behind XSP is that certain XML tags trigger the execution of given Perl routines. At a very basic level, you can use tags to delimit raw Perl code:

```
<p>
Good
<xsp:logic>
if ((localtime)[2] >= 12) {
```

```
        <i>Afternoon</i>
    }
    else {
        <i>Morning</i>
    }
    </xsp:logic>
    </p>
```

Notice that AxKit is quite happy for you to intersperse XML marked-up data with your Perl code. Because AxKit parses the XML, it knows that `<i>Afternoon</i>` is data, not Perl code, and treats it appropriately. This also means that if you have an XML guru handy, he can find a way of validating your HTML-with-embedded-XSP. In fact, since AxKit parses everything as XML, your HTML must be well-formed and valid or you won't get anything out of AxKit at all.

However, AxKit does not stop at this basic level; XSP allows you to create tag libraries with frontend Perl code. For instance, the `AxKit::XSP::ESQL` taglib provides a wrapper around the DBI libraries. These tag libraries define their own XML namespaces and place tags inside them. So your XML would use a namespace declaration to import the tag library:

```
<xsp:page
    language="perl"
    xmlns:xsp="http://apache.org/xsp/core/v1"
    xmlns:esql="http://apache.org/xsp/SQL/v2"
>
```

and this would allow you to use `<esql:...>` tags in your page:

```
<esql:connection>
<esql:driver>Pg</esql:driver>
<esql:dburl>dbname=rss</esql:dburl>
<esql:username>www</esql:username>
<esql:password></esql:password>
<esql:execute-query>
  <esql:query>
    select description, url, title from feeds
  </esql:query>
  <esql:results>
    <ul>
    <esql:row-results>
      <li>
       <a>
        <xsp:attribute name="href">
            <esql:get-string column="url"/>
        </xsp:attribute>
        <esql:get-string column="name"/>
       </a> - <esql-get-string column="description"/>
      </li>
    </esql:row-results>
    </ul>
  </esql:results>
```

```
<esql:no-results> <p> Couldn't get any results! </p> </esql:no-results>
</esql:execute-query>
</esql:connection>
```

This executes the SQL query near the top of the XML and turns it into an HTML list. The only potentially non-obvious part is where we use `<xsp:attribute>`. The key to understanding this is that a document processed by AxKit has to be 100% valid, well-formed XML. On the other hand, with `HTML::Template` and `HTML::Mason` we could get away with things like `<a href="<TMPL_VAR URL>">` or `<a href="<% $url |n%>">`—in a sense, putting tags inside tags.

But with AxKit, the whole document is parsed as XML, and then transformations are applied. With the above examples, AxKit would parse the tag as having the perfectly valid (but nonsensical) attribute values `<TMPL_VAR URL>` and `<% $url|n>` and do no more processing on them. Worse still, we can't get away with anything like `<a href=<esql:get-string column="url"/>>` as that's not even well-formed XML.

So we play a slight trick. We ask the XSP layer to rewrite the `<a>` tag, after everything has been parsed, with the appropriate `href` attribute. This keeps everything well-formed and parsable.

There are many other tag libraries that perform the same function as Template Toolkit's plugins and give the XML author access to high-level Perl functionality; my own `AxKit::XSP::ObjectTaglib` allows the programmer to easily wrap any object-oriented module into a tag library.

We're not going to implement our RSS aggregator in AxKit, as it turns out, because AxKit is a fully featured XML processor. All of the heavy lifting can be done in XSLT stylesheets, and there's almost no Perl content involved.

Instead, for more on AxKit, we'll refer you to *Perl and XML* (O'Reilly) and *http://www.axkit.org*, the AxKit home page.

Conclusion

In this chapter, we've looked at a few of the available templating tools that are commonly used in Perl; from simple formats—sprintf, and the like—on through `Text::Template` and `HTML::Template`, and then up to the more sophisticated solutions of `HTML::Mason` and Template Toolkit.

But we've missed out on one quite important question: which one should you use? As usual, the answer depends partly on what you need and partly on your tastes.

First, consider the distinction between Perl-based systems like `Text::Template` and `Text::Autoformat`, and inside-out modules like `HTML::Mason`. If the main purpose of your program is to provide some templated output, as in the case of a web-based application, then you probably want to gravitate toward the `HTML::Mason` and Template Toolkit end of the spectrum.

You also need to consider who's going to be writing the templates and whether you want to expose them to Perl code. Template Toolkit, AxKit, and HTML::Template all tend to keep the templater away from Perl, whereas HTML::Mason forces the templater to get down and dirty with it.

Second, there's the element of personal taste. I'm not a great fan of HTML::Template, preferring the way Mason does things; I find AxKit very powerful but at times very frustrating because of its insistence on clean XML; and I'm beginning to like Template Toolkit the more I use it, but prefer Mason basically because I'm more used to it.

Your tastes may differ. It's just as well, that as with so many things in Perl, there's more than one way to do it.

CHAPTER 4

Objects, Databases, and Applications

Perl programming is all about getting some data into our program, munging it around in various ways, and then spitting it back out again. So far we've looked at some interesting ways to do the munging and some great ways to represent the data, but our understanding of storing and loading data hasn't reached the same kind of level.

In this chapter, we're going to look at four major techniques for storing and retrieving complex data, and finally at *application frameworks*—technologies that pull together the whole process of retrieving, modifying, and acting on data, particularly for web applications, so that all the programmer needs to deal with is the business logic specific to the application.

For each technique, there are many CPAN modules that implement it in many different ways. We only have the space to examine one module in each section to demonstrate its approach; this is not necessarily an endorsement of the module in question as the best available. After all, there's more than one way to do it.

Beyond Flat Files

The word database might conjure up thoughts of the DBI and big expensive servers running expensive software packages,* but a database is really just anything you can get data in to and back out of.

Just a step up from the comma-separated text file is the humble DBM database. This exists as a C library in several incarnations—the most well known being the Sleepy-cat Berkeley DB, available from *http://www.sleepycat.com/download.html*, and the GNU libgdbm, from *http://www.gnu.org/order/ftp.html*. When Perl is compiled and installed, it supplies Perl libraries to interface with the C libraries that it finds and to the SDBM library, which is shipped along with Perl. I prefer to use the Berkeley DB, with its Perl interface DB_File.

---

* Or more likely, these days, commodity PCs running free software packages.

DBMs store scalar data in key-value pairs. You can think of them as the on-disk representation of a hash, and, indeed, the Perl interfaces to them are through a tied hash:

```
use DB_File;
tie %persistent, "DB_File", "languages.db" or die $!;
$persistent{"Thank you"} = "arigatou";

# ... sometime later ...

use DB_File;
tie %persistent, "DB_File", "languages.db" or die $!;
print $persistent{"Thank you"} # "arigatou"
```

DBMs, however, have a serious limitation—since they only store key-value pairs of scalar data, they cannot store more complex Perl data structures, such as references, objects, and the like. The other problem with key-value structures like DBMs is that they're very bad at expressing relationships between data. For this, we need a relational database such as Oracle or MySQL. We'll return to this subject later in the chapter to see a way of dealing with the limitations.

Object Serialization

Now we want to move on from the relatively simple key-value mechanism of DBMs to the matter of saving and restoring more complex Perl data structures, chiefly objects. These data structures are interesting and more difficult than scalars, because they come in many shapes and sizes: an object may be a blessed hash—or it might be a blessed array—which could itself contain any number and any depth of nesting of hashes, including other objects, arrays, scalars, or even code references.

While we could reassemble all our data structures from their original sources every time a program is run, the more complex our structures become, the more efficient it is to be able to store and restore them wholesale. Serialization is the process of representing complex data structures in a binary or text format that can faithfully reconstruct the data structure later. In this section we're going to look at the various techniques that have been developed to do this, again with reference to their implementation in CPAN modules.

Our Schema and Classes

To compare the different techniques here and in the rest of the chapter, we're going to use the same set of examples: some Perl classes whose objects we want to be somehow persistent. The schema and classes are taken from the example application used by Class::DBI: a database of CDs in a collection, with information about the tracks, artists, bands, singers, and so on.

We'll create our classes using the Class::Accessor::Assert module, which not only creates constructors and accessors for the data slots we want, but also ensures that relationships are handled by constraining the type of data that goes in the slots. So, for instance, the CD class would look like this:

```
package CD;
use base "Class::Accessor::Assert";
__PACKAGE__->mk_accessors(qw(
    artist=CD::Artist title publishdate=Time::Piece songs=ARRAY
));
```

This checks that artist is a CD::Artist object, that publishdate is a Time::Piece object, and that tracks is an array reference. (Sadly, we can't check that it's an array of CD::Song objects, but this will do for now.) Notice that things are going to be slightly different between the schema and the Perl code—for instance, we don't need a separate class for CD::Track, which specifies the order of songs on a CD, because we can just do that with an array of songs.

With that in mind, the rest of the classes look like this:

```
package CD::Song;
use base 'Class::Accessor';
__PACKAGE__->mk_accessors("name");

package CD::Person;
use base 'Class::Accessor::Assert';
__PACKAGE__->mk_accessors(qw(gender haircolor birthdate=Time::Piece));

package CD::Band;
use base 'Class::Accessor::Assert';
__PACKAGE__->mk_accessors( qw( members=ARRAY
                               creationdate=Time::Piece
                               breakupdate=Time::Piece ));

package CD::Artist;
use base 'Class::Accessor::Assert';
__PACKAGE__->mk_accessors(qw( name popularity person band ));

# Dispatch "band" accessors if it's a band
for my $accessor (qw(members creationdate breakupdate)) {
    *$accessor = sub {
        my $self = shift;
        return $self->band->$accessor(@_) if $self->band
    };
}

# And dispatch "person" accessors if it's a person
for my $accessor (qw(gender haircolor birthdate)) {
    *$accessor = sub {
        my $self = shift;
        return $self->person->$accessor(@_) if $self->person
    };
}
```

Now we can create artists, tracks, and CDs, like so:

```
my $tom = CD::Artist->new({ name => "Tom Waits",
                            person => CD::Person->new( ) });
```

```
$tom->popularity(2);
$tom->haircolor("black");

my $cd = CD->new({
    artist => $tom,
    title => "Rain Dogs",
    songs => [ map { CD::Song->new({title => $_ }) }
                ("Singapore", "Clap Hands", "Cemetary Polka",
                 # ...
                ) ]
});
```

The rest of the chapter addresses how we can store these objects in a database and how we can use the classes as the frontend to an existing database.

Dumping Data

One basic approach would be to write out the data structure in full: that is, to write the Perl code that could generate the data structure, then read it in, and revive it later. That is, we would produce a file containing:

```
bless( {
  'title' => 'Rain Dogs'
  'artist' => bless( {
      'popularity' => 2,
          'person' => bless( { 'haircolor' => 'black' }, 'CD::Person' ),
              'name' => 'Tom Waits'
      }, 'CD::Artist' ),
  'songs' => [
    bless( { 'title' => 'Singapore'      }, 'CD::Song' ),
    bless( { 'title' => 'Clap Hands'     }, 'CD::Song' ),
    bless( { 'title' => 'Cemetary Polka' }, 'CD::Song' ),
    # ...
  ],
}, 'CD' )
```

and later use do to reconstruct this data structure. This process is known as serialization, since it turns the complex, multidimensional data structure into a flat piece of text. The most common module used to do the kind of serialization shown above is the core module Data::Dumper.

This process of serialization is also incredibly important during the debugging process; by dumping out a representation of a data structure, it's very easy to check whether it contains what you think it should. In fact, pretty much my only debugging tool these days is a carefully placed:

```
use Data::Dumper; die Dumper($whatever);
```

If you're using the Data::Dumper module for serializing objects, however, there's a little more you need to know about it than simply the Dumper subroutine. First, by default, Dumper's output will not just be the raw data structure but will be an assignment statement setting the variable $VAR1 to the contents of the data structure.

You may not want your data to go into a variable called $VAR1, so there are two ways to get rid of this: first, you can set $Data::Dumper::Terse = 1, which will return the raw data structure without the assignment, which you can then assign to whatever you like; second, you can provide a variable name for Data::Dumper to use instead of $VAR1. This second method is advisable since having an assignment statement rather than a simple data structure dump allows Data::Dumper to resolve circular data structures. Here's an example that sets up a circular data structure:

```
my $dum = { name => "Tweedle-Dum" };
my $dee = { name => "Tweedle-Dee" };
$dee->{brother} = $dum;
$dum->{brother} = $dee;
```

If we dump $dum using the Data::Dumper defaults, we get:

```
$VAR1 = {
          'brother' => {
                         'brother' => $VAR1,
                         'name' => 'Tweedle-Dee'
                       },
          'name' => 'Tweedle-Dum'
        };
```

This is fine for debugging but cannot reconstruct the variable later, since $VAR1 is probably undef while the hash is being put together. Instead, you can set $Data::Dumper::Purity = 1 to output additional statements to fix up the references:

```
$VAR1 = {
          'brother' => {
                         'brother' => {},
                         'name' => 'Tweedle-Dee'
                       },
          'name' => 'Tweedle-Dum'
        };
$VAR1->{'brother'}{'brother'} = $VAR1;
```

Naturally, this is something that we're going to need when we're using Data::Dumper to record real data structures, but it cannot be done without the additional assignments and, hence, a variable name. You have two choices when using Data::Dumper for serialization: either you can specify the variable name you want, like so:

```
open my $out, "> dum.pl" or die $!;
use Data::Dumper;
$Data::Dumper::Purity = 1;
print $out Dumper([ $dee ], [ "dee" ]);
```

or you can just make do with $VAR1 and use local when you re-eval the code.

Data::Dumper has spawned a host of imitators, but none more successful than YAML (YAML Ain't Markup Language). This is another text-based data serialization format that is not Perl-specific and is also optimized for human readability. Using YAML's Dump or DumpFile on the Tom Waits CD gives us:

```
--- #YAML:1.0 !perl/CD
artist: !perl/CD::Artist
  name: Tom Waits
  person: !perl/CD::Person
    haircolor: black
  popularity: 2
songs:
  - !perl/CD::Song
    title: Singapore
  - !perl/CD::Song
    title: Clap Hands
  - !perl/CD::Song
    title: Cemetary Polka
  ...
title: Rain Dogs
```

This is more terse and, hence, easier to follow than the equivalent Data::Dumper output; although with Data::Dumper, at least you're reading Perl. Once you know that YAML uses key: value to specify a hash pair, element for an array element, indentation for nesting data structures, and ! for language-specific processing instructions, it's not hard.

YAML uses a system of references and links to notate circular structures; Tweedle-Dum looks like this:

```
--- #YAML:1.0 &1
brother:
  brother: *1
  name: Tweedle-Dee
name: Tweedle-Dum
```

The *1 is a reference to the target &1 at the top, stating that Tweedle-Dee's brother slot is the variable. This is much neater, as it means you can save and restore objects without messing about with what the variable name ought to be. To restore an object with YAML, use Load or LoadFile:

```
my $dum = YAML::Load(<<EOF);
--- #YAML:1.0 &1
brother:
  brother: *1
  name: Tweedle-Dee
name: Tweedle-Dum
EOF

print $dum->{brother}{brother}{name}; # Tweedle-Dum
```

Storing and Retrieving Data

As well as the text-based serialization methods, such as Data::Dumper and YAML, there are also binary serialization formats; the core module Storable is the most well known and widely used of these, but the CPAN module `FreezeThaw` deserves an honorable mention.

Storable can store and retrieve data structures directly to a file, like so:

```
use Storable;
store $dum, "dum.storable";

# ... later ...

my $dum = retrieve("dum.storable");
```

This technique is used by the `CPANPLUS` module to store a parsed representation of the CPAN module tree. This is perhaps the ideal use of serialization—when you have a very large data structure that was created by parsing a big chunk of data that would be costly to reparse. For our examples, where we have many relatively small chunks of interrelated data, the process has a problem.

The Pruning Problem

The problem is that we serialize every reference or object that we store, but the serializations don't refer to each other. It's as if each object is the root of a tree, and everything else is subordinate to it; unfortunately, that's not always the case. As a simple example, let's take our two variables in circular reference. When we serialize and store them, our serializer sees the two variables like this:

```
$dum = {
          'brother' => {
                          'brother' => $dum,
                          'name' => 'Tweedle-Dee'
                       },
          'name' => 'Tweedle-Dum'
       };
$dee = {
          'brother' => {
                          'brother' => $dee,
                          'name' => 'Tweedle-Dum'
                       },
          'name' => 'Tweedle-Dee'
       };
```

We've been serializing them one at a time, so the serializer is forced to serialize everything it needs to fully retrieve either one of these two variables; this means it has to repeat information. In the worst case, where all the data structures we store are interconnected, each and every piece of data we store will have to contain the data for the whole set. If there was some way to prune the data, so that the serializer saw:

```
$dum = {
          'brother' => (PLEASE RETRIEVE $dee FOR THIS DATA),
          'name' => 'Tweedle-Dum'
       };
$dee = {
          'brother' => (PLEASE RETRIEVE $dum FOR THIS DATA),
```

```
        'name' => 'Tweedle-Dee'
    };
```

then all would be well. But that requires a lot more organization. We'll see techniques to handle that later in the chapter.

Multilevel DBMs

Besides the pruning problem, there's another problem with the file-based serialization we've been using so far. If we're dealing with more than one data structure—which programs tend to do—we need to either put everything we want to deal with into one big array or hash and store and retrieve that, which is very inefficient, or we have a huge number of files around and we have to work out how we're going to manage them.

DBM files are one solution, as they relate one thing (an ID or variable name for the data structure) to another (the data structure itself) and hence organize individual data structures in a single file in a random-access way. However, when we last left DBMs, we were lamenting the fact that they cannot store and retrieve complex data structures, only scalars. But now that we've seen a way of turning a complex data structure into a scalar and back again, we can use these serialization techniques to get around the limitations of DBMs.

There are two ways of doing this: the new and reckless way, or the old and complicated way. We'll start with the new and reckless way since it demonstrates the idea very well.

In recent versions of Perl, there's a facility for adding filter hooks onto DBM access. That is, when you store a value into the database, a user-defined subroutine gets called to transform the data and, likewise, when you retrieve a value from the database. Your subroutine gets handed $_, you do what you need to it, and the transformed value gets used in the DBM. This filter facility has many uses. For instance, you can compress the data that you're storing to save space:

```
use Compress::Zlib;

$db = tie %hash, "DB_File", "music.db" or die $!;
$db->filter_store_value(sub { $_ = compress($_)   });
$db->filter_fetch_value(sub { $_ = uncompress($_) });
```

Or you can null-terminate your strings, for both keys and values, to ensure that C programs can use the same database file:

```
$db->filter_fetch_key  ( sub { s/\0$//    } ) ;
$db->filter_store_key  ( sub { $_ .= "\0" } ) ;
$db->filter_fetch_value( sub { s/\0$//    } ) ;
$db->filter_store_value( sub { $_ .= "\0" } ) ;
```

Or you can do what we want to do, which is to use Storable's freeze and thaw functions to serialize any references we get passed:

```
use Storable qw(freeze thaw);
```

```
$db->filter_store_value( sub { $_ = freeze($_) } );
$db->filter_fetch_value( sub { $_ = thaw($_)   } );
```

That's the easy way, but it has some disadvantages. First, it ties you down, as it were, to using Storable for your storage. It also requires the DBM filter facility, which came into Perl in version 5.6.0—this shouldn't be much of a problem these days, but you never know. The most serious disadvantage, however, is that it's unfamiliar to other programmers, which means maintainance coders may not appreciate the significance of these two lines in your program.

The way to scream to the world that you're using a multilevel DBM is to use the MLDBM module. Eventually, this ought to be rewritten to use the DBM filter hooks, but you don't need to care about that. MLDBM abstracts both the underlying DBM module and the seralization module, like so:

```
use MLDBM qw(DB_File Storable); # Use a Sleepycat DB and Storable

tie %hash, "MLDBM", "music.db" or die $!;

my $tom = CD::Artist->new({ name => "Tom Waits",
                            person => CD::Person->new( ) });
$martyn->popularity(1);

$hash{"album1"} = CD->new({
      artist => $tom,
      title  => "Rain Dogs",
      tracks => [ map { CD::Song->new({title => $_ }) }
                   ("Singapore", "Clap Hands", "Cemetary Polka", ...)
                ]
});
```

We could also choose FreezeThaw or Data::Dumper to do the serialization, or any of the other DBM drivers for the storage.

 One thing people expect to be able to do with MLDBM, but can't, is write to intermediate references. Let's say we have a simple hash of hashes:

```
use MLDBM qw(DB_File Storable); # Use a Sleepycat DB and
Storable
tie %hash, "MLDBM", "hash.db" or die $!;
$hash{test} = { "Hello" => "World" };
```

This works fine. But when we do:

```
$hash{test}->{Hello} = "Mother";
```

the assignment seems to have no effect. In short, you can't store to intermediate references using MLDBM. If you think how MLDBM works, this is quite obvious. Our assignment has done a fetch, which has produced a new data structure by thawing the scalar in the database. Then we've modified that data structure. However, modifying the data structure doesn't cause a STORE call to write the new data to the database; STORE is only called when we write directly to the tied hash. So to get the same effect, we need the rather more ugly:

```
$hash{test} = { %{$hash{test}}, Hello => "Mother" };
```

Since MLDBM uses a deep serializer, our example not only stores the CD object, but also the CD::Song objects and the CD::Artist object. When we retrieve album1 again, everything is available.

Pixie

The Pixie module from CPAN is an automated, ready-made implementation of all that we've been talking about in this section. It uses Storable to serialize objects, and then stores them in a data store—a relational database using DBI by default, but you can also define your own stores.

Pixie has two advantages over the hand-knit method we've used. First, and most important, it solves the pruning problem: it retrieves each new object in the data structure as it's referenced, rather than pulling everything in as a lump. If, for instance, we have a tree data structure where every object can see every other object, something based on MLDBM would have to read the entire tree structure into memory when we fetched any object in it. That's bad. Pixie doesn't do that.

The other advantage, and the way Pixie gets around this first problem, is that it stores each new object in the data structure separately. So when we stored our Tom Waits CD with MLDBM, we serialized the whole thing, including all the CD::Song and CD::Artist objects, into a scalar and stored that. If we stored a different CD by the same artist, we'd serialize all of its data, including the CD::Artist object, into a scalar and store that as well. We now have two copies of the same artist data stored in two different albums. This can only get worse. In the worst case of a tree structure, every object we serialize and store will have to contain the entire contents of the tree. That's bad. Pixie doesn't do that, either.

To demonstrate using Pixie, we'll use the default DBI data store. Before we can start storing objects, we first have to deploy the data store—that is, set up the tables that Pixie wants to deal with. We do this as a separate setup process before we use Pixie the first time:

```
use Pixie::Store::DBI;
Pixie::Store::DBI->deploy("dbi:mysql:dbname=pixie");
```

The deploy method creates new tables, so it will fail if the tables already exist. Now if we have pure-Perl, pure-data objects, Pixie just works. Let's take our Rain Dogs CD again, since that's what I was listening to when I wrote this chapter:

```
my $cd = CD->new({
    artist => $tom,
    title => "Rain Dogs"
    songs => [ map { CD::Song->new({title => $_ }) }
              ("Singapore", "Clap Hands", "Cemetary Polka",
               # ...
               ) ]
});
```

```
my $pixie = Pixie->new->connect("dbi:mysql:dbname=pixie");
my $cookie = $pixie->insert($cd);
```

This will store the data and return a GUID (globally unique identifier)—mine was
EAAC3A08-F6AA-11D8-96D6-8C22451C8AE2, and yours hopefully will not be. Now I can
use this GUID in a completely different program, and I get the data back:

```
use Pixie;
use CD;
my $pixie = Pixie->new->connect("dbi:mysql:dbname=pixie");
my $cd = $pixie->get("EAAC3A08-F6AA-11D8-96D6-8C22451C8AE2");

print $cd->artist->name; # "Tom Waits"
```

Notice that Pixie has not only stored the CD object that we asked it about, but it has
also stored the CD::Artist, CD::Person and all the CD::Song objects that related to it.
It only retrieves them, however, when we make the call to the relevant accessor. It's
very clever.

For our purposes, that's all there is to Pixie, but that's because our purposes are
rather modest. Pixie works extremely well when all the data belonging to an object is
accessible from Perl space—a blessed hash or blessed array reference. However,
objects implemented by XS modules often have data that's not available from Perl—
C data structures referred to by pointers, for instance. In that case, Pixie doesn't
know what to do and requires help from the programmer to explain how to store
and reconstruct the objects.

We'll use a pure Perl example, however, to demonstrate what's going on. In our
example, we have a bunch of Time::Piece objects in our storage. If these were instead
DateTime objects, we'd have to store all this every time we store a date:

```
$VAR1 = bless( {
                'tz' => bless( {
                                'name' => 'UTC'
                              }, 'DateTime::TimeZone::UTC' ),
                'local_c' => {
                                'quarter' => 3,
                                'minute' => 13,
                                'day_of_week' => 7,
                                'day' => 19,
                                'day_of_quarter' => 81,
                                'month' => 9,
                                'year' => 2004,
                                'hour' => 13,
                                'second' => 3,
                                'day_of_year' => 263
                             },
                ...,

              }, 'DateTime' );
```

This is not amazingly efficient, just to store what can be represented by an epoch time. Even though this is all pure Perl data, we can make it a bit tidier by making DateTime *complicit* with Pixie.

To do this, we implement a few additional methods in the DateTime namespace. First we use a proxy object to store the essential information about the DateTime object:

```
sub DateTime::px_freeze {
    my $datetime = shift;
    bless [ $datetime->epoch ], "Proxy::DateTime";
}
```

Now when Pixie comes to store a DateTime object, all it does instead is convert it to a Proxy::DateTime object that knows the epoch time and stores that instead.* Next, we need to be able to go from the proxy to the real DateTime object, when it is retrieved from the database. Remember that this needs to be a method on the proxy object, so it lives in the Proxy::DateTime namespace:

```
sub Proxy::DateTime::px_thaw {
    my $proxy = shift;
    DateTime->from_epoch(epoch => $proxy->[0]);
}
```

Some objects—like blessed scalars or code refs—are a bit more tricky to serialize. Because of this, Pixie won't serialize anything other than hash- or array-based classes, unless we explicitly tell it that we've handled the serialization ourselves:

```
sub MyModule::px_is_storable { 1 }
```

And that, really, is all there is to it.

Object Databases

While the methods we've seen in the previous section work very well for storing and retrieving individual objects, there are times when we want to deal with a massive collection of data with the same degree of efficiency. For instance, our CD collection may run to thousands of objects, while a simple query application—for example, to determine which artist recorded a particular track—would only use one or two of them. In this case, we don't want to load up the whole object store into memory before we run the query.

In fact, what we could really deal with is the kind of fast, efficient indexing and querying that is the hallmark of traditional relational databases such as Oracle or MySQL, but which dealt with objects in the same way as Pixie. We want an *object database*.

---

* Design pattern devotees call this the "memento" pattern.

Object Database Pitfalls

There are not many object databases on CPAN, and with good reason: writing object databases is incredibly difficult.

First, you need to worry about how to pick apart individual objects and store them separately, so that you don't end up with the pruning problem.

Second, you have to work out a decent way to index and query objects. Indexing and querying database rows in general is pretty easy, but objects? This is currently one of the areas that holds Pixie back from being an object database.

Allied with that, you need to work out how you're going to map the properties of your object to storage in a sensible way to allow such indexing; serialization-based solutions don't care about what's inside an object, they just write the whole thing into a string.

Fortunately, you don't really have to worry about these things; you can just use some of the existing solutions.

Tangram

Jean-Louis Leroy's Tangram is a mature and flexible but complex solution to mapping Perl objects onto database rows. Tangram is very explicit in terms of what the user must do to make it work. Except when it comes to filters, which we'll look at in a moment, Tangram is very short on DWIM.

For instance, Tangram relies on the user to provide a lot of class information, which it uses to decide how to map the objects onto the database. This gives you much more flexibility about how the database is laid out, but if you don't particularly care about that, it requires you to do a lot of tedious scaffolding work.

To get Tangram up and running on our CD database, we must first define the schema as a Perl data structure. This tells Tangram the classes we're interested in persisting, as well as which attributes to save and what data types they're going to be. Here's the schema for our classes:

```perl
use Tangram;
use Tangram::TimePiece;
use DBI;
use CD;
our $schema = Tangram::Relational->schema({
    classes => [
        CD => {
            fields => {
                string => [ qw(title) ],
                timepiece => [ qw(publishdate) ],
                iarray  => {
                    songs => {
                        class => 'CD::Song',
```

```
                        aggreg => 1,
                        back => 'cd',
                    },
                },
            },
        },
        'CD::Song' => {
            fields => {
                string => [ qw(name) ],
            }
        },
        'CD::Artist' => {
            abstract => 1,
            fields => {
                string => [ qw(name popularity) ],
                iset => {
                    cds => {
                        class => 'CD',
                        aggreg => 1,
                        back => 'artist'
                    },
                },
            },
        },
        'CD::Person' => {
            bases  => [ "CD::Artist" ],
            fields => {
                string => [ qw(gender haircolor) ],
                timepiece => [ qw(birthdate) ],
            },
        },
        'CD::Band' => {
            bases  => [ "CD::Artist" ],
            fields => {
                timepiece => [ qw(creationdate enddate) ],
                set => {
                    members => {
                        class => 'CD::Person',
                        table => "artistgroup",
                    },
                },
            },
        },
    ]});
    $dbh = DBI->connect($data_source,$user,$password);
    Tangram::Relational->deploy($schema, $dbh);
    $dbh->disconnect();
```

With the schema built and deployed, we can store, retrieve, and search for objects via Tangram::Storage objects, and for so-called *remote objects*, which represent a class of objects of a particular type in storage.

Tangram CRUD: create, read, update, delete

We can create and insert objects, like so:

```perl
my ($cd, @songs, $band, @people);
my $tom = CD::Band->new
    ({ name => "Tom Waits",
       popularity => "1",
       cds => Set::Object->new
       (
        $cd =
        CD->new({title => "Rain Dogs",
                 songs => [
                 @songs = map {CD::Song->new({ name => $_ })}
                 "Singapore", "Clap Hands", "Cemetary Polka", ...
                          ],
                }),
       ),
    });

# stick it in
my $storage = Tangram::Storage->connect($schema, $data_source, $username, $password);
my $oid = $storage->insert($tom);
my $id = $storage->export_object($tom);
```

Later, we can retrieve objects either by their object ID, or by class and ID:

```perl
# Object ID
$band = $storage->load($oid);

# Class and ID - polymorphic select
$band = $storage->import_object("CD::Artist", $id);
```

The import_object method is *polymorphic*, meaning that it can load the CD::Artist object with ID $id, even though that object is actually a CD::Band object.

However, selecting by storage ID is not enough to get us by. We also need to be able to query objects based on some specification of which objects we want.

With Tangram, you first fetch a remote object, representing a *database-side object*. In its blank state, this remote object could represent any object in the database of that type. You then write expressions that refer to a subset of those objects with regular Perl operators:

```perl
my $r_artist = $storage->remote("CD::Artist");

my @artists = $storage->select
    ( $r_artist,
      $r_artist->{name} eq "Tom Waits" );
my $r_cd = $storage->remote("CD");
```

It may look like that second parameter to select is going to return a single (false) value and the select isn't going to work; however, Tangram is more magical than that. First, the remote object doesn't represent a single artist—it represents all the possible artists. Second, $r_artist->{name} returns an overloaded object, and just as we saw in the first chapter, we can use overloading to determine how objects behave in the presence of operators like eq. Here, the Tangram::Storage class overloads all the comparison operators to return Tangram::Filter objects; these objects store up all the comparisons and use them to represent a WHERE statement in the SQL select.

Tangram's query filters are extremely expressive:

```
my $join = ($r_cd->{artist} eq $r_artist);
my $query =
    ( $r_artist->{name}->upper( )->like(uc("%beat%"))
      | $r_cd->{title}->upper( )->like(uc("%beat%")) );

my $filter = $join & $query;
my $cursor = $storage->cursor ( $r_cd, $filter );

my @cds=( );
while ( my $cd = $cursor->current ) {
    print("found cd = " ,$cd->title,
          ", artist = ", $cd->artist->name, "\n");
    $cursor->next;
}
```

Note that in the above example, we built the query keeping join conditions and query fragments seperate, combining them to pass to the Tangram::Storage function. Tangram uses a single & for AND and a single | for OR (see Tangram::Expr). We also used a Tangram::Cursor to iterate over the returned results, rather than slurping them all in at once. Finally, the CD::Artist object corresponding to each CD object is fetched via a *back-reference*.

A back-reference is an example of a third method of traversing a Tangram stored object structure: through the relationships of the object. Tangram ships with seven types of object relationship classes: many-to-one relationships (references), one-to-many relationships (intrusive or foreign key relationships, with three variants: Sets, Arrays, and Hashes), as well as many-to-many relationships (relationships connected via a link table—again with three variants of Set, Array, and Hash).

So, once we have the @artists, we can retrieve the associated information just by following the Perl object structure. This is implemented via *on-demand storage references*.

```
@cds = $artists[0]->cds->members;  # Set::Object
my @tracks = @{ $cds->[0]->songs };   # Array
```

So, we've covered create and read—what about updates? Updates are performed by $storage->update:

```
my ($pfloyd) = $storage->select
    ( $r_artist,
      $r_artist->{name} eq "Pink Floyd" );

$cd;
$pfloyd->cds->insert
    ($cd=
```

```
CD->new({ title => "The Dark Side of The Moon",
          publishdate => Time::Piece->strptime("2000-04-06", "%y-%m-%d"),
          songs => [ map { CD::Song->new({ name => $_ }) }
                       "Speak To Me/Breathe", "On The Run",
                     "Time", "The Great Gig in the Sky",
                       "Money", "Us And Them",
                       "Any Colour You Like", "Brain Damage",
                       "Eclipse",
                   ],
        })
  );
$pfloyd->popularity("legendary");
$storage->update($pfloyd);
$storage->id($cd);
```

So far we've demonstrated three points about Tangram's update facilities. The final aspect of Tangram's CRUD—deleting objects—is done with $storage->erase( ):

```
my (@gonners) = $storage->select
    ($r_artist,
     $r_artist->{popularity} eq "one hit wonder");

$storage->erase(@gonners);
```

Tangram has excellent transaction support, mature object caching abilities, functions to deal with short-term dirty read problems, and the orthogonal ability to perform schema migration using two database handles. Its debugging output, selected with the environment variable TANGRAM_TRACE or by setting the Perl variable $Tangram::TRACE to a filehandle, provides a clear picture of what queries are being run by your program.

Its major downsides are that it does not support partially reading objects (only complete rows), it cannot easily be queried with raw SQL expressions, and it does not deal with indexing (the assumption being that the database administrator can set up appropriate indexes, or that creating such indexes happens independently of the normal schema deployment).

Database Abstraction

Tangram has given us a way to store and retrieve objects in a database. The other side of the coin is the situation of having an existing database and wanting to get a view of it in terms of Perl objects. This is a very subtle distinction, but an important one. In the case of Tangram (and indeed, Pixie), we didn't really care what the database schema was, because the database was just an incidental way for Tangram to store its stuff. It could create whatever tables and columns it wanted; what we really care about is what the objects look like. In the current case, though, we already have the database; we have a defined schema, and we want the database abstraction tool to work around that and tell us what the objects should look like.

There are several good reasons why you might want to do this. For many people, database abstraction is attractive purely because it avoids having to deal with SQL or the relatively tedious process of interacting with the DBI; but there's a more fundamental reason.

When we fetch some data from the database, in the ordinary DBI model, it then becomes divorced from its original database context. It is no longer live data. We have a hash reference or array reference of data—when we change elements in that reference, nothing changes in the database at all. We need a separate step to put our changes back. This isn't the paradigm we're used to programming in. We want our data to do something, and data that do something are usually called *objects*—we want to treat our database rows as objects, with data accessors, instantiation and deletion methods, and so on. We want to map between relational databases and objects, and this is called, naturally, *object relational mapping*.

SQLite

SQLite (*http://www.hwaci.com/sw/sqlite/*) is a self-contained relational database that works on a simple file in the filesystem, and it's getting ever more sophisticated. It's also incredibly fast. Instead of having a separate database daemon that listens for and responds to queries, SQLite takes the DBM approach of providing a C library that acts on the data directly. If you install the DBD::SQLite module from CPAN, you'll have everything you need to use relational databases without the hassle of installing one of the bigger database engines:

```
use DBI;
my $dbh = DBI->connect("dbi:SQLite:dbname=music.db");
$dbh->do("CREATE TABLE cds ( ... )");
```

Trivial Mapping

We'll demonstrate some of the principles of an object-relational mapper by creating a very, very simple object-relational mapper that is read-only—it doesn't allow us to make changes to the database. Then we'll show how to add this functionality, and look at Class::DBI, a very similar mapper that does it all for us.

Before I heard of Class::DBI, I actually implemented something like this in production code. The basic idea looks like this:

```
package CD::DBI;
our $dbh = DBI->connect("dbd:mysql:music");

sub select {
    my ($class, $sql, @params) = @_;
    my $sth = $dbh->prepare($sql);
    $sth->execute(@params);
```

```
        my @objects;
        while (my $obj = $sth->fetchrow_hashref()) {
            push @objects, (bless $obj, $class);
        }
    }

    package CD;
    use base 'CD::DBI';

    package CD::Artist;
    use base 'CD::DBI';
    #...

    package main;

    my @cds = CD->select("SELECT * FROM cd");
```

fetchrow_hashref is a very useful DBI method that returns each row as a hash:

```
    {
        id => 180,
        title => "Inside Out",
        artist => 105,
        publishdate => "1983-03-14"
    }
```

This looks rather like our CD objects, so we simply bless this into the right class, and all the accessors work as normal. This is actually very close to what we want. There are two things we can improve: artist now returns an ID instead of a CD::Artist object and any changes we make don't get written back to the database.

So, to deal with the first problem, we can modify the artist accessor like so:

```
    package CD;
    sub artist {
        my $self = shift;
        my ($artist) = CD::Artist->select(
            "SELECT * FROM artist WHERE id = ?",
            shift->{artist}
        );
        return $artist;
    }
```

This time, we retrieve an individual record from the artist table and bless it into the CD::Artist class. We can write similar accessors for other relationships. For instance, to get all the tracks belonging to a specific CD:

```
    sub tracks {
        my $self = shift;
        CD::Track->select("SELECT * FROM track WHERE cd = ?",
                          $self->{id}
                          );
    }
```

To make this whole system read-write instead of read-only, we need to update our accessors again, something like this:

```
package CD;
sub title {
    my ($self, $title) = @_;
    if ($title) {
        $CD::DBI::dbh->do("UPDATE cd SET title = ? WHERE id = ?",
                          undef, $title, $self->{id});
    }
    $self->SUPER::title($title);
}
```

But here we're writing a lot of code; the purpose of using automated accessor generators was to avoid going through all this rigmarole. Perhaps there should be a module that generates database-aware accessors....

Class::DBI

By far my favorite of the object-relational mapping modules is Michael Schwern and Tony Bowden's Class::DBI. It is very easy to learn and to set up, highly extensible, and supported by a wide range of auxilliary modules. It is also, not entirely coincidentally, rather like the simple mapper we just created. To set it up, we subclass Class::DBI to create a driver class specific to our database:

```
package CD::DBI;
use base 'Class::DBI';
__PACKAGE__->connection("dbi:mysql:musicdb");
```

We do this so that when we implement the table classes, they all know where they're connecting to. Now let's take the first table, the artist table:

```
package CD::Artist;
use base 'CD::DBI';
__PACKAGE__->table("artist");
__PACKAGE__->columns(All => qw/artistid name popularity/);
```

Here we're using our own CD::Artist class and the other classes we will generate, instead of the classes we wrote in the earlier chapter. The interface will be just the same as our original CD::Artist, because Class::DBI uses the same Class::Accessor way of creating accessors.

It also adds a few more methods to the CD::Artist class to help us search for and retrieve database rows:

```
my $waits = CD::Artist->search(name => "Tom Waits")->first;
print $waits->artistid; # 859
print $waits->popularity; # 634

my $previous = CD::Artist->retrieve(858);
print $previous->name; # Tom Petty and the Heartbreakers

# So how many Toms are there?
```

```
my $toms = CD::Artist->search_like(name => "Tom %")->count;
print $toms; # 6

for my $artist ( CD::Artist->retrieve_all ) {
    print $artist->name, ": ", $artist->popularity, "\n";
}
```

We can also create a new artist by passing in a hash reference of attributes:

```
$buff = CD::Artist->create({
    name => "Buffalo Springfield",
    popularity => 10
});
```

Class::DBI automatically creates data accessors for each of the columns of the table; we can update columns in the database by passing arguments to the accessors. Here's a program that uses Mac::AppleScript to ask iTunes for the currently playing artist, and then increments the artist's popularity:

```
use Mac::AppleScript qw(RunAppleScript;
my $current = RunAppleScript(<<AS);
  tell application "iTunes"
    artist of current track
  end tell
AS

my $artist = CD::Artist->find_or_create({ name => $current });
$artist->popularity( $artist->popularity() + 1 );
$artist->update;
```

This uses find_or_create to first search for the name, then retrieve the existing row if there is one, or create a new one otherwise. Then we increment the popularity—normally we'd think about race conditions when updating a database like this, but in this case, we know that nothing else is going to be updating the library when the script is run. We explicitly update the row in the table with a call to update. I dislike doing this, so I often tell Class::DBI to do it automatically with autoupdate:

```
package CD::Artist
use base 'MusicDB::DBI';
__PACKAGE__->table("artist");
__PACKAGE__->columns(All => qw/artistid name popularity/);
__PACKAGE__->autoupdate(1);
```

Now we can dispense with the update calls—updates to accessors are instantly reflected in the database.

Class::DBI often wants me to set up things by hand that the computer should be able to do for me. For instance, I feel I shouldn't have to specify the columns in the table. Thankfully, there are numerous database-specific extensions for Class::DBI on CPAN that know how to interrogate the database for this information:

```
package CD::DBI;
use base 'Class::DBI::mysql';
__PACKAGE__->connection("dbi:mysql:musicdb");
```

```
__PACKAGE__->autoupdate(1);

package CD::Artist;
use base 'CD::DBI';
__PACKAGE__->set_up_table("artist");
```

This uses the mysql extension to query the database for the columns in the table.

Once we've set up all our tables, we can start declaring the relationships between them.

Relationships

Class::DBI supports several types of database relationships. The two most common are has_a and has_many. It also allows you to use or write plug-in modules to declare other relationship types.

The diagram in Figure 4-1 illustrates the difference between has_a and has_many.

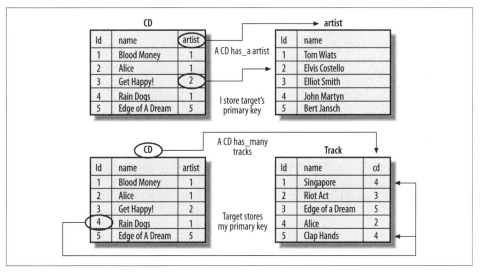

Figure 4-1. has_a versus has_many

We've already seen the use of a has_a relationship between CDs and artists—each CD has_a artist. We've also already written some code to implement a nice Perlish interface to it: when we ask a CD object for its artist, it takes the artist's primary key, finds the row in the artist table with that ID, and returns the appropriate object. However, in Class::DBI, instead of writing our own accessor, we just declare the relationship:

```
CD->has_a(artist => "CD::Artist");
CD::Track->has_a(song => "CD::Song");
# ...
```

The nice thing about this is that we can also declare relationships to classes that are not Class::DBI based but that follow the same general pattern: find the column in the database, do something to it, and turn it into an object. For instance, the publishdate column needs to be turned into a Time::Piece object:

```
CD->has_a(publishdate => 'Time::Piece',
            inflate => sub { Time::Piece->strptime(shift, "%Y-%m-%d") },
            deflate => 'ymd',
        );
```

As before, we relate a column to a class, but we also specify a subroutine that goes from the data in the database to an object, and a method to go the other way, to serialize the object back into the database.

A has_many relationship is also easy to set up; instead of writing the tracks accessor as we did before, we ask Class::DBI to do it for us:

```
CD->has_many(tracks => "CD::Track");
```

Now, for instance, to dump all the tracks in the database, we can say:

```
for my $cd (CD->retrieve_all) {
    print "CD: ".$cd->title."\n";
    print "Artist: ".$cd->artist->name."\n";
    for my $track ($cd->tracks) {
        print "\t".$track->song->name."\n";
    }
    print "\n\n";
}
```

For more complex relationships, such as the way an artist is either a person or a group, we can use a plug-in relationship like Class::DBI::Relationship::IsA:

```
use Class::DBI::Relationship::IsA;
CD::Artist->is_a(person      => 'CD::Person');
CD::Artist->is_a(artistgroup => 'CD::Artistgroup');
```

The is_a relationship does the right thing: it inherits the accessors of the class that we're referring to. If we ask a CD::Artist for haircolor, it transforms this into a call to $artist->person->haircolor.

Plug-in relationships for Class::DBI are a relatively new concept, and there are not many on CPAN at the moment. HasVariant allows you to use one column to inflate to more than one kind of object; so, for instance, you could have your $cd->artist return a CD::Person or CD::Artistgroup directly depending on the data in the column. There's also HasManyOrdered, which is similar to has_many but allows you to specify how the results should be returned; we should, for instance, ensure that the tracks returned by $cd->tracks are returned in their track number on the CD.

Class::DBI extensions

The other great thing about `Class::DBI` is that there are so many additional modules that make it easier to use. For instance, in the same way that `Class::DBI::mysql` asked the database for its rows, you can set up all your classes at once by asking the database for its tables as well. The `Class::DBI::Loader` module does just this:

```
my $loader = Class::DBI::Loader->new(
    dsn => "dbd:mysql:music",
    namespace => "MusicDB"
);
```

With our database, this will set up classes called `MusicDB::CD`, `MusicDB::Artist`, and so on. All we need to do is set up the reltionships between the classes.

For very simple relationships, `Class::DBI::Loader::Relationship` can help set these up as well:

```
$loader->relationship("a cd has an artist");
$loader->relationship("a cd has tracks");
# ...
```

There's also `Class::DBI::DATA::Schema` to define database tables from schemas placed in the DATA section of a class, `Class::DBI::Plugin::RetrieveAll` adds the functionality to easily do a `SELECT *` with various ordering and restrictions, and we'll meet a few more plug-in classes later in the chapter.

Other Contenders

I've just demonstrated `Class::DBI` here, but there are many more object-relational mapping tools on CPAN. I believe that `Class::DBI` has the cleanest and the simplest interface, which makes it ideal for demonstrating the principles of object-relational mapping, but there are those who would contend that this simplicity limits what it can do. Some of the other tools available make different trade-offs between complexity and power.

For instance, one limitation of `Class::DBI` is the difficulty of creating complex multi-table joins that are executed in one SQL statement, letting the database do the work. `Class::DBI` leaves it to programmers to do this kind of work in Perl or build their own abstracted SQL using `Class::DBI` hooks and extensions. On the other hand, something like `DBIx::SearchBuilder` excels at constructing SQL in advance. Search-Builder is the foundation of the Request Tracker problem tracking system, perhaps one of the most widely deployed and complex enterprise Perl applications; so Search-Builder is clearly up to the job.

Other modules you should know about include SPOPS and Alzabo, both mature and fully featured relational mappers. There's also interesting work going on in `Class::PINT` to apply Tangram-style object persistence on top of `Class::DBI`.

Practical Uses in Web Applications

One of the more popular ways of creating web-based applications these days is called the *MVC Pattern*—it's a design pattern where you have three components: a model of your data, a view that displays it, and a controller that routes requests and actions between the other two. It's a design pattern that first appeared in graphical applications in the Smalltalk programming language, but has translated reasonably well over to the Web. The key point of MVC is that, if you do it properly, your data model, your view, and your controller can be completely independent components, and you only need to worry about what goes on at the edges.

Now, the kind of templating system we looked at in the previous chapter looks very much like a view class: it abstracts out a way of presenting data. Similarly, the ways of treating database rows as objects look very much like model classes. Almost for free, using CPAN modules, we've got two of the three parts we need for a web application. The upshot is that, if you follow the MVC strategy, you have a very cheap way of writing web applications in which you delegate presentation to a templating library, you delegate data representation to an ORM library, and all you need to care about is what the darned thing actually does.

While this strategy can be applied to pretty much any of the tools we've talked about in the past two chapters, I want to look particularly at using Class::DBI and Template Toolkit; partly for the sake of example, partly because I personally think they fit together extremely well, and partly for another reason that will become apparent shortly.

Class::DBI and the Template Toolkit

The magic coupling of CDBI and TT, as they're affectionately known, was first popularized around 2001 by Tony Bowden, who'd just taken over maintaining Class::DBI. The idea spread through the mailing lists and Perl-mongers groups until, in 2003, Kate Pugh wrote a perl.com article (*http://www.perl.com/lpt/a/2003/07/15/nocode.html*) expounding the concept. Why? Because, as Pugh says, CDBI and TT work extremely well together.

Part of the reason for this is that, when templating database applications, you often want to display your objects and their attributes. Class::DBI allows you to get at their attributes by simple method calls, and Template Toolkit provides an easy way of making method calls in the templates. Your data goes straight from the database to the template without much need for any code in the middle.

For instance, for the simple job of viewing a CD, we can have a CGI script like so:

```
use CD;
use CGI qw/:standard/;
use Template;
print header();
```

```
my $id = param("id");
if (!$id) {
    print "<h1> You must supply an ID! </h1>"; exit;
}
my $obj = CD->retrieve($id);
Template->new()->process("view.tt", { cd => $obj });
```

This takes the ID of a CD from the CGI form variables, retrieves the relevant CD, and passes it through to the template, which might look like this:

```
<html>
    <head> <title>[% cd.name %]</title> </head>
<body>
    <h1> [% cd.name %] </h1>
    <h2> [% cd.artist.name %] </h2>

<ul>
[% FOR track = cd.tracks %]
    <li> [% track.song.name %] </li>
[% END %]
</ul>
</body>
</html>
```

To view a list of CDs, we simply pass more objects to the template. However, if we want to avoid hitting the user's browser with the data on several hundred CDs, we can restrict the number of items on a page with Class::DBI::Pager:

```
use CD;
package CD;
use Class::DBI::Pager;

package main;
use CGI qw/:standard/;
use Template;
print header();
use constant ITEMS_PER_PAGE => 20;

my $page = param("page") || 1;
my $pager = CD->page(ITEMS_PER_PAGE, $page);
my @cds = $pager->retrieve_all;
Template->new()->process("view.tt", { cds => \@cds, pager => $pager });
```

Class::DBI::Pager is a mix-in for Class::DBI-based classes that allows you to ask for a particular page of data, given the number of items of data on a page and the page number you want. Calling page returns a Data::Page object that knows the first page, the last page, which items are on this page, and so on, and can be used in our template for navigation:

```
[% IF pager.previous_page %]
<A HREF="?page=[%pager.previous_page%]"> Previous page </A> |
```

```
[% END %]
Page [% pager.current_page %]
[% IF pager.next_page %]
| <A HREF="?page=[%pager.next_page%]"> Next page </A>
[% END%]
```

The `Class::DBI::FromCGI` and `Class::DBI::AsForm` modules make it easy to construct forms for editing or creating records and then processing those changes in the database.

Of course, similar tricks can be done with templating languages other than 'Template Toolkit, such as `HTML::Mason`, but TT allows relatively complex constructs, such as method calls, without requiring the template writer to learn a fully fledged programming language. In an ideal world, the database can be handed off to a database team to populate, the templates given to web designers to create, and all that you as a programmer need to write are the kind of short scripts given above.

Or maybe even less....

Maypole

At the beginning of 2004, a few ideas relating to CDBI and TT came together in my head, and I found myself writing lots of web applications that all did more or less the same sort of thing—they determined a set of CDBI objects to retrieve, got them out of a database, performed some action on them, and placed them into a template. I did what every good programmer should do on feeling that they've had to do something twice—I abstracted it out. The result was Maypole.

Maypole has two complementary but very distinct goals. Its first goal is to be a way of rapidly designing web applications by providing all the common code and templates for a standard frontend to a database: if you need a way to simply add, delete, view, and update records in a relational database, you can do it in no more than 20 lines of Perl code.

The second goal of Maypole is to be a generic controller method for all web applications. By default, it hooks into CDBI as a model class and TT as a template class to provide all the scaffolding code for a web application; all that you need to do is write the logic specific to what your application should do. And so the first goal—a web frontend to a database—uses this generic controller with a load of metadata from the model class and a set of carefully designed default templates to produce an application that does the right thing.

Let's demonstrate Maypole by putting a quick frontend onto our `Class::DBI` record database. The code is simple enough:

```
package CDPole;
use base 'Maypole::Application';
use CD;
CDPole->config->model("Maypole::Model::CDBI::Plain");
```

```
CDPole->setup([qw/ CD CD::Artist CD::Track /]);
CDPole->config->uri_base("http://localhost/cdpole/");
CDPole->config->template_root("/home/simon/modules/Apache-MVC/templates/");
1;
```

We first say that we are based on `Maypole::Application`, a special class that determines whether this application should be CGI-based or Apache `mod_perl`-based, and sets up the inheritance appropriately. In our case, we're going to run this as a `mod_perl` application.

Next, we say that we're using a plain `Class::DBI` data source. If we didn't say this, Maypole would default to using `Class::DBI::Loader` to automatically read the tables from our data source. We also tell the application about the classes—that is, the tables—that we want to use. Finally, we configure the application, telling it where it will live and where the templates are. With no change to the default templates, our application looks like Figure 4-2.

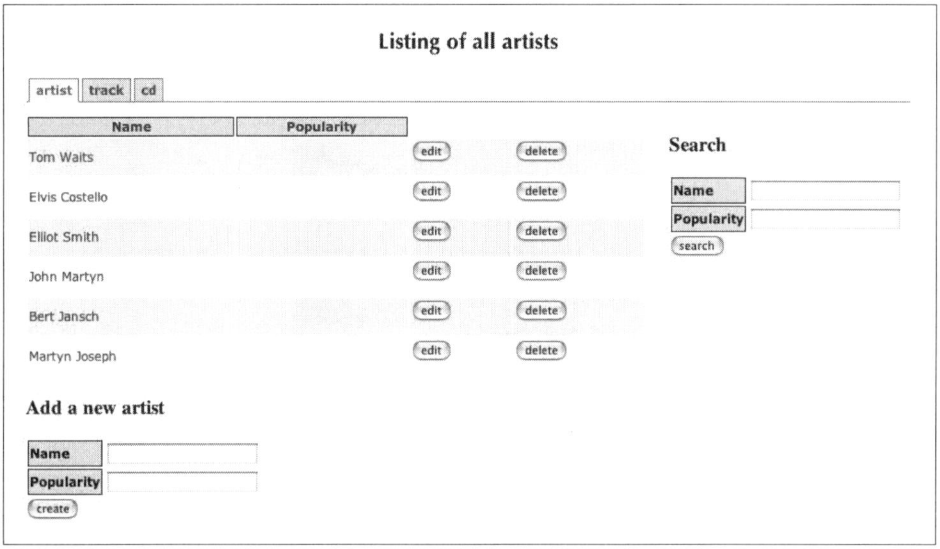

Figure 4-2. Viewing artists in Maypole

Of course, we don't always want to use the default templates; in fact, we should hardly ever use them, although they are useful for having something up and running quickly to interface to a database. Maypole allows us to override the templates in several ways. To understand these, we need to look at the basic principles of how Maypole works. Now we are moving from the first goal, the database interface, to the second goal, the application framework.

Maypole applications are made up of *actions*, which pull together some Perl code from the model side of the application with a template from the view side. The action we saw in the figure above was a `list` action on the `artist` class. Maypole, in effect, called `CD::Artist->list( )` and put the results into a suitable `list` template. A more complicated action would be triggered by the URL *http://localhost/cdpole/ artist/edit/110*. This would select artist ID 110 (Joni Mitchell), call `CD::Artist->` edit with that artist object as a parameter, and then find an `edit` template. We can view the whole Maypole process pictorially in Figure 4-3.

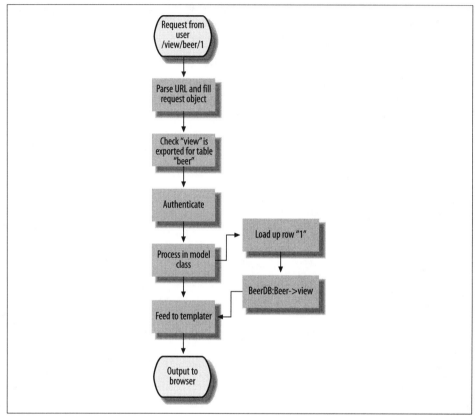

Figure 4-3. The Maypole work flow

To find the appropriate template, Maypole looks in three directories: first, a directory named after the table. So for `/artist/edit/110`, it would look for `artist/edit`. If this is not found, it looks in a directory specific to your application, which is called custom; that is, `custom/edit`. If again this is not found, Maypole falls back to the factory-supplied template in `factory/edit`.

As well as designing your own templates, you can also design your own actions by specifying that a particular class's method is exported and can be called from the web. This is done with the `:Exported` attribute:

```
package CD::Artist;

sub all_tracks :Exported {
    my ($self, $r, $artist) = @_;
```

```
        $r->template_args->{tracks} = [ map { $_->tracks } $artist->cds ]
    }
```

This method receives the Maypole request object and the artist object. We get a list of all the tracks on all the CDs that this artist has recorded and feed that to the template. The artist/all_tracks template might look like this:

```
[% PROCESS macros %]
[% INCLUDE header %]
<h2> All tracks for [% artist.name %] </h2>

<ul>
[% FOR track = tracks %]
<li> [% maybe_link_view(track) %] </li>
[% END %]
</ul>
[% INCLUDE footer %]
```

That's all it takes to add a new action to the application. These are the basics of Maypole and enough to construct reasonably sophisticated web applications. Maypole has a full manual available at *http://maypole.perl.org/*.

We've seen Maypole in relation to Class::DBI and Template Toolkit, but its model and view classes are abstracted out such that you can use it with Alzabo or SPOPS, or with HTML::Mason or any other templating or database abstraction class you wish. This brings us onto the whole range of other application frameworks available for Perl.

Other Application Frameworks

Maypole is not the only player in the application framework space.

OpenInteract is Chris Winters's application framework using the SPOPS database abstraction layer. It's a fully featured framework, with session handling, LDAP support, authentication, groups, caching, cookies, and all sorts of other bits in the core.

PageKit is not tied to any object mapper, but it does require you to use either HTML::Template for your templates or XSLT.

OpenFrame has no relation to OpenInteract. It is something more than a web application framework; it works around the concept of pipelines, similar to the Maypole workflow we saw above, but in a much more generic way. Unlike the other tools, it doesn't provide any link with a data store; you have to code all that up yourself.

CGI::Application is an interesting idea that is parallel to these other kinds of application frameworks; it provides a way of reusing components of CGI applications (such as a package that provides a web-to-email form) so that you can recombine them in whatever way you want. It's another way of quickly creating web applications, but again it doesn't provide any MVC functionality or any direct link to a data store.

Conclusion

Storing and retrieving data is the backbone of programming, so it shouldn't be much of a surprise that there are so many techniques available to make it easier. We've looked at ways of storing keyed data using DBMs, extended that with serialization of objects to create a way to store objects in DBMs, then used Pixie to organize our object store. This brought us on to looking at Tangram as a more flexible and powerful object database. Next, we turned the problem over and tried to make databases look like objects, using `Class::DBI`. Finally, we showed how this view of databases works in concert with the templating techniques we looked at in Chapter 3 to create application frameworks like Maypole, allowing you to write large web applications with very little code.

## CHAPTER 5

Natural Language Tools

Sean Burke, author of *Perl and LWP* and a professional linguist, once described artificial intelligence as the study of programming situations where you either don't know what you want or don't know how to get it.

Natural-language processing, or NLP, is the application of AI techniques to answer questions about text written in a human language: what does it mean, what other documents is it like, and so on. As Perl is often described as a text-processing language, it shouldn't be much of a surprise to find that there are a great many modules and techniques available in Perl for carrying out NLP-related tasks.

But as we've seen so far in this book, the real strength of Perl is not in the ease with which we can program particular techniques, but that so many of the techniques we need—techniques to break texts into sentences and words, to correctly strip the endings off inflected words, to put the right endings back on again, and so on—have already been implemented and placed on CPAN. So in this chapter we're going to take a tour of the natural language section of CPAN, and see how we can use its modules to slice and dice any language text we need to deal with.

Perl and Natural Languages

There's an especially good reason why Perl is used for handling natural language problems—Perl was created with natural languages in mind. In fact, Perl's creator, Larry Wall, has a joint degree in natural and artificial languages and sees Perl as influenced by both branches of his education.

For instance, as Larry says, it is "officially OK" to program in a restricted subset of Perl, a sort of baby Perl. Much as no one is expected to learn the entirety of a human language before speaking it, Perl's ability to express programming concepts in multiple ways allows for a wide range of abilities to get the same job done.

This is also why Perl folk aren't particularly worried about the ambiguities in the grammar of the language—natural languages *need* ambiguity.* Perl can work out whether / is the division operator or the start of a regular expression based on context, the way humans do.

You can read more about the natural language concepts that influenced (and continue to influence) the design of Perl at Larry's site: *http://www.wall.org/~larry/ natural.html*.

Handling English Text

Most of the time when dealing with natural-language processing we don't really need any heavy, state-of-the-art language manipulation algorithms. Indeed, most of what we're doing with Perl involves merely throwing around different chunks of text.

Pluralizations and Inflections

Our introduction to handling English text comes from the perennial user interface disaster:

```
You have 1 messages.
```

If you've been using (or perhaps writing) bad code for long enough, you might not see anything wrong with that, but it is actually somewhat grammatically lacking. Everyone at some point has written code that gets around the problem, perhaps a little like this:

```
print "You have " . $messages . " message" . ($messages == 1 ? "" : "s") . ".\n";
```

This itself should already be looking like a candidate for modularization, but the problem gets worse:

```
You have 2 messages in 2 mailboxs.
```

Another oops. We surely meant mailboxes. We could write another special case for the word mailbox, but what's really needed is a generic routine to make things agree with a number. Unfortunately, of course, due to the hideous complexity of the English language, this is a near-impossible task. Thankfully, the great Dr. Damian Conway speaks Australian English, simplifying the problem dramatically, and has produced the Lingua::EN::Inflect module.

This provides a whole host of subroutines, but perhaps the most useful for us are the PL, NO, and NUMWORDS routines.

---

* The aforementioned Sean Burke has a linguistic conjecture that says all natural languages tend toward some element of grammatical ambiguity; ambiguous languages are easier to learn. This may explain the relative difficulty of learning highly regularized artificial languages, such as Lojban.

The first subroutine, PL, provides a way to get at the plural form of a given word:

```
% perl -MLingua::EN::Inflect=PL -le 'print "There are 2 ",PL("aide-de-camp")'
There are 2 aides-de-camp
```

Additionally, you can pass in a number as well as a word to be pluralized, and PL will only do the pluralization if the number requires a plural.

```
use Lingua::EN::Inflect qw(PL);
for my $catcount (0..2) {
    print "I saw $catcount ", PL("cat", $catcount), "\n";
}

# I saw 0 cats
# I saw 1 cat
# I saw 2 cats
```

Now we're closer to solving our message/mailbox problem:

```
print "You have $message ", PL("message", $message), " ",
    " in $mailbox ", PL("mailbox", $mailbox), "\n";
```

This is a little smarter, although there's a certain amount of repetition in there. This is where we move onto the next subroutine, NO. This combines the number with the appropriate plural and, additionally, translates "0" into the slightly more readable "no":

```
use Lingua::EN::Inflect qw(NO);
my $message = 0; my $mailbox = 4;

print "You have ".NO("message", $message). " in ".
    NO("mailbox", $mailbox)."\n";

# You have no messages in 4 mailboxes
```

I prefer a slightly more refined approach, which takes advantage of the fact that people find it easier to read numbers from one to ten in running text if they're spelled out. For this, we need to bring in the NUMWORDS subroutine, which converts a number to its English equivalent. My preferred pluralization routine looks like this:

```
sub pl {
    my ($thing, $number) = @_;
    return NUMWORDS($number). " ".PL($thing, $number)
        if $number >= 1 and $number <= 10;

    NO($thing, $number);
}
```

This handles "no cats," "one cat," "two cats," and "65 poets-in-residence" all perfectly well.

Converting Words to Numbers

The handy `NUMWORDS` subroutine from `Lingua::EN::Inflect` turns a number into English text for human-friendly display. A bunch of other modules on CPAN do roughly the same thing, including `Lingua::EN::Numbers`, `Lingua::EN::Nums2Words`, and `Lingua::Num2Word`.

However, if we're really doing natural language work and trying to extract meaning from a chunk of text, we are often called to do precisely the opposite—turn some English text representing a number into its computer-friendly set of digits. The best Perl module for this on CPAN is Joey Hess's `Lingua::EN::Words2Nums`.

Although it doesn't give you a regular expression for extracting numbers directly, once you have your number, it does a very thorough job of turning it into a digit string. The module exports the `words2nums` function, which does all the hard work:

```
% perl -MLingua::EN::Words2Nums -e 'print words2nums("twenty-five")'
25
```

I particularly like this module because it caters to the fact that I can't spell. So, if I misspell forty-two, `words2nums` still returns the desired result:

```
% perl -MLingua::EN::Words2Nums -e 'print words2nums("fourty-two")'
42
```

However, the fact that it can't scan through a text and return the first number it sees can be a bit of a pain. It's all very well if we're using it when prompting for a number:

```
my $times;
do {
    print "How many times should we repeat the process? ";
    $times = words2nums(scalar <STDIN>);
    last if defined $times;
    print "Sorry, I didn't understand that number.\n";
} while 1;
```

But if, for instance, we want to write a supply chain program that automatically processes customer orders by email, we need to be able to scan through the text of the email to extract the numbers, so we can turn "I would like to buy forty-five copies of *Advanced Perl Programming*" into:

```
$order = { quantity => 45, title => "Advanced Perl Programming" };
```

As it stands, Lingua::EN::Words2Nums won't let us do this; it wants the numbers pre-extracted. So we have to do a bit of trickery. Looking at how Lingua::EN::Words2Nums works, we see that it builds up a regular expression from a set of words:

```
our %nametosub = (
    naught =>   [ \&num, 0 ],   # Cardinal numbers, leaving out the a
    nought =>   [ \&num, 0 ],
    zero =>     [ \&num, 0 ],   # ones that just add "th".
    one =>      [ \&num, 1 ],   first =>    [ \&num, 1 ],
...

);

# Note the ordering, so that eg, ninety has a chance to match before nine.
my $numregexp = join("|", reverse sort keys %nametosub);
$numregexp=qr/($numregexp)/;
```

This is a big help, but we can't, unfortunately, steal this regexp directly, for two reasons. First, it's in a private lexical variable, so we can't easily get at it. Second, Words2Nums also does some munging on the text separate to the regular expression, removing non-numbers like "and," hyphens, and so on. But we'll start by grabbing the expression and passing it through the wonderful Regex::PreSuf module to optimize it. This module generates a regular expression from a list of words that matches the same words as the original list. The result looks like this:

```
(?-xism:((?:b(?:akers?dozen|illi(?:ard|on))|centillion|d(?:ecilli(?:ard|on)|
ozen|u(?:o(?:decilli(?:ard|on)|vigintillion)|vigintillion))|e(?:ight(?:een|
ieth|[yh])?|leven(?:ty(?:first|one))?|s)|f(?:i(?:ft(?:een|ieth|[yh])|rst|ve)|
o(?:rt(?:ieth|y)|ur(?:t(?:ieth|[yh]))?))|g(?:oogol(?:plex)?|ross)|hundred|mi
(?:l(?:ion|li(?:ard|on))|nus)|n(?:aught|egative|in(?:et(?:ieth|y)|t(?:een|
[yh])|e)|o(?:nilli(?:ard|on)|ught|vem(?:dec|vigint)illion))|o(?:ct(?:illi
(?:ard|on)|o(?:dec|vigint)illion)|ne)|qu(?:a(?:drilli(?:ard|on)|ttuor
(?:decilli(?:ard|on)|vigintillion))|in(?:decilli(?:ard|on)|tilli(?:ard|on)|
vigintillion))|s(?:core|e(?:cond|pt(?:en(?:dec|vigint)illion|illi(?:ard|on))|
ven(?:t(?:ieth|y))?|x(?:decillion|tilli(?:ard|on)|vigintillion))|ix(?:t(?:ieth|
y))?)|t(?:ee?n|h(?:ir(?:t(?:een|ieth|y)|d)|ousand|ree)|r(?:e(?:decilli(?:ard|
on)|vigintillion)|i(?:gintillion|lli(?:ard|on)))|w(?:e(?:l(?:fth|ve)|nt(?:ieth|
y))|o)|h)|un(?:decilli(?:ard|on)|vigintillion)|vigintillion|zero|s)))
```

It's a start. Now we have to extend this to allow for all the munging that words2nums does on the text. The important bits of the code are:

```
s/\b(and|a|of)\b//g; # ignore some common words
s/[^A-Za-z0-9.]//g;  # ignore spaces and punctuation, except period.
```

This is fine if we can change the text we're matching, but we don't necessarily want to do that. Instead, we have to construct a regular expression around our big optimized list of numbers that allows for and silently ignores these words and spaces. We also need to remember that we want to find numbers that are not in the middle of a word ("zone" does not mean a "z" followed by the number 1) so we use Perl's regular expression boundary condition (\b) to surround the final regexp. Here's what it looks like:

```
my $ok_words = qr/\b(and|a|of)\b/;
my $ok_things = qr/[^A-Za-z0-9.]/;
my $number = qr/\b(($numbers($ok_words|$ok_things)*)+)\b/i;
# Where $numbers is the big mad expression above.
```

Bundling this into a package with a couple of utility functions gives you the Lingua::EN::FindNumber CPAN module:

```
use Lingua::EN::FindNumber;
print numify("Fourscore and seven years ago, our four fathers...");
```

which prints out:

```
87 years ago, our 4 fathers...
```

To go the other way, and turn numbers into words, there is a whole family of modules named Lingua::XX::Numbers where XX is the ISO language code of the language you want your numbers in: Lingua::EN::Numbers for English, for instance. There's also Lingua::EN::Numbers::Ordinate to turn "2" into "2nd". Similar modules exist for other languages.

Modules for Parsing English

Parsing ordinary written text is perhaps the ultimate goal of any natural-language processing system, and, to be honest, we're still a long way from it at the moment.

Even so, there are a good number of modules on CPAN that can help us deal with understanding what's going on in a chunk of text.

Splitting Up Text

There are many scenarios in which a large document needs to be split up into some kind of chunks. This can vary from splitting out individual words, to splitting out sentences and paragraphs, and right up to splitting a document into logical subsections—working out which sets of paragraphs refer to a common topic and which others are unrelated.

We'll begin with splitting up sentences, since there are a variety of ways to do this. The naive approach is to assume that a period, question mark, or exclamation mark followed by whitespace or the end of text is the end of a sentence, and to use punctuation and capitals to help this determination. This is what Text::Sentence does, and it's not bad:

```
use Text::Sentence qw( split_sentences );
my $text = <<EOF;
This is the first sentence. Is this the second sentence? This is the
third sentence, with an additional clause!
EOF
print "#$_\n\n" for split_sentences($text);
```

This prints out:

```
#This is the first sentence.

#Is this the second sentence?

#This is the third sentence, with an additional clause!
```

This punctuation-based assumption is generally good enough, but screws up messily on sentences containing abbreviations followed by capital letters, e.g., This one. It incorrectly identifies the boundary between the punctuation and the capital letter as a sentence boundary:

```
#This punctuation-based assumption is generally good enough, but screws
up messily on sentences containing abbreviations followed by capital
letters, e.g.,

#This one.
```

Thankfully, the exceptions are sufficiently rare that even if you're doing some kind of statistical analysis on your sentences, with a big enough corpus the effect of the assumption failing is insignificant. For cases where it really does matter, though, Shlomo Yona's Lingua::EN::Sentence does a considerably better job:

```
use Lingua::EN::Sentence qw( get_sentences add_acronyms );
my $text = <<EOF;
This punctuation-based assumption is generally good enough, but screws
up messily on sentences containing abbreviations followed by capital
letters, e.g., This one. Shlomo Yona's Lingua::EN::Sentence does a
considerably better job:
EOF
my $sentences=get_sentences($text);
foreach my $sentence (@$sentences) {
    print "#", $sentence, "\n\n";
}
```

The result of this example is:

```
#This punctuation-based assumption is generally good enough, but screws
up messily on sentences containing abbreviations followed by capital
letters, e.g., This one.

#Shlomo Yona's Lingua::EN::Sentence does a considerably better job:
```

For things that aren't sentences, my favorite segmentation module is Lingua::EN::Splitter; this can handle paragraph- and word-level segmentation, and its cousin Lingua::Segmenter::TextTiling takes a stab at clustering paragraphs into discrete sections of a document.

The paragraph and word segmentation are done using fairly simple regular expressions, but the paragraph clustering is done using a technique invented by Marti Hearst called TextTiling. This measures the correlation of particular words in order to detect sets of paragraphs with distinct vocabularies.

We'll use Lingua::En::Splitter's words routine often in this chapter. It's an excellent building block for analyzing texts, as in this simple concordancer for generating histograms of word-frequency:

```
use Lingua::EN::Splitter qw(words);

my $text = "Here is Edward Bear, coming downstairs now, bump, bump,
bump, on the back of his head, behind Christopher Robin.";

my %histogram;
$histogram{lc $_}++ for @{ words($text) };
use Data::Dumper; print Dumper(\%histogram);
```

This example correctly counts up three occurrences of bump, and one each of the other words:

```
$VAR1 = {
            'robin' => 1,
            'here' => 1,
            'edward' => 1,
            'now' => 1,
            'bear' => 1,
            'coming' => 1,
            'head' => 1,
            'his' => 1,
            'downstairs' => 1,
            'of' => 1,
            'bump' => 3,
            'on' => 1,
            'the' => 1,
            'behind' => 1,
            'back' => 1,
            'is' => 1,
            'christopher' => 1
        };
```

Stemming and Stopwording

Of course, merely building up a histogram of words isn't enough for most serious analyses; our job is complicated by two main factors. First, there's the fact that most languages have some system of inflection where the same root word can appear in multiple forms.

For instance, if you're trying to analyze a mass of scientific articles to find something about what happens when volcanos erupt, you want to find all those that speak about "volcanic eruption," "volcano erupting," "volcanos erupted," and so on.

While these are quite obviously different words, we want them all to be treated the same for the purposes of searching.

The usual process for doing this is to stem the words, pruning them back to their roots: all of the "volcanos erupting" phrases should be pruned back to "volcano erupt" or similar. Porter's stemming algorithm, invented by Martin Porter at Cambridge University and first described in the paper *An algorithm for suffix stripping* is by far the most widely used algorithm for stemming English words.[*]

Benjamin Franz has implemented a generic framework for stemmers such as the Porter algorithm in Lingua::Stemmer; it contains stemming algorithms for many languages, but we'll look at Lingua::Stem::En for the moment.

For a module later in this chapter, I needed to know if a particular word was a dictionary word, as opposed to some kind of personal noun. Of course, thanks to inflections, there are plenty of "dictionary" words that aren't in the dictionary. I employed a Porter stemmer to catch these.

First we need to stem all the words in the dictionary, or else they aren't going to match the stemmed versions we're looking for:

```perl
sub stem {
    require Lingua::Stem::En;
    my ($stemmed) = @{ Lingua::Stem::En::stem({ -words => [shift] }) };
}

while (<DICT>) {
    chomp;
    next if /[A-Z]/;
    $wordlist{stem($_)}=1;
}
```

We actually make %wordlist a tied hash to a DBM file, so that we only need to stem the dictionary once, no matter how many times we look up words in it. Once that's done, we can now remove all the dictionary words from a list:

```perl
my @proper = grep { !$wordlist{$_} }
    @{ Lingua::Stem::En::stem({ -words => \@words }) };
```

Similarly, the Plucene Perl-based search engine has an analyzer that stems words so that searches for "erupting" and "erupt" give the same results.

The second problem that arises is that there are a large number of English words that don't carry very much semantic content. For instance, you probably wouldn't miss much from that previous sentence if it were transformed into "The second problem

---

[*] That doesn't mean, of course, that it's particularly good. Porter himself says: "It is important to remember that the stemming algorithm cannot achieve perfection. On balance it will (or may) improve IR [information retrieval] performance, but in individual cases it may sometimes make what are, or what seem to be, errors."

However, as with the infamous Brill part of speech tagger, once something gets established as the de facto standard tool in NLP, it's very hard to shift it.

arises large number English words don't carry semantic content." Words like "are," "that," and "very" are called *stopwords*.

Stopwords don't add much to the underlying meaning of an utterance. In fact, if we're trying to wade through English text with Perl, we probably want to get rid of any such words and concentrate on the ones that are left.

The `Lingua::EN::StopWords` module contains a handy hash of stopwords so that you can quickly look up whether a word has weight:

```perl
use Lingua::EN::StopWords qw(%StopWords);

my @words = qw(the second problem that arises is that there are a
large number of English words that don't carry very much semantic
content);

print join " ", grep { !$StopWords{$_} } @words;

second problem arises large number English words don't carry
semantic content
```

By combining these two modules and `Lingua::EN::Splitter`, we can get some kind of a metric of the similarity of two sentences:

```perl
use Lingua::EN::StopWords qw(%StopWords);
use Lingua::Stem::En;
use Lingua::EN::Splitter qw(words);
use List::Util qw(sum);
print compare(
    "The AD 79 volcanic eruption of Mount Vesuvius",
    "The volcano, Mount Vesuvius, erupted in 79AD"
    );

sub sentence2hash {
    my $words   = words(lc(shift));
    my $stemmed = Lingua::Stem::En::stem({
                    -words => [ grep { !$StopWords{$_} } @$words ]
                });
    return { map {$_ => 1} grep $_, @$stemmed };
}

sub compare {
    my ($h1, $h2) = map { sentence2hash($_) } @_;
    my %composite = %$h1;
    $composite{$_}++ for keys %$h2;
    return 100*(sum(values %composite)/keys %composite)/2;
}
```

The compare subroutine tells us the percentage of compatibility between two sentences—in this example, 83%. The sentence2hash subroutine first splits a sentence into individual words, using `Lingua::EN::Splitter`. Then, after grepping out the stopwords, it stems them, makes sure there's something left after stemming (to get rid of non-words like "79"), and maps them into a hash.

The compare subroutine simply builds up a hash that contains all the stemmed words and the number of times they appear in the two sentences. If the sentences mesh perfectly, then each word will appear precisely twice in the composite hash, and so the average value of the hash will be 2. To find the compability of the sentences, we divide the average by 2, and multiply by 100 to get a percentage.

In this case, our two sentences only differed by the fact that the Porter stemmer didn't stem "volcano" to "volcan" as it did for "volcanic." It's not perfect, but it's good enough for NLP.

Categorization and Extraction

It is no exaggeration to say that the most widely used application of NLP, and also the one with the greatest research effort these days, is the fight against spam—deciding on the basis of the content whether a particular email is wanted or unwanted. Some anti-spam software, such as SpamAssassin, takes a relatively straightforward approach to the problem: an email gets points if it contains certain words or phrases, and this is combined with the use of relay blacklists and other non-textual evidence.

However, anti-spam authors are increasingly taking an altogether different, and generally more successful, approach. They take one corpus of mail that is known to be spam and one that is known to be not spam (ham), and use statistical means to identify attributes that make a particular message more spammy or more hammy. When a new message comes in, the same statistical analysis is performed to determine its likely spamminess.

This is an application of the field of natural-language processing called document categorization. We have two categories—spam and ham—and want to determine which category a new document is likely to fall into. Naturally, this can be used for many other purposes, although the fight against spam is arguably the most urgent: automatically determining the language of a document; helping to route enquiries to the most appropriate department of a company; even organizing recipe collections.

We'll look at a few applications of document categorization, and the related field of information extraction.

Bayesian Analysis

Here's one application of document categorization that I found particularly useful. As we saw in the last chapter, I'm a big fan of receiving news and stories from web pages via RSS aggregation. The problem with subscribing to a variety of RSS feeds is that the quality and interest level of the stories varies wildly. While I like to know about upcoming Perl conferences through *http://use.perl.org*, I don't really care to be told about Perl Mongers meetings on the other side of the world.

So there are a set of news stories I find interesting and a set I find boring. I should not be having to make the decision about whether something is interesting or boring when I have several thousand dollars of processor power in front of me. This is a document categorization problem, not too dissimilar to the spam problem, so we can use the same techniques to solve it.

One technique that's found favor in anti-spam circles recently is Bayesian analysis. This is a very old technique, an application of the Bayesian theory of probability. It is used to invert conditional probabilities.

Bayes and Predicting Diseases

A quick introduction to Bayes's theorem is in order. For example, the chance that someone who has a particular rare genetic disease will test positive to a clinical test is 99%. Let's say John takes the test, and he tests positive. What are the chances that he has the disease? It's not 99%. Nothing like it. The short answer is that, at the moment, we can't say. We need more information.

Now suppose we know that the test yields a 5% false-positive rate. That is, if John doesn't have the disease, there's a 5% chance he'll test positive anyway. We also need to know how common the disease is; let's say it's 0.5% prevalent in the general population. (We'll say $P(D) = 0.005$ for the probability of the disease.)

Now we can work out the probability that any given test will be positive $(P(T))$. This is the combination of two situations: that the test is positive for someone who has the disease (0.005 * 0.99) and that the test is positive for someone who doesn't (0.995 * 0.05). This adds up to 4.975% + 0.495% = 5.47%. Should John be worried about this?

To find out, we use Bayes's theorem. This allows us to turn on its head the probability that a person tests positive given that he has the disease $(P(T|D) = 0.99)$ and gives us $P(D|T)$, the probability that he has the disease given that he tests positive.

Bayes's formula is:

$$P(D|T) = [P(T|D) \times P(D)] / P(T)$$

And plugging in the numbers, we find that John is only 9.05% likely to have the disease. Bayes's theorem is important because it forces us to take into account everything we know—even though there was a relatively high chance that the test was accurate, we need to factor in the relative rarity of the disease in the general population.

We want to find out the probability that a document is interesting given the particular set of words in it. We know the probability that any document is interesting, regardless of its words; just count up the number of documents that are interesting, count up all the documents, and divide. We can work out the probability that an interesting document contains a given set of words, and so all that's left is a lot of tedious mathematics.

Thankfully, the `Algorithm::NaiveBayes` module can help to hide that away. It includes an analyzer that takes a number of attributes and corresponding weights, and associates them with a set of labels. Typically, for a text document, the attributes are the words of the document, and the weight is the number of times each word occurs. The labels are the categories under which we want to file the document.

For instance, suppose we have the news article:

> The YAPC::Taipei website is now open and calls for registration. Welcome to Taipei and join the party with us!

We split that up into words, count the occurrence of the relevant words, and produce a hash like this:

```
my $news = {
    now => 1, taipei => 2, join => 1, party => 1, us => 1,
    registration => 1, website => 1, welcome => 1, open => 1,
    calls => 1, yapc => 1
};
```

Then we add this article to our categorizer's set of known documents:

```
my $categorizer = Algorithm::NaiveBayes->new;
$categorizer->add_instance( attributes => $news,
                            label      => "interesting" );
```

When we've added a load of documents, the categorizer has a good idea of what kind of words make up stories that I would categorize as interesting. We then ask it to do some sums, and we can find out what it thinks about a new document:

```
$categorizer->train;
my $probs = $categorizer->predict( attributes => $new_news );
```

This returns a hash mapping each category to the probability that the document fits into that category. So once we have our categorizer trained with a few hand-categorized documents, we can say:

```
if ( $probs->{interesting} > 0.5 ) {
    # Probably interesting
}
```

Of course, now the main problem is getting the document into the hash of words and weights. We use our now-familiar `Lingua::EN::Splitter` and `Lingua::EN::StopWords` techniques to produce a subroutine like this:

```
sub invert_string {
    my ($string, $weight, $hash) = @_;
    $hash->{$_} += $weight for
        grep { !$StopWords{$_} }
        @{words(lc($string))};
}
```

This inverts a string, adding its component words into a hash. In our RSS aggregator example, the stories will be hashes extracted from `XML::RSS` objects. We want to give more weight to words that appear in the title of a story than those that appear in the body, so we end up with this:

```perl
sub invert_item {
    my $item = shift;
    my %hash;
    invert_string($item->{title}, 2, \%hash);
    invert_string($item->{description}, 1, \%hash);
    return \%hash;
}
```

With these subroutines in place, we can now train our analyzer on two carefully constructed RDF sources:

```perl
#!/usr/bin/perl

use XML::RSS;
use Algorithm::NaiveBayes;
use Lingua::EN::Splitter qw(words);
use Lingua::EN::StopWords qw(%StopWords);

my $nb = Algorithm::NaiveBayes->new();

for my $category (qw(interesting boring)) {
    my $rss = new XML::RSS;
    $rss->parsefile("$category.rdf");
    $nb->add_instance(attributes => invert_item($_),
                      label       => $category) for @{$rss->{'items'}};
}

$nb->train; # Work out all the probabilities
```

And now we can ask it how we feel about the articles in a third source:

```perl
my $target = new XML::RSS;
$target->parsefile("incoming.rdf");
for my $item (@{$target->{'items'}}) {
    print "$item->{title}: ";

    my $predict = $nb->predict(attributes => invert_item($item));
    print int($predict->{interesting}*100)."% interesting\n";
}
```

If we train the categorizer from two weblogs written by Bob (interesting) and George (boring) as the data sources and then compare it with the Slashdot feed from a random day, it predicts the following:

```
Elektro, the Oldest U.S. Robot: 12% interesting
French Court Orders Google to Stop Competing Ad Displays: 0% interesting
Personal Spaceflight Leaders Form New Federation: 43% interesting
Symantec Antivirus May Execute Virus Code: 0% interesting
Open-Source Technique for GM Crops: 99% interesting
North Korea Admits to Having Nuclear Weapons: 19% interesting
```

```
Judge Slams SCO's Lack of Evidence: 24% interesting
Sci-Fi Channel Renews Battlestar Galactica: 0% interesting
Tecmo Sues Game Hackers Under DMCA: 15% interesting
Identifying World's Species With Genetic Bar Codes: 32% interesting
```

This is a very simple case of categorization where we've only really used one dimension—interesting versus boring. Now we'll look at a more complex example, using multiple dimensions and a more sophisticated algorithm.

Keyword Extraction and Summary

One extremely common task in language processing is the reduction of a text down to essential keywords or phrases. Perl people are busy people and don't want to read through masses of documents if they don't need to. Why not get a computer to do the bulk of the reading for them?

There are two ways to getting a sense of what a document is about. The first is to extract what appear to be key sentences and strip away anything that doesn't seem so important. This is particularly good for summarizing scientific or factual input. The second is to look for particularly important keywords, nouns, and noun phrases that recur frequently in a text. This doesn't give a readable overview of the sense of the text, but it is often enough to give a good overview of the key concepts involved.

Lingua::EN::Summarize is the module for the first approach, extracting key sentences. Digging into the source, we see it takes a relatively naive approach by looking for clauses that could be declarative:

```
my $keywords = "(is|are|was|were|will|have)";
my @clauses = grep { /\b$keywords\b/i }
              map { split /(,|;|--)/ } split_sentences( $text );
```

It then tries to trim them to a required length. To be honest, it isn't great. If we run the summarize subroutine on the first part of this chapter:

```
use Lingua::EN::Summarize;
print summarize($chapter5, maxlength => 300, wrap => 70);
```

it produces the following summary:

```
Is the application of AI techniques to answer questions about text
written in a human language: what does it mean. What other documents
is it like. As Perl is often described as a text-processing
language. It shouldn't be much of a surprise to find that there are a
great many modules and techniques available in Perl for carrying out
NLP-related tasks.
```

To make a better text summarizer, we need to turn to the academic literature, and there's a lot of it. A paper by Kupiec, Pedersen, and Chen[*] uses a Bayesian categorizer, like the one we used to categorize RSS stories, to determine whether or not a given sentence would be in a summary. Implementing this using `Algorithm::NaiveBayes` should be a relatively straightforward exercise for the interested reader.

Another technique (by Hans Peter Luhn[†]) uses something called Zipf's Law of Word Distribution, which states that a small corpus of words occur very frequently, some words occur with moderate frequency, and many words occur infrequently. To summarize a text, you take the sentences that contain words that appear very frequently. Unfortunately, this requires a very large corpus of related material, in order to filter out relatively common phrases, but let's implement this in Perl.

I grabbed a bunch of technical papers on computational linguistics from *http://www.arxiv.org* and built up background and document-specific frequency histograms using the usual techniques:

```
use Lingua::EN::Splitter qw(words);
use Lingua::EN::Sentence qw(get_sentences);
use File::Slurp;
use Lingua::Stem::En;
use Lingua::EN::StopWords qw(%StopWords);
use List::Util qw(sum);
use strict;
my %base;
my %per_file;

my $amount = shift;
for my $file (<*.txt>) {
    my $sentences = get_sentences ( scalar read_file($file) );
    for my $sentence (@$sentences) {
        my @words = grep { !$StopWords{$_} } @{words(lc $sentence) };
        for my $word (@{ Lingua::Stem::En::stem({ -words => \@words }) }) {
            $base{$word}++;
            $per_file{$file}{$word}++;
        }
    }
}
```

Now we convert these histograms into frequency tables, by dividing the count for each word by the total number of hits in the hash:

```
my $sum = sum values %base; $base{$_} /= $sum for keys %base;
my %totals;
```

---

[*] Julian Kupiec, Jan O. Pedersen, and Francine Chen. 1995. "A Trainable Document Summarizer." In *Research and Development in Information Retrieval,* pages 68-73. Available at *http://www.dcs.shef.ac.uk/~mlap/teaching/kupiec95trainable.pdf.*

[†] Hans Peter Luhn. 1958. "The Automatic Creation of Literature Abstracts." *IBM Journal of Research and Development,* 2(2):159-165. Reprinted in *H.P. Luhn: Pioneer of Information Science, Selected Works.* Edited by Claire K. Schultz. Spartan Books, New York. 1968.

```
for my $file (keys %per_file) {
    $sum = sum values %{$per_file{$file}};
    $per_file{$file}{$_} /= $sum for keys %{$per_file{$file}};
}
```

Now that we have our frequencies of words relative to the corpus as a whole and relative to individual documents, we can start our second pass: look over a document and score each sentence in terms of the average relative unusualness of its constituent words. We begin as before:

```
for my $file (<*.txt>) {
    print $file,":\n";
    my $sentences = get_sentences (scalar read_file($file) );
    my %markings;
    my $order = 0;
    for my $sentence (@$sentences) {
        my @words = grep { !$StopWords{$_} } @{words(lc $sentence) };
```

But this time we want to mark the sentence with its order in the document and a score for each word; this is the ratio between the expected frequency and the observed frequency:

```
        my @words = grep { !$StopWords{$_} } @{words(lc $sentence) };
        $markings{$sentence}->{order} = $order++;
        if (!@words) {
          $markings{$sentence}->{score} = 0;
          next;
        }
        for my $word (@{ Lingua::Stem::En::stem({ -words => \@words }) }) {
            my $score = $per_file{$file}{$word} / $base{$word};
            $markings{$sentence}->{score} += $score;
        }
```

Finally, we divide the sentence's score by the number of words to find the average and so that we're not unfairly favoring longer sentences.

```
        $markings{$sentence}->{score} /= @words;
    }
```

Now we have a score for each sentence in the document. We can sort the sentences by score to find the 10 highest-scoring, then re-sort them by order so that they appear in the original order:

```
    my @sorted = sort
                { $markings{$b}->{score} <=> $markings{$a}->{score} }
                keys %markings;
    my @selected = sort
                { $markings{$a}->{order} <=> $markings{$b}->{order} }
                @sorted[0..9];
    print "@selected\n\n";
}
```

And that's all we need for a simple frequency-based summarizer. To take an example of the output, the summarizer reduced a 2,000-word paper on language generation down to the following abstract:

> This paper introduces the neca mnlg; a Multimodal Natural Language Generator. The neca mnlg adopts the conventional pipeline architecture for generators (Reiter and Dale, 2000). Feature structures are also used in the fuf/surge generator. See *http://www.cs.bgu.ac.il/surge/*. Matching trees might in turn have incomplete daughter nodes. These are recursively expanded by matching them with the trees in the repository, until all daughters are complete. The module is based on the work of Krahmer and Theune (2002). The negation is passed on to the VP subtree via the feature. The attributes x and y allow us to capture unbounded dependencies via feature perlocation. The value of the attribute is passed on from the mother node to the daughter nodes. The neca mnlg has been implemented in prolog.

Keyword extraction

The second approach to document summary, extracting keywords, is a little easier, and it is instructive to have a look at the Lingua::EN::Keywords module and how its techniques evolved.

The first versions of Lingua::EN::Keywords were very simple. They split the text into words manually, then counted up the frequency of each word, and returned the top five most frequent words. This was, of course, pretty bad.

The second set of versions used a hardwired stopword list, which was a little better, but still not good enough. The third series used the Lingua::EN::StopWords techniques we've seen several times in this chapter. The fourth iteration used the same technique as "Keyword Extraction and Summary" earlier in this chapter to detect and score proper names that wouldn't appear in the dictionary, rather than ordinary words that would. This was because proper nouns are more easily identifiable as the topic of a document.

And there it sat for a while as I looked for ways to extract not just words but key phrases. There are various academic papers about how to do this, but, to be honest, I couldn't get any of them to work accurately. Finally, something caught my eye: Maciej Ceglowski and his team at Middlebury College released Lingua::EN::Tagger, a rather nice English part-of-speech tagger, which contained a noun-phrase extractor. This produces histograms of all the nonstop words in the text, but also tries to group together nouns into phrases:

```
use Lingua::EN::Tagger;
my $tag = Lingua::EN::Tagger->new(longest_noun_phrase => 5,
                                  weight_noun_phrases => 0);

my %wordlist = $tag->get_words("This is a test of the emergency warning
system. This is only a test. If this had been an actual emergency, you
would have been instructed to tune to either Cable Channel 3 or
local emergency radio stations.");
```

This produces the following histogram in our word list %wordlist:

```
'emergency warning system' => 1,
'emerg' => 3,
'cable channel' => 1,
'warn' => 1,
'radio stations' => 1,
'actual emergency' => 1,
'local emergency radio stations' => 1,
'radio' => 1,
'emergency radio stations' => 1,
'emergency radio' => 1,
'channel' => 1,
'warning system' => 1,
'emergency warning' => 1,
'station' => 1,
'system' => 1,
'test' => 2
```

As you can see, individual words (emergency) are stemmed (emerg), but noun phrases are kept together. If we collate these histograms over a large document, nouns that appear together as a phrase will rise to the top. For instance, if the document always talks about "local football leagues," then that phrase will be ranked highly. However, if there's a relatively even split between "local football leagues" and "local football matches," then "local football" will be the most frequent phrase.

With this module available, Lingua::EN::Keywords just becomes a matter of collating the histograms and spitting back the most common phrases, with one slight exception. The problem is that when we constructed the histogram, we stemmed the words. To present these words to the user, we need to unstem them, but that's not very easy. The way we do this in Lingua::EN::Keywords is to cache every stemming in a hash, then reverse the hash to go from a stemmed word to the original. By subclassing Lingua::EN::Tagger, we can override the stem method, and provide another method to get access to the cache:

```
package My::Tagger;
use base 'Lingua::EN::Tagger';
my %known_stems;
sub stem {
    my ( $self, $word ) = @_;
    return $word unless $self->{'stem'};
    return $known_stems{ $word } if exists $known_stems{$word};
    my $stemref = Lingua::Stem::En::stem( -words => [ $word ] );

    $known_stems{ $word } = $stemref->[0] if exists $stemref->[0];
}

sub stems { reverse %known_stems; }
```

Now we can write a trivial unstem routine that looks up the original word from its stem in the reversed hash, shown in the next block of code.

```
use My::Tagger;
my $tag = My::Tagger->new(longest_noun_phrase => 5,
                          weight_noun_phrases => 0);

sub unstem {
    my %cache = $tag->stems;
    my $stem = shift;
    return $cache{$stem} || $stem;
}
```

This isn't a perfect solution. If two different words have the same stem, the distinction is lost in the reverse operation. A few modifications to the stems subroutine can keep a record of the exact variations found in the original text if that information is important. Finally, the keyword subroutine is as simple as:

```
sub keywords {
    my %wordlist = $tag->get_words(shift);
    my %newwordlist;
    $newwordlist{unstem($_)} += $wordlist{$_} for keys %wordlist;
    my @keywords = sort { $newwordlist{$b} <=> $newwordlist{$a} } keys %newwordlist;
    return $keywords[0..4];
}
```

This generates a Lingua::EN::Tagger histogram from the single string argument. It then creates a new hash combining the counts from the original histogram with the unstemmed keywords. It sorts the keywords by frequency and returns the five most common keywords. If we pass the keywords subroutine the same text as the first example in this section, the first two results are emergency and test. The remaining three keywords of the top five aren't in a predictable order because they're all equally frequent.

Extracting Names and Places

An extension of the principle of extracting keywords from text involves what's known in the trade as *named-entity extraction*. A named entity is any proper noun, such as a place, a person's name, an organization's name, and so on. Extracting these proper nouns and categorizing them is a good first step to retrieving pertinent information from a particular source text.

There are any number of well-documented algorithms for named-entity extraction in the academic literature, but, being Perl hackers, we're interested in a quick, easy but efficient ready-made solution.

There are two modules that perform named-entity extraction for English text: GATE::ANNIE::Simple and Lingua::EN::NamedEntity. GATE::ANNIE::Simple is an Inline::Java wrapper around the GATE[*] project's ANNIE[†] named-entity extraction engine. The

---

[*] General Architecture for Text Engineering (*http://www.gate.ac.uk*).

[†] A Nearly-New Information Extraction system. When it comes to acronymic naming schemes, academics can be just as bad as hackers.

GATE documentation talks of this use of ANNIE as a "textual sausage machine"—
you feed text in at one end, and out the other end comes a categorized set of entities.
This is the sort of solution we're looking for.

```
use GATE::ANNIE::Simple;
$text = <<EOF;
The United States is to ask the United Nations to approve the creation
of a multinational force in Iraq in return for ceding some political
authority, US officials say.
EOF
%entities = annie_extract($text);
```

This results in the following entries in the %entities hash:

```
'Iraq' => 'Location',
'United Nations' => 'Organization',
'US' => 'Location',
'United States' => 'Location'
```

ANNIE has very high recall and categorization accuracy, meaning that it can find
most of the relevant entities in a document (and doesn't find too many things that
aren't actually named entities) and can decide whether the entity is a person, a place,
an organization, and so on. It can also extract dates, numbers, and amounts of
money. The downside of ANNIE is its complexity, requiring a bridge to Java, and its
speed—before the first set of extraction, ANNIE must first load all its rulesets into
memory, something that can take a matter of minutes even on a fast machine.

When looking at alternatives to ANNIE for the purposes of writing this chapter, I
started writing about a relatively naive approach:

- First, extract all phrases of capitalized words, storing the context two or three
  words before and two or three words after.

- Second, trim out those that are purely sentence-initial dictionary words, using a
  stemmer (see above) to remove inflections.

- Third, allocate a score to each entity in each of the following categories: person,
  place, organization. If the first word in the entity is found in a lexicon of fore-
  names, score it up as a person, and so on.

Then I realized that by the time I'd finished describing this heuristic in English, I could
have already written it in Perl, and Lingua::EN::NamedEntity was born. It was originally designed to be a benchmark against which more academically correct solutions
could be measured. Although it doesn't have the same precision as ANNIE, Lingua::
EN::NamedEntity actually turned out to be good enough for most named-entity work.

When you install the module from CPAN, it sets up a series of files in the .namedentity
subdirectory of your home directory, precomputing the forename and lexicon databases to speed up their loading. Once it's all installed and set up, you can use the
extract_entities subroutine to produce a list of named entities.

As with most information-extraction techniques, named-entity recognition works well on reasonably long documents, so I ran it on a Perl 6 Summary:

```
use File::Slurp;
use Lingua::EN::NamedEntity;

my $file = read_file("summary.txt");
for my $ent (extract_entities($file)) {
    print $ent->{entity}, ": ", $ent->{class}, "\n";
}
```

The results weren't perfect, as you'll see:

```
Go Melvin: person
Larry and Damian: organisation
Hughes: place
Perlcentricity: place
Jonathan Worthington: person
Melvin Smith: person
Meanwhile Melvin Smith: person
Piers Cawley: person
Austin Hastings: person
Perl Foundation and the Perl: organisation
Simon Cozens: person
Robin Redeker: person
Simon: person
Right Thing: person
Leo T: person
Leon Brocard: person
Payrard: place
Perl: place
London: place
...
```

However, one thing to note is that Lingua::EN::NamedEntity ends up erring on the side of recklessness, much more so than ANNIE—it will extract a lot of entities, and usually end up catching all the entities in a document, even if it does extract a few things that aren't really entities.

There are three main plans for future work on the module. The first is to tighten up the categorization somewhat and extend the number of categories. At the moment, for instance, it filed Perl as a place, because the summary talks so much about things being "in Perl."

The second is to remove some false positives by checking for supersets of supersets of entities: for instance, seeing "Melvin Smith" as an entity should make it less likely that "Meanwhile Melvin Smith" is really a person. Conversely, the third plan is to correlate subsets—not only should it know that "Melvin Smith" and "Melvin" are the same person, but it should use the combined ranking to strengthen its certainty that both belong in the person category.

Conclusion

In this chapter, we've looked at just a few of the available tools for working with natural language data. Many more are available on CPAN, including modules for localization, machine translation, guessing the language of a text, and formatting text or numbers in ways unique to a language. If you have a language-related problem to solve, you'll do well looking through the `Lingua::*`, `Locale::*`, and `Text::*` namespaces on CPAN.

CHAPTER 6

Perl and Unicode

Over the last couple of major releases, Perl has gained more advanced support for Unicode data manipulation. With the Perl 5.8 series, this support is now mature, so it's worth taking some time to look at what Unicode means for your applications and what tools Perl hands you to deal with it.

Terminology

It's a good idea to take a little time out, before we think about what Unicode is and what problem it solves, to clarify in our minds a few terms that have been widely used and abused in the programming world. In particular, the term *character set* is more troublesome than it might appear.

We often talk about the ASCII character set, but this relates to many different ideas—it could mean the actual suite of characters involved, or the order in which they are placed in that suite, or the way that a piece of text is represented in bytes. In fact, when people talk about text from an ASCII system, it may not even be ASCII. The potential for confusion comes because ASCII is a seven-bit character set, whereas for the past 25 years or so, computers have had eight-bit bytes. ASCII only defines the meaning of the first 128 entries in the set, so what should be done with the other 128? Rather than leave them unused and wasted, nearly every ASCII system chooses to define them in some way, usually with accented characters and extra symbols. Many manufacturers chose to make their machines use one of the range of national sets as defined by ISO standard 8859. Of these sets, ISO-8859-1—generally called "Latin 1"—was the most popular because it provides all the accented letters needed by most Western European languages. It is also the default encoding assumed by protocols such as HTTP. So prior to Unicode, many computers supposedly using ASCII actually produced text using all 8 bits and assumed that any machine that they exchanged data with also happened to associate the same meaning for the 128 non-ASCII characters. You can see the potential for mistakes here, and that's just with the data. There's also ambiguity about what the term *character set* means, so really we want avoid it altogether and replace it with some more precise terms:

character

A *character* is somewhat easier to define; it is the abstract description of a symbol, devoid of any formatting expectations. There are any number of ways that one might format the character that Unicode calls LATIN SMALL LETTER A: a, a, *a*, **a**, and so on. However, they all represent the same character. This is distinct from a *glyph*.

glyph

A glyph is the physical, visual representation of a character. A glyph concerns itself with shape, typeface, point size, boldness, slant, and so on; a character does not. "a" and "a" are the same character, but different glyphs.

Unicode does not concern itself with glyphs in any way; it does not determine how its characters should *look*, just what they *are*. On the other hand, character repertoires such as the Japanese standards JIS *do* specify not just the collection of characters used, but also their appearance.

character repertoire

A *character repertoire* is a collection of characters. Latin 1 has a character repertoire of 256 characters. The character repertoire itself does not specify the order in which the characters appear, nor does it map characters to codepoints. (See below.)

character code

The order and the mapping is specified by the *character code*. This is what tells us that, for instance, the Unicode character LATIN SMALL LETTER B comes directly after LATIN SMALL LETTER A.

codepoint

A character's *codepoint* is the number relating to the position of a character in a given character code. The Perl function to get a character's codepoint is ord.

character encoding

When dealing with a 256-character repertoire such as Latin 1, it is easy to see how the codepoints should be represented to a computer—each codepoint is simply encoded as one byte. When we get to 65,536 characters and above, on the other hand, we need to specify rather precisely how we're going to represent each character as a sequence of bytes. This is the *character encoding* of our data.

Unicode typically uses a set of well-specified character encodings it calls *Unicode Transformation Formats* or UTFs. We'll look at the most commonly used UTFs later on in the chapter.

What Is Unicode?

In the bad old days of data handling, if you wanted to work with text in a different language, you'd probably have to deal with a different character set. This could mean a different character repertoire, or a different character encoding, or both. Applications that needed to process Japanese data had to deal with at least two major character sets in any of three encodings—more if you needed to deal with Latin 1, as well. Each encoding would need special-case code to handle it, and programming was not fun.

Unicode—or, more formally, the *Unicode Standard*—is an attempt to put that right. The core of the Unicode Standard defines a universal character repertoire; it then also defines standard encodings for that repertoire. The Unicode Standard is augmented by a series of *Unicode Technical Reports* (UTRs), which provide additional information: more encodings, additions, and corrections to the standard; algorithms for collation; and so on.

The Unicode effort started in the late '80s—the term Unicode was first used in 1987—by programmers working at Xerox and Apple. The first edition of the Unicode Standard was released in 1990.

Unicode is based on four primary design principles (quoted from Tony Graham's book *Unicode: A Primer*):

    a. *Universal*. The character repertoire should be large enough to encompass all characters likely to be used in general text interchange.

    b. *Efficient*. Plain text, composed of a sequence of fixed-width characters, is simple to parse, and software does not need to maintain state, look for special escape sequences, or search forward or backward through text to identify characters.

    c. *Uniform*. A fixed-length character code allows efficient sorting, searching, display and editing of text.

    d. *Unambiguous*. Any given 16-bit value always represents the same character.

These goals were obtained by a combination of an extensive character repertoire and a fixed-width native coding scheme, UTF-16.

What Is UCS?

At the same time as the Unicode teams at Apple and Xerox were putting together a universal character set, the ISO standards organization was developing an international character set standard, ISO 10646. Realizing the futility of having *two* standard, universal character sets, the Unicode team and the ISO working group (ISO/IEC JTC1/SC2/WG2) agreed in 1991 to join forces. This has ensured that the industry standard, Unicode, and the international standard, ISO 10646, have remained—to all intents and purposes—identical.

However, since we have two cooperating standards, we have two sets of terminology to deal with—unfortunately, ISO standards tend to use different terms from industry standards. Hence, the Unicode character repertoire, as defined by the Unicode Standard, is known as the Universal Character Set, or UCS in ISO legalese. UCS is also slightly different: while it is character-for-character identical with the Unicode character repertoire, it allows for much more expansion.

As far as the Unicode Standard is concerned, the character repertoire consists of a maximum of 65,536 characters. This was initially thought to be far more than required for all the world's languages. By the time the second edition of the Unicode Standard was published, there were still 18,000 unassigned codepoints; by Unicode 3.0, there were 8,000 code points to go. This is obviously not enough, especially with the thousands of rare Chinese and Japanese characters that have been submitted for inclusion. The Unicode way of coping with this is to extend to two characters by means of the *surrogate pair* extension mechanism. In ISO 10646, however, the 65,536 characters form something called the Basic Multilingual Plane (BMP) and the UCS is made up of multiple planes.

The UCS is conceptually a series of cubes, or groups. There are 256x256 cells in a plane, and 256 planes in a group. There are 128 groups in total, allowing UCS to encode a massive 256x256x256x128 = 2,147,483,648 characters. These will never all be assigned, of course; Unicode's native encoding format UTF-16, with its surrogate pair mechanism, can only encode 16 planes (1,048,576 characters).

The ISO standard also defines two encoding mechanisms for UCS: UCS-2 and UCS-4. UCS-2 is conceptually identical to UTF-16. We will examine both encodings in the section on UTFs later in this chapter.

What is the Unicode Consortium?

After the ISO and Unicode efforts merged, a consortium of interested parties was set up to manage and develop the Unicode portion of the combined standard. The Unicode Consortium was founded in 1990 and incorporated as Unicode, Inc., in 1991.

The technical work of the consortium is carried out by the Unicode Technical Committee (UTC), which publishes the Unicode Standard and also issues Unicode Technical Reports.

The consortium also maintains many mailing lists, FAQs, and other resources available from *http://www.unicode.org/*, the Unicode Consortium web site.

Membership in the consortium is open to anyone, and there are a variety of membership levels. Perl is a member of the consortium, represented at associate member level, the first programming language to be independently represented to the consortium.

Why Should I Care?

The most important thing that this chapter can teach you about Unicode is that you should find out more about it and start being aware of it in your own programs. Unicode is coming.

If you're already working with data in various languages, you'll know the hell you need to go through to get everything working. Unicode makes it a lot easier.

If you're not already working with different languages, you will. Unicode can help you internationalize and localize your programs; Unicode awareness and support can make multinationalization a great deal more straightforward—once your program is Unicode-aware, common tasks such as sorting, searching, and regular expression matching just work in any language.

And if you don't think you will ever work with different languages, you still need to know about Unicode. Will you be receiving data from external sources? There's a growing possibility this data will be in Unicode, and you're going to need to know how to handle it.

If you're a Perl module author, there's absolutely no excuse; you have no idea how people will use your module or what data they might throw at it. If it can't cope with that data, it's broken, and people will blame you.

Finally, even if you're sure you'll never ever touch data that's not in good ol' ASCII, it does you good to know about Unicode anyway, since it is the way the world's going. Unicode support is very easy to achieve, especially in Perl, and it makes you a better programmer. The Perl value of laziness is important, but good laziness means you'll take the time to make your programs Unicode-aware first, so you won't need to make any changes when the time comes to support non-ASCII data.

Unicode Transformation Formats

As we've mentioned, with hundreds of thousands of characters in a character repertoire now, it's no longer possible to fit one character into one byte. We've introduced the concept of UTF-16, the native character encoding for Unicode, but there are several other standard encodings. Those starting with UTF are defined by the Unicode Standard or associated Unicode Technical Reports; the two UCS encodings are defined by the ISO 10646 standard.

UCS-2

UCS-2 is the two-byte ISO 10646 encoding. Recall that ISO defines the UCS in terms of groups and planes, where planes consist of 256 rows and 256 columns. In UCS-2, the first byte encodes the row, and the second encodes the column. Hence, UCS-2 can only encode the 65,536 characters in the Basic Multilingual Plane; furthermore,

ISO does not recognize the surrogate pair extension mechanism, so UCS-2 cannot be used to access any characters outside the BMP.

UTF-8

Formerly known as File System Safe UCS Transformation Format, UTF-8 is the Unicode encoding supported natively by Perl. It is an integral part of the Unicode Standard and is recognized by the ISO standard.

Unlike all the other UTFs, UTF-8 is a variable-width encoding; this is regarded as a compromise, as you may remember that one of the Unicode design goals was that encodings should be fixed width.

One redeeming feature of UTF-8, however, is that it is a superset of seven-bit ASCII. That is, data that is purely seven-bit ASCII—containing no bytes 128 or above—is valid UTF-8. Additionally, UTF-8 encodes codepoints 128 and above using only bytes 128 and above, so that the bytes 0 to 127 in a UTF-8 encoded string only ever correspond to the codepoints 0 to 127 (the ASCII characters). This means that any application that gives special meaning to some ASCII characters but is unaware of UTF-8 cannot be confused or tricked, such as a filesystem that allows bytes 0 to 255 in filenames and treats "/" as a directory separator.

UTF-8's encoding algorithm is slightly complex, because the algorithm used depends on the codepoint. For codepoints up to 128 (U+007F), the character is encoded as in ASCII: one byte per codepoint. From U+0080 up to U+07FF, the codepoint is converted to its bit pattern, and this bit pattern is split over two bytes. For instance, U+0169 LATIN CAPITAL LETTER U WITH TILDE has the bit sequence 0000000101101001. The six least significant bits and the next five significant bits are 101001 and 00101. We prefix the five with 110 to make 11000101, and the six with 10 to make 10101001. Hence, our character in UTF-8 is encoded as 11000101 10101001; that is, character 197 and character 169. The following Perl code demonstrates this technique and extends it to characters requiring three or four bytes to encode:

```
$d = "";
if ($uv < 0x800) {
    $d .= chr(( $uv >> 6)    | 0xc0);
    $d .= chr(( $uv & 0x3f) | 0x80);
    return $d;
}
if ($uv < 0x10000) {
    $d .= chr(( $uv >> 12)          | 0xe0);
    $d .= chr((($uv >>  6) & 0x3f) | 0x80);
    $d .= chr(( $uv        & 0x3f) | 0x80);
    return $d;
}
if ($uv < 0x200000) {
    $d .= chr(( $uv >> 18)          | 0xf0);
    $d .= chr((($uv >> 12) & 0x3f) | 0x80);
    $d .= chr((($uv >>  6) & 0x3f) | 0x80);
```

```
    $d .= chr(( $uv        & 0x3f) | 0x80);
    return $d;
}
```

UTF-16BE

Unicode's own native encoding is the two-byte UTF-16. This is available in big-endian and little-endian flavors; data sent over a network is expected to be in network order (big-endian).

UTF-16 is very similar to UCS-2; in fact, any UCS-2 encoded data is valid UTF-16BE. However, UTF-16 is extended to characters beyond the BMP by the use of surrogate pairs.

The surrogate pair mechanism uses two characters, one from the High Surrogate Zone, which ranges from U+D800 to U+DBFF, and one from the Low Surrogate Zone, which stretches from U+DC00 up to U+DFFF. The codepoint of a pair of characters so used is calculated as (HIGH - 0xD800) * 0x400 + (LOW - 0xDC00) * 0x10000. With 1024 high and 1024 low surrogates, the surrogate pair mechanism extends UTF-16 with another 1,048,576 characters.

UTF-16LE

UTF-16LE is the little-endian version of UTF-16BE.

UCS-4

UCS-4 is the four-byte ISO 10646 encoding. Whereas UCS-2 encoded just the row and column coordinates of a character cell in the BMP, UCS-4 encodes the four-dimensional coordinates of group, plane, row, and column; within the BMP, the first two bytes of each character will be zero. The advantage of UCS-4 is that it can encode every single codepoint in the UCS; the disadvantage is that every single character requires four bytes.

UTF-32

UTF-32 is, roughly speaking, the Unicode equivalent of ISO's UCS-4. The only difference is that UTF-32 is restricted to encoding the same range of codepoints as UTF-16; it even uses the surrogate pairs mechanism to extend its range beyond those codepoints. It can therefore be thought of as a wide form of UTF-16, and, like UTF-16, comes in big-endian and little-endian flavors. Nobody seems to know what it's for.

UTF-EBCDIC

UTF-EBCDIC is the encoding method designed for EBCDIC systems; it is specified in Unicode Technical Report 15. It's not intended as an open interchange format and should only be used internally to EBCDIC machines. Unless you're exchanging data with or using an EBCDIC system, you're unlikely to need this.

UTF-7

UTF-7 is another of those UTFs you'll probably never need. It's used in environments where eight-bit cleanliness is not guaranteed, such as passing mail through a VAX. Ergh. But fear not, Perl versions 5.8.1 and higher know how to translate it.

Handling UTF-8 Data

So much for theory. Let's now look at what Unicode means for Perl.

Let's suppose we've got some text encoded in UTF-8, and we want to mess about with it in Perl. You'd think we could just open the file and it would all magically work, but fortunately, Perl's not that clever. I say fortunately because we don't actually want Perl to automatically treat data as UTF-8; imagine, for instance, handling a piece of binary data, such as a JPEG image, and Perl obliviously tries to treat it as UTF-8.

Instead, Perl has two distinct processing modes for data—byte mode and character mode. The default is byte mode, and this works equally well for binary data and text encoded in a system that requires one byte per character, such as ordinary Latin 1. Character mode, on the other hand, treats the data as UTF-8. What does this mean in practice? Well, let's suppose we have the following text file, encoded in UTF-8:

```
Üñîçöðè
```

The UTF-8 representation of that string is:

```
C3 9C C3 B1 C3 AE C3 A7 C3 B6 C3 B0 C3 A8 0A
```

(0x0A is the newline at the end.)

So we can see that the file itself is 15 bytes long. And if we don't inform Perl, we get 15 bytes:

```
% perl -e 'open IN, "foo.utf8"; $a = <IN>; print length ($a)'
15
```

But we also know that, although there are 15 bytes in the file, there are only 8 UTF-8 characters. So we tell Perl to open the file as UTF-8, and now:

```
% perl -e 'open IN, "<:utf8", "foo.utf8"; $a = <IN>; print length ($a)'
8
```

Once you have your UTF-8 data correctly treated as UTF-8, everything works as you would expect; Perl converts the UTF-8 data to its internal Unicode format* on input, and you can use length (as demonstrated), substr, index, and all other built-in Perl functions on character data, and they'll use character positions instead of byte positions.

If you get your input and output correct, most of the rest of your problems go away. Convert your input to Unicode right away, as it enters the program. Convert your output to the desired encoding at the last possible point, just as it leaves your program. This ensures all the data inside your program is Unicode and doesn't need to be converted. If you add conversions somewhere inside your dataflow, you run the risk of performing the conversions more than once, or wrongly concatenating data in two different encodings. The most common symptom of this kind of problem is outputting double encoding—that is, the UTF-8 encoding of the UTF-8 encoding of a Unicode string. This is similar to entity-encoding text in a web page that's already entity-encoded, so a literal > would give you &lt; in the HTML source instead of the correct <. Convert at the boundaries and let Perl keep track of things internally—it's what it's good at.

Entering Unicode Characters

We've looked at how to read in UTF-8 data from external sources (filehandles); how about generating Unicode from inside our program? There are three main ways to do this.

The first way is perhaps the most obvious: functions like chr are automatically extended to produce Unicode strings when they need to. In fact, for lack of a decent Unicode editor, I generated some of my test files for this chapter using code like this:

```
binmode(STDOUT, ":utf8");
print chr $_ for
(0x30b8, 0x30a7, 0x30c3, 0x30cb, 0x306f, 0x5927, 0x597d, 0x304d, 0xff01);
```

In the same way that we told Perl to treat data from a particular input filehandle as UTF-8, we also need to tell it that a particular output filehandle expects UTF-8 data. The call to binmode in the previous example sets this UTF-8 handling on a filehandle that's already open.

The second way of entering Unicode data is as string literals. In this case the \x notation is extended beyond \xFF by means of curly braces:

```
binmode(STDOUT, ":utf8");
print "\x{30B8}\x{30A7}...";
```

---

* Perl's internal Unicode format happens to be UTF-8, but you don't need to know these implementation details to be able to use Unicode in Perl unless you write XS code. Use a recent 5.8.x release and simply treat the internals as a black box.

And third, if your Unicode characters happen to have names defined in the Unicode Standard, you can use the \N literal notation in conjunction with the charnames pragma.

```
use charnames ":full";
binmode(STDOUT, ":utf8");

print "I \N{HEAVY BLACK HEART} Unicode\n";
```

Writing the full names can be tedious sometimes, particularly when you're entering characters from particular alphabets. Instead, charnames provides a shorter form to access characters from particular Unicode blocks:

```
use charnames ":short";
binmode(STDOUT, ":utf8");

print "\N{hebrew:alef} \N{greek:omega}\n";
```

This only works where the Unicode name is of the form *SCRIPT* LETTER *NAME* or *SCRIPT* CAPITAL/SMALL LETTER *NAME*. Capitals can be obtained, intuitively, by starting the character name with a capital:

```
use charnames ":short";
binmode(STDOUT, ":utf8");

print "\N{greek:Sigma}\N{greek:iota}\N{greek:mu}\N{greek:omicron}\N{greek:nu}";
```

But as you can see, this also gets tedious if you're working in the same alphabet. The charnames pragma allows you to import particular alphabets, like so:

```
use charnames qw(greek hebrew);
binmode(STDOUT, ":utf8");

print "\N{Sigma}\N{iota}\N{mu}\N{omicron}\N{nu}\n";
print "\N{alef}\N{bet}\N{gimel}\n";
```

On a Unicode terminal, this may output:

```
Σιμον
אבג
```

Notice that although Perl outputs the Hebrew characters in alphabetical order, the terminal is responsible for handling the right-to-left aspects of the Hebrew output.

Of course, perhaps the most intuitive way of all for getting Unicode characters into Perl literals is simply to dump them into the middle of a string. You can do this, so long as you use the utf8 pragma. Perl allows you to use Unicode characters for string literals, comments, and, if you feel so inclined, the names of Perl identifiers.

Unicode Regular Expressions

Perl's regular expression engine supports what it calls polymorphic regular expressions; when matching against Unicode data, regular expression operators have character semantics, and when matching against non-Unicode data, the same regular expressions have byte semantics. No change to your code is needed to make regular expressions do the right thing in each context.

What does it mean for a regular expression to have character semantics? The first and most obvious thing is that operators such as . don't just match a single byte, but match an entire Unicode character:

```
use charnames qw(katakana);
binmode(STDOUT, ":utf8");

$x = "\N{sa}\N{i}";

$x =~ /(.)$/;
print $1;
```

This prints ✦, the last character in the string, instead of the last byte in the UTF-8 representation, which is \xA4. So far so good—Perl does what you mean.

If this isn't what you mean, and you do want to slice up a string into its component bytes, you have two ways of doing so; the first is the lexically scoped use bytes pragma, which pretends we are in 5.005 land, where Unicode does not even exist:

```
use charnames qw(katakana);
binmode(STDOUT, ":utf8");

$x = "\N{sa}\N{i}";

{
  use bytes;
  $x =~ /(.)$/;
  printf "\\x%X\n", $1;
}
```

This one does, indeed, print out \xA4. Your other alternative is to use the new \C match operator, which matches an individual byte.* Both of these methods require some caution, as they make it easy to generate ill-formed UTF-8.

Other properties of Unicode regular expressions are much friendlier. For instance, character classes such as \d and \w take their definitions from the Unicode Standard; we now know about more numbers than just our Arabic digits:

```
use charnames qw(:full);
binmode(STDOUT, ":utf8");

$x = "Some numbers: \N{DEVANAGARI DIGIT TWO}\N{DEVANAGARI DIGIT SIX}";

print "Found a number: $1" if $x =~ /(\d+)/;

Found a number: २ ६
```

---

* \C was named, perhaps unwisely, after C's char data type—char, of course, is a byte, not a character.

Sadly, there's no easy way to get at the digit value yet, and non-Arabic numbers do not convert between strings and numbers in the usual Perl way. You cannot (yet) say "\N{DEVANAGARI DIGIT TWO}" + 3 to get 5.

The Unicode Standard also declares that particular characters have particular properties, and regular expressions can match against these properties using the \p{...} notation. For instance, $, ¥, and € all have the Unicode CurrencySymbol property so /\p{CurrencySymbol}/ matches against them. A negated version, \P{...}, matches all characters that don't have the named property.

Finally, Perl provides the \X shortcut for matching complete decomposed characters. Many characters in the Unicode character repertoire can combine with a myriad variety of accents, marks, voicings, and other decorations; naturally, it's not practical for the character repertoire to include all possible combinations of marks on each character. Instead, base characters can be followed by combining characters that should all be treated as a single unit. For example, as Table 6-1 shows, the polytonic Greek character ὔ can be broken down (decomposed) into three constituent parts.

Table 6-1. Decomposing Unicode characters

υ	+	¨	+	´
GREEK SMALL LETTER UPSILON		COMBINING DIAERESIS		COMBINING ACUTE ACCENT

\X allows you to match these single decomposed units:

```
% perl -le 'my $x = chr(0x03c5).chr(0x0308).chr (0x0301); $x=~/(\X)/ and print length
$1'

3
```

In general, you should use \X rather than . to pick out individual, meaningful characters; for example, I was recently asked to write some code that displayed names vertically by putting a newline in between each character.* Doing this with print "$_\n" for $name =~/(.)/g led to the occasional surprise with decomposed data:

```
L
o
i
¨
s
```

The right answer, of course, was to use /(\X)/g:

```
L
o
ï
s
```

---

* Thankfully, I was guaranteed that the names would not be in any of the right-to-left or top-to-bottom scripts, which would have led to a whole world of pain.

The most important thing for most people to know about handling Unicode data in Perl, however, is that if you don't ever use any Unicode data—if none of your files are marked as UTF-8 and you don't use UTF-8 locales—then you can happily pretend that you're back in Perl 5.005_03 land; the Unicode features will in no way interfere with your code unless you're explicitly using them. Sometimes the twin goals of embracing Unicode but not disturbing old-style byte-oriented scripts has led to compromise and confusion, but it's the Perl way to silently do the right thing, which is what Perl ends up doing.

Encode

Life would be so much easier if everything in the world was already Unicode. We'd have this one standard data interchange format, data processing would be trivial, world peace would be easily achievable, and Perl programmers could get back to finding cures for cancer and watching *Buffy the Vampire Slayer* DVDs.

Sadly, that hasn't happened yet, and we still have to deal with a wide variety of character encodings in existing data. Based on initial work by Nick Ing-Simmons, Dan Kogai has produced the Encode family of modules, which do an admirable job of converting data between various character encodings and Perl's own internal format. We'll examine these modules in a little more detail later in the chapter.

Suppose I have some text in Shift JIS, the standard Japanese encoding for Windows machines, and I want to manipulate it in Perl. I can read the bytes from a file into the scalar $text, but Perl sees opaque bytes, rather than a sequence of Unicode characters. So I need to start by changing it into Perl's internal format, using the Encode function decode:

```
use Encode;
my $intern = decode("shiftjis", $text);
```

The text in $intern is Unicode characters, which Perl can understand. Internally, Perl stores them as UTF-8, but unless you're dealing directly with Perl's internals, the representation of Unicode characters isn't important. Because ASCII is a strict subset of UTF-8, $intern is also a valid ASCII string if the input happened to contain only characters in the ASCII range (though, given that it was initially Japanese, this is unlikely here). Indeed, on a UTF-8 terminal, I can now print out $intern as Unicode text:

```
binmode(STDOUT, ":utf8");
print $intern;
```

Or, I can perform the same conversion on the command line using the -C command-line option to set STDOUT to UTF-8:

```
% perl -C2 -MEncode -MFile::Slurp\
    -e 'print decode("shiftjis", read_file("japanese.sjis"));'
```

パールは大好き！

The -C command-line option sets UTF-8 handling on STDIN, STDOUT, STDERR, @ARGV, and the PerlIO layer. The PERL_UNICODE environment variable is equivalent and takes the same options as -C. These are available in Perl Versions 5.8.1 and higher. Read more in the *perlrun* documentation file.

There's also a corresponding function called encode for turning data from Perl's internal representation into another representation; we can use these two functions to make a cheap and cheerful character set convertor:

```
#!/usr/bin/perl -n0 -MEncode
BEGIN{($from, $to) = splice @ARGV,0,2};

print encode($to, decode($from, $_));
```

This allows us to say, for instance:

```
% transcode shiftjis euc-jp < japanese.sjis > japanese.euc
```

to convert a file between two of the more common Japanese encodings. (*Transcoding* is the jargon for converting from one encoding to another.)

The conversion direction of the two functions encode and decode isn't instantly memorable. It may help to remember that the Perl interpreter only understands UTF-8 and subsets of UTF-8 (ASCII, Latin 1), and so anything else needs decoding before the interpreter can understand it as text.

How do we know what encodings are available? Well, we can ask Encode to tell us:

```
% perl -MEncode -le 'print for Encode->encodings(":all")'

7bit-jis
AdobeStandardEncoding
AdobeSymbol
AdobeZdingbat
ascii
...
```

We use the :all parameter to include not just the standard set of encodings that Encode provides, but also those defined in any Encode::* modules that it's been able to find; for instance, many of the Japanese encodings are stored in Encode::JP.

There's also a handy shorthand for transcoding, called from_to. The only thing to note about this is that it converts the string in-place, modifying its input.

The PerlIO Trick

Perl 5.8.0 came with a very neat feature called PerlIO, which is a complete standard I/O library written exclusively for Perl. Normally, this would only excite really hardcore Perl maintainers (I must confess to being pretty baffled by most of it), but it provides a number of useful hooks to allow Perl modules to play about with any data going through the I/O system.

The upshot is that you can tell Perl to automatically encode and decode data as it's read from and written to a filehandle. If we want to transcode a file from Shift-JIS to EUC, we can just say:

```
use Encode;
open IN,  "<:encoding(shiftjis)", "data.jis" or die $!;
open OUT, ">:encoding(euc-jp)",   "data.euc" or die $!;
print OUT <IN>;
```

Anything read from IN will be decoded from Shift-JIS into Perl's internal format; similarly, anything written to OUT will be encoded as EUC.

The Gory Details

 You should probably not read this section unless you're either working with XS code that handles Unicode data, or if you're doing extremely clever things with Unicode and you can't get Encode to do what you want.

There are two dirty secrets about Encode and handling Unicode data in Perl. The first dirty secret is that Perl knows very little about Unicode, but it knows a lot about UTF-8. That's to say, Perl primarily cares about whether or not a string is UTF-8 encoded, and it cares little about the string's actual character code; knowing that a string is encoded in UTF-8 does *not* tell you whether it's Unicode, Latin 1, or anything else. Perl does not keep track of the character code anywhere, but assumes, for the purposes of regular expression matching, that things that are marked as UTF-8 will be Unicode. Many of the problems that people have with Unicode come about by thinking that once they've got data in UTF-8, they can do Unicode things with it; that's not the case. Similarly, you can't assume anything about the character coding of a string that *isn't* UTF-8. It might be Latin 1, but it might be something else entirely.

 UTF-8 is just a character encoding, and it implies nothing about character repertoires.

The other dirty secret is how Perl decides how to treat a string. There isn't a global setting as to whether we're in byte or character mode; the decision about what to do with a string is made on a string-by-string basis. Each Perl string has a flag inside it that determines whether it's in UTF-8 encoding or not. There's only one flag to determine both whether a string is internally stored as UTF-8, and whether a string is to be treated with Unicode semantics by the regular expression engine and functions such as lc. So, if a string is converted to UTF-8 internally, it will be treated as Unicode.[*]

This has historically led to some interesting conundrums with what to do when data of one type meets data of another. Take this piece of Perl code:

```
my $acute = chr(193);
print $acute;

$identity = $acute . chr(194); chop $identity;
print $identity;

$itentity = $acute . chr(257); chop $identity;
print $itentity;
```

Character 193 in Latin 1 is a capital A with acute accent (Á), so when I run this, I would expect to see ÁÁÁ. This works nicely on Perl 5.8.0, but on Perl 5.6.0, I see ÁÁĀ.

This is a leakage of what's going on inside Perl's Unicode support. When our non-UTF-8 string ($acute) meets the UTF-8 string chr(257), Perl has to recode the original character in UTF-8 before concatenating it. This is to avoid situations where the original string contains valid UTF-8 representations of a completely different character. It's similar to the situation where you have to escape text before putting it inside HTML, as symbols like <, >, and & have different meanings there.

So our Á is now encoded in UTF-8, and when Perl 5.6.0 comes to print it out, it prints the UTF-8 bytes. The first byte is character 195, Ã. Oops. Perl 5.8.0 corrects this by attempting to downgrade strings from UTF-8 to Latin 1 when they're output to filehandles not explicitly marked as UTF-8, but it gives you an idea of the shenanigans that are required to make the byte-character duality work.

What does this mean for troubleshooting Unicode problems? Well, the most common problems occur when a scalar's internal UTF-8 flag is incorrectly set and Perl treats the string with the wrong semantics. If the flag is wrongly turned off, then Perl treats what should be a Unicode string as a sequence of bytes. These bytes are the UTF-8 encoding of the Unicode characters, because Perl's internal representation of Unicode has been accidentally exposed. If the flag is wrongly turned on, then Perl provides Unicode semantics for that scalar and treats whatever sequence of bytes were in the scalar as UTF-8. Perl's internals will expect the bytes to be valid UTF-8, and will issue loud warnings if they are not. The easiest way to get this internal flag incorrect is by marking a filehandle as UTF-8 when it is not, or forgetting to mark it when it is.

---

[*] Arguably this is a bug, but it's one we have to live with until Perl 6.

For instance, writing this chapter, I had my sample file containing ŭñíçöðè, encoded in UTF-8, and I ran the following code in a UTF-8-aware terminal:

```
open IN, "<:utf8", "foo.utf8" or die $!;
$a = <IN>;
print $a;
```

I was mildly surprised to get gibberish thrown back at me—since I know how the internals store Unicode—until I remembered what was going on: standard output was not marked as expecting UTF-8, so Perl automatically downgraded the string to Latin 1 on printing it. The downgraded string was not valid UTF-8, so my terminal went mad. The upshot is that this new-fangled Unicode-aware Perl code didn't work on a new-fangled Unicode-aware terminal, although it works just fine on an old-fashioned Latin 1 terminal.

The Encode module allows you to generate the UTF-8 encoding of any Perl string with encode("utf8", $string).

```
use Encode;

open IN, "<:utf8", "foo.utf8" or die $!;
$a = <IN>;
$b = encode("utf8", $a);
print $b;
```

This made my UTF-8 terminal happy again, because Perl's output is a string of bytes that is valid UTF-8. Perls doesn't know (or care) that the characters $b contains happen to be UTF-8. They're just characters between 0 and 255, and as standard output is taking bytes (the default), it will output one byte per character. If we were to ask Perl for the lengths of the two strings, we'd see that $a had 8 characters and $b had 15. As internals gurus we know that they are probably stored in memory as the same sequence of bytes, but the interface Perl presents to the programmer is that strings are built from characters, and how those characters are stored should remain hidden.

If you have the opposite problem—data that you believe to be Unicode but which Perl is still storing as a sequence of UTF-8 bytes—you can convert a string to Unicode using decode("utf8", $string). These functions can be handy for ensuring that data coming into or going out of your routines will be in the form you expect.

So far we haven't worked out how to determine whether any given string uses byte or character semantics, because the Perl way is that you shouldn't have to care and Perl should transparently do the right thing. But since we're discussing how to deal with situations where Perl is not doing the right thing, let's look at how to deal with the UTF-8 flag directly.

Encode provides three internal-use functions that we can import on demand: is_utf8, _utf8_on, and _utf8_off.

Let's suppose we've just read some data from an I/O socket, using read. By default, Perl will assume that this data has byte semantics. The only thing that can determine whether the string is bytes or UTF-8 encoded characters is the specification for the protocol that we're reading—are we expecting to see UTF-8 data? If we are, then we can take advantage of our knowledge that Perl stores its Unicode strings internally as UTF-8. We just need some way of telling Perl to treat the data that it just read as Unicode. _utf8_on comes to our rescue here:

```
use Encode qw(_utf8_on);
my ($length, $data);
read(SOCKET, $length, 2);
read(SOCKET, $data, $length);
_utf8_on($data);
```

Now we can use $data with the correct semantics. There is another way to achieve the same effect without using Encode; whether it is considered more or less ugly is a matter of taste. It relies on the new U modifier to pack—pack("U", $number) is now equivalent to chr($number). The difference is that if U is the first template in the call to pack, it is guaranteed to return a UTF-8-on string:

```
use Encode qw(is_utf8);

$s1 = chr(70);
print "String 1 is ", (is_utf8($s1) ? "" : "not "), "UTF-8 encoded\n";

$s2 = pack("C", 70);
print "String 2 is ", (is_utf8($s2) ? "" : "not "), "UTF-8 encoded\n";

$s3 = pack("U", 70);
print "String 3 is ", (is_utf8($s3) ? "" : "not "), "UTF-8 encoded\n";
```

This produces:

```
String 1 is not UTF-8 encoded
String 2 is not UTF-8 encoded
String 3 is UTF-8 encoded
```

To force a string to be treated as containing Unicode characters, we create a pack format that begins with U, but packs zero characters. Internally, pack creates a string with the UTF-8 flag set. Then we fill the string up with ordinary characters using the C* pattern—this special pattern tells pack to ignore whether the scalars are internally encoded as UTF-8 and to directly use the raw bytes stored, so it will fill up the string with whatever UTF-8 encoded bytes you throw in. You're directly manipulating the internal representation of scalars here, so you need to be sure of what you're doing—pack won't check that the UTF-8 sequence it is building is valid. In this case, as long as we pass in valid UTF-8 byte sequences, all will be fine. The end result is to turn on Perl's internal UTF-8 flag without changing the raw bytes, which makes Perl treat those bytes as Unicode characters. The code to do this looks like this:

```
$string = pack("U0C*", unpack("C*", $string));
```

Another useful feature is the bytes pragma, which lexically turns off any kind of UTF-8 processing and allows you to see *any* string as its byte representation, no matter what:

```
open IN, "<:utf8", "foo.utf8" or die $!;
$a = <IN>;
chomp $a;

print length $a; # 8

{
  use bytes;
  print length $a; # 15
}
```

This can be handy if we're dealing with data that has to be sent over a network connection, or packed into a fixed-length structure.

Unicode for XS Authors

If you write XS routines, Unicode means a whole new set of rules for processing strings. Standard C tricks for iterating over the characters in a string no longer work in the Unicode world. Instead, Perl provides a series of functions and macros that make handling Unicode strings a little easier.

Traversing Strings

The first problem everyone comes across is that they have a large amount of legacy code that assumes that everything is in some seven- or eight-bit character encoding, and they can write:

```
while (*s++) {
    /* Do something with *s here */
}
```

Along comes a string that has its data encoded in UTF-8, and it all goes horribly wrong. What can we do about this situation?

First, we should take note that this situation means we can no longer pass raw char* strings around; we need to know whether or not such a C string is encoded in UTF-8. The most obvious way to do that is to pass around SVs instead of char*s, but where this isn't possible, you either need to use an explicit interface convention between the functions of your XS code, or pass around a boolean denoting the UTF-8 encoding of the string.

Once we have a string and know whether it's supposed to be encoded in UTF-8, we can use some of Perl's Unicode handling functions to help us walk along it. The most obviously useful one is utf8_to_uvchr, which pulls a code point out of a string:

```
STRLEN len;
while (*s) {
```

```
        UV c = utf8_to_uvchr(s, &len);
        printf("Saw a character with codepoint %d, length %d\n", c, len);
        s += len;
}
```

Perl deals with Unicode codepoints as UVs, unsigned integer values. This actually gives Perl support for UTF-8 characters beyond the range that the Unicode Standard provides, but that's OK. Maybe they'll catch up with us one day.

If you want to avoid extra work in the case of *invariant* characters—those that look just the same in UTF-8 and in byte encodings—you can use the UTF8_IS_INVARIANT( ) macro to test for this:

```
while (*s) {
    if (UTF8_IS_INVARIANT(*s)) {
        /* Use *s just like in the good old ASCII days */
        s++;
    } else {
        STRLEN len;
        UV c = utf8_to_uvchr(s, &len);
        /* Do the Unicode thing. */
        s += len;
    }
}
```

If you're not interested in looking at the Unicode characters, you can just skip over them, but you have to do this in a sensible way. If you just skip the first byte in the character, you can end up horribly misaligned and seeing characters that aren't there. Instead, use the UTF8SKIP( ) macro to fetch the length of the character, and use that to skip over it:

```
while (*s) {
    if (UTF8_IS_INVARIANT(*s)) {
        /* Use *s just like in the good old ASCII days */
        s++;
    } else {
        /* Don't care about these scary high characters */
        s += UTF8SKIP(*s);
    }
}
```

Encoding Strings

As well as getting data out of strings, we might occasionally find ourselves wanting to put Unicode characters into a string. We can do this in a number of ways. First, we can enter characters one codepoint at a time, much in the same way as we traversed strings one character at a time. When getting Unicode codepoints out of strings, we used utf8_to_uvchr, so it should be no surprise that to put Unicode codepoints into strings, we can use uvchr_to_utf8. As UTF-8 is a variable-length encoding, we cannot infer the number of bytes needed to store our string from the number of characters, so allocating the correct amount of memory is tricky. The easiest thing to do is loop twice, once to work out the number of bytes needed, and once to act.

```
/* Convert an array of numbers into a Unicode string */
I32 len, i;
STRLEN strlen = 0;
SV* sv;
char* s;

len = av_len(av) + 1;

for (i = 0; i < len; i++) {
    SV** sav = av_fetch(av, i, 0);
    if (! sav) continue;
    strlen += UNISKIP(SvUV(*sav));
}

/* Allocate space for the string */
sv = newSV(strlen);
s = SvPVX(sv);

for (i = 0; i < len; i++) {
    SV** sav = av_fetch(av, i, 0);
    if (! sav) continue;
    s = uvchr_to_utf8(s, SvUV(*sav));
}

/* Perl internally expects a NUL byte after every buffer, so write one */

s = '\0';

/* Tell Perl how long our scalar is, that it has a valid string
buffer, and that the buffer holds UTF-8 */

SvCUR_set(sv, strlen);
SvPOK_on(sv);
SvUTF8_on(sv);
```

As can be seen from this example, uvchr_to_utf8 returns the advanced pointer after the new character has been added. This is the recommended UTF-8-aware way of adding a character to a buffer, unlike *s++ = c;, which assumes all characters are the same size. The UNISKIP function returns the number of bytes required to UTF-8-encode a Unicode codepoint.

If we have a string that is Unicode but stored as bytes instead of UTF-8, you can use the sv_utf8_upgrade function, which converts an existing SV to UTF-8. Conversely, if you have a string that is valid UTF-8 but Perl doesn't know that fact yet, you can use the SvUTF_on(sv) macro to turn on the UTF-8 flag:

```
sv_gets(sv, fp, 0);
/* But we expect that to be Unicode */
SvUTF8_on(sv);
```

Of course, the problem here is that we haven't checked that the data really is valid UTF-8 before telling Perl that it is. We can do this with is_utf8_string to avoid problems later:

```
STRLEN len;
char *s;

sv_gets(sv, fp, 0);
s = SvPV(sv, len);
if (is_utf8_string(s, len)) {
    SvUTF8_on(sv);
} else {
    /* Not really UTF-8—what is going on? */
}
```

Transcoding with XS is quite tricky, and you would be best doing that stage in Perl. There are plans to allow easy transcoding from C in the future, but for the moment, the only available option is to do something like this to get an Encode::XS object:

```
ENTER;
SAVETMPS;

PUSHMARK(sp);
XPUSHp("euc-jp", 6);
PUTBACK;
call_pv("Encode::find_encoding", G_SCALAR);
SPAGAIN;
encoding_obj = POPs;
PUTBACK;
```

And then use this object to perform decoding and encoding:

```
PUSHMARK(sp);
XPUSHs(encoding_obj);
XPUSHs(euc_data);
XPUSHi(0);
PUTBACK;
if (call_method("decode", G_SCALAR) != 1) {
    Perl_die(aTHX_ "panic: decode did not return a value");
}
SPAGAIN;
uni = POPs;
PUTBACK;
```

It isn't pretty, but it works. The code in *ext/PerlIO/encoding/encoding.xs* in the Perl source tree is probably the only example of this around at the moment.

Conclusion

Perl's Unicode support has developed slowly and steadily over the past few versions, but it is now at a point where one can write major programs with core Unicode components. Hopefully this chapter has shown you some of the things that Perl's Unicode support can allow you to do and how deploying Unicode can save a lot of hassle with alternate character repertoires.

We've looked at the differences between Unicode and legacy encodings, and the various different UTF encodings. As we have noted, Perl speaks UTF-8 internally but tries hard to allow users to use Unicode features without knowing anything about the internal representation.

Perl's support for Unicode extends to distinguishing between character and byte semantics, providing Unicode character escapes and names, and transcoding modules to allow easy input of legacy data.

We've also seen what to do if Unicode doesn't behave as you might expect, and how to convert old XS code to support Unicode data.

## CHAPTER 7

POE

In this chapter, we're going to look at what Mark-Jason Dominus called "the most interesting development in Perl 5": the Perl Object Environment. POE has many goals and many uses; to give a few of them:

- Provide a cooperative scheduling and multitasking environment rivalling threads and IPC
- Simplify the development of protocol-driven network clients and servers
- Provide an architecture for creating state machines
- Abstract away a lot of the boring I/O details from complex programs

As you can see, POE is a difficult thing to describe,* but the main point is that POE attempts to hide the menial details of event-driven programming.

Programming in an Event-Driven Environment

If you've ever programmed a graphical application using something like Tk or Gtk, you'll know that it's a little different than ordinary procedural programming. In normal programming, you write a sequence of things you'd like the program to do, and it does them. However, GUIs don't work like that—instead, you set up an environment (a window, for instance) that responds to certain events (clicking a button or selecting a menu item). This is called the *event-driven paradigm*.

It's not just GUIs that use this paradigm. For example, a network server does not *do* a sequence of events, but it sits waiting for a connection (an event), and then services the connection depending on the input from the client. When the client is done and disconnects, it goes back to waiting for the next event.

---

* It's been described as a small operating system implemented in Perl, and this isn't too far from the truth—it has kernel, which contains a scheduler; it has I/O abstraction layers; and so on.

Similarly, you could write something that watches over a directory; it sits around watching, periodically looking at the files in the directory, and as it detects changes made to the files, it fires off certain responses.

The core of the event-driven paradigm is the event loop, sometimes called the *main loop*. Tk has one, the Event module has one, and POE, an event-driven environment, has one. POE's event loop is handled by the POE *kernel*.

As we've said, POE can be thought of as a minute operating system, and so the name kernel is no coincidence. When an ordinary operating system's kernel has finished setting up the working environment, it too sits back and waits for events. These can be system calls from user space, or they can be hardware interrupts. As well as servicing events, it takes care of passing messages between different components—typically communication between processes (IPC).

POE's kernel also services events and handles communications between different parts of the POE world, although the equivalent of processes are called *sessions*.

Hello, POE

There's been a lot of talk so far and very little code, so let's rectify this with a brief example.

```perl
use POE;
POE::Session->create(
    inline_states => {
        _start  => \&start,
        hello   => \&hello,
    },
);

print "Running Kernel\n";
$poe_kernel->run();
print "Exiting\n";
exit(0);

sub start {
    my ($kernel) = $_[KERNEL];
    print "Setting up a session\n";
    $kernel->yield("hello");
}

sub hello { print "Hello, world\n"; }
```

This is the POE equivalent of the famous Hello World program. If we're going to continue to think in operating system terms (which will shortly become unhelpful, but will do for now) then we're starting up a machine's kernel and creating a single process that prints out Hello World and then exits. Let's look at the different pieces of this in turn.

```
use POE;
print "Running Kernel\n";
$poe_kernel->run();
print "Exiting\n";
exit(0);
```

This is the core of any POE program; the variable $poe_kernel is provided by the POE module and represents the POE kernel itself. In many cases the call to run will never return; for instance, a network server should sit in a loop accepting new connections until something awful happens. In our case, however, we're only setting up one brief session that soon terminates. Newer code may prefer to say POE::Kernel->run, which is pretty much the same.

```
POE::Session->create(
    inline_states => {
    _start => \&start,
    hello  => \&hello,
    },
);
```

This creates a session. A session can be thought of as a state machine with multiple states, or as a handler for multiple events—the two representations are equivalent. In state-speak, the preceding example defines two states in the inline_states parameter passed to the constructor. States whose names begin with an underscore are predefined by POE, whereas all other states are user-defined. The session automatically enters the _start state after it has been successfully constructed.

If you prefer an event-driven explanation, then we say that our session responds to the _start event and the hello event, and POE posts a _start event to the session as soon as it has been created.

There are other predefined events, most of which are to do with parent/child relationships and signals; there's the _stop event, which is posted when a session is due to finish. Let's now see how we handle the events that we've defined:

```
sub start {
    my ($kernel) = $_[KERNEL];
    print "Setting up a session\n";
    $kernel->yield("hello");
}

sub hello { print "Hello, world\n"; }
```

We pass our start handler a number of parameters, one of which is a handle on the POE kernel. We extract this from the parameter list using the KERNEL constant. For the sake of efficiency, POE uses constants like this for indexes into @_, rather than a parameter hash. You'll often see POE state handlers that start something like this:

```
my ($kernel, $heap, $session) = @_[KERNEL, HEAP, SESSION];
```

This is just an ordinary array slice with constant indexes, returning the POE kernel, the heap, and the current session object. The heap is a place where a session can store its private, per-session stuff. We'll come back to what sort of stuff is good to store in a heap later.

Now that we have the kernel, what do we do with it? Well, we tell it that we want to be in another state, the hello state:

```
$kernel->yield("hello");
```

We're yielding because we're posting an event to the current session; if we had stored a handle to another session, we could communicate with it by posting an event to it using the post method. We'll see examples of this later on.

So our start-up state has told the POE kernel that soon we want to move to the hello state. This will not happen, however, until the next time POE runs over its event loop. Once we run the loop with $poe_kernel->run, the kernel looks at its list of pending tasks, finds that the first thing it needs to do is move our session into the hello state, and fires off the appropriate handler. Then it prints our Hello, world! message.

Hello, Again, POE!

Suppose we now want the message to repeat every five seconds. We could, of course do this:

```
sub hello {
    my ($kernel) = $_[KERNEL];
    print "Hello, world!\n";
    sleep 5;
    $kernel->yield("hello");
}
```

However, this is no way to behave in a cooperative multitasking environment. We can't simply hog the whole kernel for five seconds, because other sessions may have things to do: there might be things coming in from the network that need immediate servicing, and so in. Instead, we need to allow the kernel to schedule the hello state for five seconds in the future. We do this with the delay_set method to the kernel:

```
sub hello {
    my ($kernel) = $_[KERNEL];
    print "Hello, world!\n";
    $kernel->delay_set("hello", 5);
}
```

Now we're a little more polite. Let's now see what we can do with two different sessions running. Here's some code lightly modified from Matt Sergeant's wonderful POE tutorial (*http://www.axkit.org/docs/presentations/tpc2002/poe/*):

```
use POE;

for my $session_no (1..2) {
  POE::Session->create(
```

```
      inline_states => {
        hello => \&hello,
        _start => sub { $_[KERNEL]->alias_set("session_" . $session_no) },
      });
    }

    $poe_kernel->post("session_1", "hello", "session_2");
    $poe_kernel->run();
    exit(0);

    sub hello {
      my ($kernel, $session, $next) = @_[KERNEL, SESSION, ARG0];
      print "Event in ", $kernel->alias_list($session), "\n";
      $kernel->post($next, "hello", $session->ID);
    }
```

We've seen much of this before; we create a session (this time, we create two of them) that has a start handler and a handler for the hello event. Notice that both sessions are sharing the code for the two handlers (_start and hello), although the data passed to the code will be quite different in each case.

This time, the start handler does something a little different from the previous program. It tells the kernel to register an *alias* for this session. Each session has an internal ID (which we also use later in the program) but that's really known only to POE when the sessions are created. By registering a programmer-friendly alias, we get a handle by which we can refer to the session later in the program.

Again in order to be programmer-friendly, we can ask the kernel for a session's alias in order to output our messages in an understandable manner:

```
    print "Event in ", $kernel->alias_list($session), "\n";
```

Now that we have two sessions going on, we need to tell the kernel which of them is going to start the action, and we do this by posting a hello event to session 1, referred to by its alias:

```
    $poe_kernel->post("session_1", "hello", "session_2");
```

When we're posting or yielding events, we can pass additional parameters with the event, which get passed in to the event's handler. These arguments arrive in @_ starting at position ARG0. If we had many arguments, we could say something like this to collect them all up:

```
      my ($kernel, $session, @args) = @_[KERNEL, SESSION, ARG0..$#_];
```

But here we are only interested in the first argument, which is the name of the next session to call. Session 1 passes control to session 2, and vice versa. Now that we're up and running, we don't need to be programmer-friendly any more, so we can identify the next session to run by its internal session ID:

```
    $kernel->post($next, "hello", $session->ID);
```

This says "I'm calling you now, and next time around you call me (by ID)."

With these two sessions running, we now have a cooperative multitasking environment:

```
Event in session_1
Event in session_2
Event in session_1
Event in session_2

...
```

However, if we're going to do anything interesting with our newfound environment, we have to start looking at POE's provisions for more complex I/O.

Wheels

Wheels are the driving force (hah, hah) of POE's I/O system. A *wheel* is a connection to the outside world that generates events. You can think of wheels as POE's equivalent to filehandles, but there's more to them than that.

The simplest wheel to understand is POE::Wheel::FollowTail, which follows an ever-growing file. You give a filename to the wheel, and it generates events when that file has more data in it. Here's a nice compact example:

```perl
use POE qw(Wheel::FollowTail);

POE::Session->create(
  inline_states => {
    _start => sub {
        my ($heap) = $_[HEAP];
        my $log_watcher = POE::Wheel::FollowTail->new(
            Filename => "my_log_file.txt",
            InputEvent => "got_record",
        );

        $heap->{watcher} = $log_watcher;
    },
    got_record => sub { my $record = $_[ARG0]; print $record,"\n"; }
  }
);

$poe_kernel->run();
```

First, notice the compact way of loading up multiple POE modules; any parameters to use POE will be interpreted as module names under POE:: and use'd in turn.

As before, we have two states. The got_record state is nice and easy to understand: it prints its argument. Let's have a look at the _start state in a little more detail, though:

```perl
my $log_watcher = POE::Wheel::FollowTail->new(
    Filename => "my_log_file.txt",
    InputEvent => "got_record",
);
```

The job of our start state is to set up our wheel. We tell the wheel to watch the file *my_log_file.txt* and post a got_record event every time it sees a new line.

What do we do with our wheel? We'd like it to persist for the duration of the session—else it's pretty useless—but as it's just an ordinary Perl object, it'll be destroyed at the end of the current block if we don't store it somewhere. Now we see the immediate value of having a per-session storage area, the *heap*:

```
my ($heap) = $_[HEAP];
  . . .
$heap->{watcher} = $log_watcher;
```

And this is all we need; the wheel happily sits there watching the file and generating events, and our event handler prints out the line that was seen. Now let's add another wheel into the equation.

Let's suppose, for some reason, our log file is actually binary data and we want to print out new lines in hexadecimal using the hexdump command.*

The POE::Wheel::Run wheel handles I/O with regard to external programs. We can simply create a wheel that calls hexdump, and feed it the data we get:

```
use POE qw(Wheel::FollowTail Wheel::Run);

POE::Session->create(
  inline_states => {
    _start => sub {
      my ($heap) = $_[HEAP];
      my $log_watcher = POE::Wheel::FollowTail->new(
        Filename    => "my_log_file.txt",
        InputEvent  => "redirect",
      );
      my $dumper = POE::Wheel::Run->new(
        Program     => "/usr/bin/hexdump",
        StdoutEvent => "print"
      );

      $heap->{watcher} = $log_watcher;
      $heap->{dumper}  = $dumper;
    },
    redirect => sub {
      my ($heap, $data) = @_[HEAP, ARG0];
      $heap->{dumper}->put($data);
    },
```

---

* If you don't have a hexdump command in your operating system, demand one! You can also mock one with Perl, of course. Something like this ought to do the trick:

```
my $i = -16;
binmode(STDIN);
my $data; $|++;
printf "%07x ". ("%02x%02x "x8)."\n", $i+=16, map ord, split//,$data
    while read STDIN, $data, 16;
```

```
            print => sub { my $record = $_[ARG0]; print $record, "\n"; }
        }
    );
```

Let's look at a diagram of what's going on in Figure 7-1.

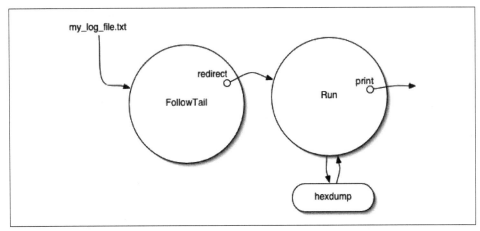

Figure 7-1. Filtered log tailing

The FollowTail wheel feeds data into the program and sends it to the session, which sends it straight back out to the Run wheel, which in turn generates print events and prints the data. Wonderful.

Except it doesn't work. If we try and run this with an ordinary Unix hexdump, all our data disappears into the ether and is never seen again. But here's an interesting thing: if we use our makeshift Perl hexdump, it works just fine. Can you guess why this is?

The key is in the magic $|++ in our version. The system's hexdump buffers its output completely if it senses that it's connected to a pipe. Since our program isn't supposed to terminate, hexdump just sits there buffering data until we break, at which point everything is lost. We need to trick hexdump into thinking that it's connected to a real terminal. Unsurprisingly, POE provides a way to do this:

```
        my $dumper = POE::Wheel::Run->new(
            Program      => "/usr/bin/hexdump",
            Conduit      => "pty",
            StdoutEvent  => "print"
        );
```

There are various other wheels you can fit together like this: POE::Wheel::Curses reads data using the non-blocking Curses interface library, whereas POE::Wheel::ReadLine uses Term::ReadKey to implement a line-based editable console input interface. POE::Wheel::ListenAccept is a low-level socket-based listener. We'll look at two of the more important wheels in our next example, POE::Wheel::ReadWrite and POE::Wheel::SocketFactory.

A Port Forwarder

You know the story. You're at work. You're behind an aggressive firewall that won't let you IRC. You simply can't work without IRC, so you perform some nasty shenanigans. You're going to set up some forwarders so that when you connect to port 6667 on your local machine, it heads off to port 80 (which is allowed through the firewall) on your hosted box out in the real world. Then another forwarder will listen on port 80 of that machine and forward connections through to port 6667 on the IRC server. You set your IRC client to connect to localhost, and, boom, you're connected right through. Let's see how POE can help you lose your job.

 This example was inspired by the wonderful POE Cookbook (*http://poe.perl.org/?POE_Cookbook*) and a certain large accounting company's overly restrictive firewall.

Let's start by setting up the server that listens for connections:

```
my $office = shift;

my ($local_address, $local_port, $remote_address, $remote_port);
($office ? $remote_address : $local_address) = "mybox.real-world.int";
($office ? $local_port     : $remote_port)  = 6667;
($office ? $remote_port    : $local_port)   = 80;

if ($office) {
   $local_address = "127.0.0.1";
} else {
   $remote_address = "irc.perl.org";
}

POE::Session->new
  ( _start => \&server_start,
    client_connected => \&client_connected,
    [ $local_address, $local_port, $remote_address, $remote_port ]
  );
$poe_kernel->run;
```

Once we've worked out whether we're the forwarder from the office to the hosted machine or from the hosted machine to the eventual server, we set up the various addresses and ports, and create a new session with the appropriate parameters. This one session starts up all the other sessions we need. As we're dealing with three parties in this forwarding exchange—the socket we bind to, the client that connects to us, and the server that we tunnel to—we need three sessions and three wheels.

We've omitted a lot of error handling in this and later sessions, partly for clarity of the explanation, and partly because if an error does happen while, say, accepting a connection, there's very little you can do about it other than ignore it and wait for the next successful connection.

But you shouldn't do that, of course. Even just logging an error and then doing nothing about it shows you've thought it through a little.

The first wheel comes in the server's start state; this has to set up a listener on the appropriate address and port, which we'll do with the SocketFactory wheel:

```perl
sub server_start {
    my ( $heap, $local_addr, $local_port, $remote_addr, $remote_port )
      = @_[ HEAP, ARG0,       ARG1,        ARG2,         ARG3 ];

    # Store our parameters
    $heap->{local_addr}  = $local_addr;
    $heap->{local_port}  = $local_port;
    $heap->{remote_addr} = $remote_addr;
    $heap->{remote_port} = $remote_port;

    # Create and store a wheel
    $heap->{server_wheel} = POE::Wheel::SocketFactory->new
      ( BindAddress  => $local_addr,
        BindPort     => $local_port,
        Reuse        => 'yes',
        SuccessEvent => 'client_connected'
      );
}
```

When the SocketFactory wheel accepts a connection and posts a client_connected event, it passes the socket and the peer address and port like so:

```perl
sub client_connected {
    my ( $heap, $socket, $peer_addr, $peer_port ) =
      @_[ HEAP, ARG0,    ARG1,       ARG2];
}
```

Now we have a server that listens for and accepts connections, but what do we do once we've accepted one? In an ordinary, non-POE application, we'd probably fork here or create a new thread to service the request so we can immediately get back to listening for new connections. In POE terms, we create a new session to handle the client. Remembering that we've stored our connection parameters in the first session's heap, we can pass these on to the new session.

```perl
sub accept {
    my ( $heap, $socket, $peer_addr, $peer_port ) =
      @_[ HEAP, ARG0,    ARG1,       ARG2];

    POE::Session->new
      ( _start => \&forwarder_start,
        server_connect => \&connected_to_other_side,
```

```
        client_input   => \&forward_outbound,
        server_input   => \&forward_inbound,

        [ $socket, $peer_addr, $peer_port,
          $heap->{remote_addr}, $heap->{remote_port} ]
    );
}
```

When this session starts up, it needs to set up the connection to the final destination and get ready to read and write data from the client. We do this by passing the client $socket we received to our second wheel, POE::Wheel::ReadWrite, POE's generic I/O wheel. Just like in a non-POE environment, we reuse the socket that we've been using to handle the connection as a filehandle to read from and write to.

Let's stop for a moment and look at a diagram of what we've got so far in Figure 7-2.

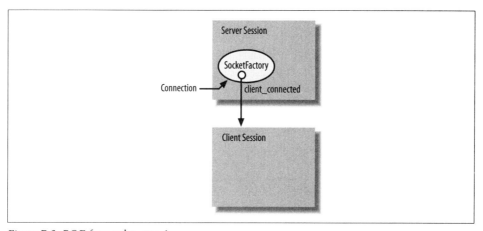

Figure 7-2. POE forwarder: step 1

So far we've taken care of the client that has connected to us; we also want another wheel to connect us to the server at the other end of the forwarding tunnel.

```
sub forwarder_start {
    my ( $heap, $session,
         $socket, $peer_host, $peer_port, $remote_addr, $remote_port
       ) =
       @_[ HEAP, SESSION, ARG0, ARG1, ARG2, ARG3, ARG4 ];

    $heap->{qw(peer_host    peer_port   remote_addr   remote_port)} =
             ($peer_host, $peer_port, $remote_addr, $remote_port);

    $heap->{wheel_client} = POE::Wheel::ReadWrite->new
      ( Handle => $socket,
        Filter     => POE::Filter::Stream->new,
        InputEvent => 'client_input',
      );

    $heap->{wheel_server} = POE::Wheel::SocketFactory->new
```

```
( RemoteAddress => $remote_addr,
  RemotePort   => $remote_port,
  SuccessEvent => 'server_connect',
);
}
```

We'll add one slight detail to that; since we're trying to do everything as asynchro-
nously as possible, we have to look out for the case where we're still establishing a
connection to the server, but we've received some data from the client. We add a
queue to store any data we get before the connection is set up:

```
$heap->{state} = 'connecting';
$heap->{queue} = [ ];
```

Now let's see what happens when data comes in from the client. If we're still await-
ing the connection, it gets put in the queue. Otherwise, we send it out through the
other wheel to the server:

```
sub forward_outbound {
    my ( $heap, $input ) = @_[ HEAP, ARGO ];

    if ( $heap->{state} eq 'connecting' ) {
        push @{ $heap->{queue} }, $input;
    }
    else {
        $heap->{wheel_server}->put($input);
    }
}
```

Once we have set up the connection with the other side, we need to do the same sort
of thing again and turn the socket into our third wheel, another ReadWrite wheel.

```
sub connected_to_other_side {
    my ( $kernel, $session, $heap, $socket ) = @_[ KERNEL, SESSION,
HEAP, ARGO
];

    $heap->{wheel_server} = POE::Wheel::ReadWrite->new
      ( Handle => $socket,
        Driver      => POE::Driver::SysRW->new,
        Filter      => POE::Filter::Stream->new,
        InputEvent => 'server_input',
      );
}
```

We can now run the queue in case anything has built up while we were connecting:

```
$heap->{state} = 'connected';
foreach my $pending ( @{ $heap->{queue} } ) {
    $kernel->call( $session, 'client_input', $pending );
}
$heap->{queue} = [ ];
```

For each bit of data we receive, we post the data back to the client_input event; however, this time we are no longer connecting, and the event will pass the data onto the server.

Finally, we need to move data received from the server back down the tunnel to the client, by filling in the forward_inbound subroutine:

```
my ( $heap, $input ) = @_[ HEAP, ARG0 ];
$heap->{wheel_client}->put($input);
```

Let's take a look at a final diagram of the whole forwarder, in Figure 7-3, before we start to look at how to make this even simpler.

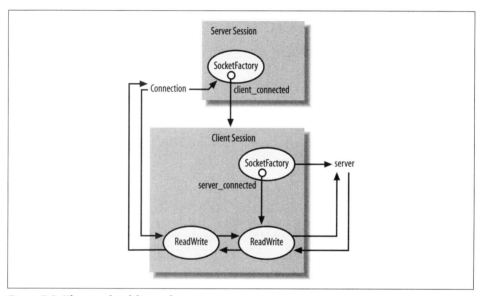

Figure 7-3. The completed forwarder

Top-Level Pieces: Components

The examples we've seen so far in this chapter go part way to abstracting out some of the I/O logic in a program, but not all of it; and they certainly don't relieve us of some of the problems of higher layers of program design, such as the protocol layer. If POE is going to help us concentrate purely on the logic of our particular application, we need another layer of abstraction on top—fortunately, we have such a layer, and it's provided by POE's Components.

Components are modules, usually in the POE::Component:: namespace (often abbreviated to PoCo:: in POE documentation), that provide very high-level functionality to an application. There are components that act as SOAP or XML/RPC servers, provide the basics of a mail server, speak Jabber or Yahoo! IM, receive syslog messages, play MP3s, and many other things. We'll start by looking at one of the protocol-level components, such as PoCo::Client::HTTP, and then move up to look at components that provide the whole core of an application for us.

Medium-Level Components

One of the ideas behind POE components is to hide the more repetitive parts of setting up I/O from the user, to abstract even wheels away. (One of the reasons wheels are called wheels is because they so often get reinvented.)

The most-used components are those that deal with TCP clients and servers; the server component knows how to bind to sockets, accept connections, talk to clients, and so on. Let's convert our port forwarder to use PoCo::Client::TCP and PoCo::Server::TCP instead of doing the work ourselves.

First, we have the same idea of a server where we're listening for connections, but this is handled somewhat differently:

```
POE::Component::Server::TCP->new(
    Port => 6667,
    ClientConnected => \&spawn_client_side,
    ClientInput => sub {
        my ( $kernel, $heap, $input ) = @_[ KERNEL, HEAP,  ARG0 ];
        $kernel->post( $heap->{client_id} => send_stuff => $input );
    },
    InlineStates => {
        _child => sub {
            my ( $heap, $child_op, $child ) = @_[ HEAP, ARG0, ARG1 ];
            $heap->{client_id} = $child->ID
              if $child_op eq "create";
        },
        send_stuff => sub {
            my ( $heap, $stuff ) = @_[ HEAP, ARG0 ];
            $heap->{client}->put($stuff);
        }
    },
);
```

We start by saying we want to listen on port 6667, and once a client has connected, we'll head off and set up the client's component. The ClientInput state says that when the client sends us something, we post a send_stuff event to the client session, which sends it off to the other side of the tunnel.

But wait! How do we know what the client session is? Well, this is what the _child state is for. When something happens to a child session, when it gets created or destroyed, POE automatically tells our session about it. So using the _child state, we can store the client's ID so we can talk to it later.

And that's all we need to do for that part of the session. Now what happens to spawn the client?

```
sub spawn_client_side {
    POE::Component::Client::TCP->new(
        RemoteAddress => 'mybox.real-world.int',
        RemotePort    => 80,

        Started => sub { $_[HEAP]->{server_id} = $_[SENDER]->ID; },
        ServerInput => sub {
            my ( $kernel, $heap, $input ) = @_[ KERNEL, HEAP, SESSION, ARGO ];
            $kernel->post( $heap->{server_id} => send_stuff => $input );
        },

        InlineStates => {
            send_stuff => sub {
                my ( $heap, $stuff ) = @_[ HEAP, ARGO ];
                $heap->{server}->put($stuff);
            },
        },
    );
}
```

This session is a POE::Component::Client::TCP, and the first two parameters set up where it's talking to. We store the ID of the server that spawned the new session, so we can send it stuff.

Now, things are about to get a little tricky to describe, because we have a server that's just spawned a client, but that client opens a TCP connection to a completely different server. So let's have a quick look at a diagram in Figure 7-4 to explain what's going on here.

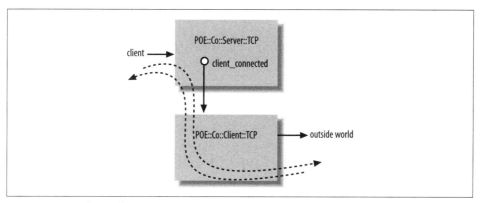

Figure 7-4. Port forwarder, mark 2

When we receive something from the other end of the tunnel (port 80 of the remote host), we post it as a send_stuff event to the server component, which, as we've seen, sends it to the end user. Conversely, when the server component tells us to send stuff arriving on port 6667 of the local host, we want to send it down the POE::Wheel::ReadWrite connection to port 80 of the remote host. PoCo::Client::TCP stores the wheel in the heap as $heap->{server}, so we just call put on that to send the data across. And that's all there is to it—50 lines of code, all told.

Using components has greatly simplified the process of handling network servers and clients, but we can go much further even than this.

A POE Web Server

The POE component POE::Component::Server::HTTP implements the business end of a web server in POE; it handles all the network and protocol layers and leaves us a callback to provide content in response to a request. This couldn't be simpler: we get an HTTP::Request object, and we have to send back an HTTP::Response object. This is how programming is meant to be—all we need to do is decide on how we're going to create our content.

We could write an extremely simple server using PoCo::Server::HTTP, but we'll be slightly more advanced and create a file server that serves up files under a given directory. Here's all it takes to fire up our web server:

```
use strict;
use POE::Component::Server::HTTP;
use POE;

my $datadir = "/Users/simon/";
POE::Component::Server::HTTP->new(
    ContentHandler => { '/' => \&callback },
    Port => 8000
);
$poe_kernel->run;
```

Next comes the actual callback that responds to the request:

```
use URI::Escape;
use HTTP::Headers;
use File::Spec::Functions;
use File::MMagic;

sub callback {
    my ($request, $response) = @_;
    my $path = catfile($datadir,canonpath(uri_unescape($request->uri->path)));

    return error($response, $request, RC_NOT_FOUND) unless -e $path;
    return error($response, $request, RC_FORBIDDEN) unless open OUT, $path;

    $response->code(RC_OK);
    my $magic = File::MMagic->new();
    $response->push_header("Content-type", $magic->checktype_filename($path));
    local $/; $response->content(scalar <OUT>);
    close OUT;
    return $response;
}
```

Let's briefly pause to examine this function. Most of the magic is done in the second line:

```
my $path = catfile($datadir,canonpath(uri_unescape($request->uri->path)));
```

This first extracts the path part of the request URI, turning *http://www.foo.int:8000/some/file* into */some/file*. Then, as this is a URI, it may contain characters encoded in the percent-encoding scheme, so we unescape those using the uri_unescape function from URI::Escape.

Now we have a valid local part; however, we have to be careful at this point. If we blindly tack this onto the end of our data directory, */Users/simon*, some joker will come along and request */../../etc/passwd.* The canonpath function, from File::Spec:: Functions, will tidy this up as though it were an absolute path, and remove leading .. sequences.

Once we add our document root to the beginning of this path, we've got something that turns *http://www.foo.int:8000/some/file* into */Users/simon/some/file*—this one line has done the rough equivalent of Apache's URL mapping phase.

We must now check whether our file actually exists and is readable:

```
return error($response, $request, RC_NOT_FOUND) unless -e $path;
return error($response, $request, RC_FORBIDDEN) unless open OUT, $path;
```

We'll define the error routine in a second; we use the codes from HTTP::Headers to represent the 404 (Not Found) and 403 (Forbidden) status codes. If we get past these two statements, we have a readable file and an active filehandle, so we can return a 200 (OK) status code. The next stage is to establish the MIME type of the file, which we do using a similar trick to Apache's mod_mime_magic—the File::MMagic module gives us a method that looks at the first few bytes of a file to determine its content type.

```
$response->push_header("Content-type", $magic->checktype_filename($path));
```

To complete the request, we spit out the contents of the file in a relatively straight-forward way:

```
local $/; $response->content(scalar <OUT>);
close OUT;
return $response;
```

And, finally, the error response subroutine is equally straightforward:

```
sub not_found {
    my ($response, $request, $code) = @_;
    my $uri = $request->uri;
    my $message = status_message($code);
    my $explanation = $code == RC_FORBIDDEN ? "accessible" : "found";
```

---

* And, of course, he'll find that since this is a Macintosh, that information won't help him much. But it's the principle of the thing.

```
    $response->code($code);
    $response->push_header("Content-type", "text/html");
    $response->content(<<EOF);
<!DOCTYPE HTML PUBLIC "-//IETF//DTD HTML 2.0//EN">
<HTML><HEAD>
<TITLE>$code $message</TITLE>
</HEAD><BODY>
<H1>$message</H1>
The requested URL $uri was not $explanation on this server.<P>
</BODY></HTML>
EOF
    return $response;
}
```

The key to this is the status_message routine provided by HTTP::Headers, which turns a numeric status code (404) into a message (Not Found).

When we put this all together, we have a very simple file server in fewer than 50 lines of Perl code. The vast majority of these lines are actually taken up with error handling; perhaps that's the way it should be.

I hope you've noticed that when we've been looking at this web server, we've not really talked about POE at all. This is deliberate; the idea of POE components is to make the POE part almost invisible and allow you to concentrate on the program logic.

Highest-Level Components

As we mentioned at the beginning of this section, there are a wealth of components out there, and after awhile one can begin to think that most programming with POE is just a matter of sticking the appropriate bits together.

In Chapter 2, we looked at several implementations of an RSS aggregator and renderer. Now we'll look at a related problem: a realtime RSS newswire, which periodically checks a bunch of RSS sources and informs us of any new headlines.

How would you go about this without POE? Maybe use LWP to fetch a list of URLs, determine which have changed since the last fetch, parse with XML::RSS, work out the new articles, report these to the user, then go back to sleep for a while. Sounds easy, but when you get down to the details of working out the changed feeds and new headlines, you're probably looking at about 200 lines of code, at least. If you're lucky, you might find XML::RSS::Feed, which does some of this, but it's still not a 10-minute job.

Now that you know about POE, you might think you can use POE::Component::Client::HTTP to handle queuing and scheduling the HTTP fetches, and have a response state grab the responses and parse them. That takes some of the pressure away, but it's still way too much work. Can't we get a component to do this?

Here's a simple RSS newswire using `POE::Component::RSSAggregator`. We'll start by setting up our arrays of feeds using `XML::RSS::FeedFactory`:

```
use XML::RSS::Feed::Factory;

my @feeds = feed_factory(
    {   url  => "http://slashdot.org/slashdot.rss",
        name => "Slashdot",
      delay => 60 },
    {   url  => "http://blog.simon-cozens.org/blosxom.cgi/xml",
        name => "Simon Cozens",
      delay => 60 },
    {   url  => "http://use.perl.org/perl-news-short.rdf",
        name => "Perl news",
      delay => 60 }
);
```

Now we can simply pass this array of feeds to `POE::Component::RSSAggregator`, and most of the work is done:

```
my $aggie = POE::Component::RSSAggregator->new(
            feeds    => \@feeds,
            callback => \&new_headlines
);
POE::Kernel->run;
```

This sets up the relevant sessions to take care of getting the summaries from the feeds; all that's left is to decide what to do each time some RSS arrives:

```
sub new_headlines {
    my ($feed) = shift;
    return unless my @newnews = $feed->late_breaking_news;
    for my $headline (@newnews) {
        print $headline->headline . ": " . $headline->url . "\n";
    }
}
```

`XML::RSS::Feed` automatically keeps track of what headlines we've seen, so we can return immediately unless there's something new for us to see. When there is something new, we get an `XML::RSS::Headline` object we can interrogate.

Again, POE components have abstracted away the generic pieces of our application—fetching and parsing feeds, and keeping track of what headlines we've seen—and allowed us to concentrate on the specific parts: what we want to do with new headlines.

Conclusion

As we've seen, POE is a fantastic module for taking away the complexity in creating event-based programs. The huge range of POE-related modules on CPAN allows you to choose precisely how high or low a level you wish to program at, and can make a great deal of repetitive code, particularly protocol-specific code, disappear in a puff of abstraction. POE also helps when writing nonblocking or multitasking code by offering a task scheduler and event loop.

POE itself is multilayered, with sessions passing messages between each other, wheels providing I/O abstraction, and filters wrapping a higher level around wheels.

Finally, POE components represent the very highest level of abstraction, containing major units of functionality. I'd recommend looking at POE for any event-based program where nonblocking I/O or multitasking is important.

## CHAPTER 8

Testing

Every programmer likes writing code, but only a brave and masochistic few actually like writing tests for their code. However, with the rise of XP, Agile programming, and other programming methodologies, it has become more important for programmers to write complete test suites for the code they produce.

Not only that, but thanks to the efforts of the Perl Kwalitee Assurance team, headed by Michael Schwern, there's a good deal of social pressure for CPAN module writers to come up with thorough automated test plans for their modules.

Thankfully, Schwern and others have also produced a bunch of modules that make producing such test plans relatively painless. We'll take a look at the more popular and useful modules in this chapter.

Test::Simple

Back in the mists of time, around the late 1990s, test plans were very simple indeed; you had a program that spat out "ok" or "not ok" followed by a test number, and an automated testing harness would go through, run your tests, and pick out the tests that failed.

So, programmers would write test scripts that looked something like this:

```
print "1..10\n";

print (( 1 + 1 == 2  ? "": "not "), "ok 1\n");
print (( 2 + 2 != 7  ? "": "not "), "ok 2\n");
if (foobar() ) {
    print "ok 3\n";
} else {
    print "not ok 3\n";
}
...
```

Then some programmers realized they didn't want to keep score of the test numbers themselves, so they used a variable instead:

```
print "1..10\n";

my $i = 1;
print (( 1 + 1 == 2  ? "": "not "), "ok ", $i++, "\n");
print (( 2 + 2 != 7  ? "": "not "), "ok ", $i++, "\n");
...
```

The next logical advance would be to put the test into a subroutine that spat out the appropriate string. Some people came up with their own idiosyncratic way of skipping tests, marking known failures, and providing names for their tests so that they wouldn't have to go through and count to find the failing test.

Eventually, we ended up in the situation where every test suite looked more or less the same but somehow subtly different from the others. It was out of this chaos that the original Test module was born. Test provided an ok subroutine that compared one thing with another, and reported the result and an automated test number.

However, Test wasn't very flexible, and along came its modern replacement, Test::Simple. It works on exactly the same principle: you have an ok function that runs a test and prints out the appropriate output. Here's a simple test plan with Test::Simple.

```
use Test::Simple tests => 3;

ok( 1 + 1 == 2 );
ok( 2 + 2 != 7, "Two and two are not seven" );
ok( foobar() );
```

The first line states how many tests are going to run, so that the automated test harness will know if the test script completed successfully or died halfway through. Then come the three tests. Test::Simple provides the ok subroutine to emit a test result. If the first parameter to ok is true, then the test was successful. The second parameter is an optional description to display along with the test result. When you're viewing the output, the description makes it much easier to understand what the test is for and also helps to locate which tests are failing. Running the preceding three tests on the command line has the following result:

```
1..3
ok 1
ok 2 - Two and two are not seven
ok 3
```

If the first parameter to ok is false, then the test failed. When you test a false value:

```
ok( 1 == 2, "One is two" );
```

The test output includes your description, the name of the test file, and the line number where the test failed to help you locate which test is failing:

```
not ok 1 - One is two
#     Failed test (simple.t at line 5)
```

These results are interpreted by the test harness to total up successes and failures. And this, basically, is all there is to Test::Simple, and all that most people need to know about testing. Test::Simple was, as its name implies, deliberately made really, really easy, so that there'd be no excuse* for not writing a decent test plan.

Test::More

If you want a little more than the appropriately named Test::Simple, you can move on to the equally appropriately named Test::More.

The first useful thing this module provides is a number of different ways to compare a value against another. First, you can provide two values and ask Test::More if they're the same:

```
is( test_function( ), 1234, "Checking whether test_function returns 1234");
```

or if they're different:

```
isnt( MyClass->new( ), undef, "new method should succeed");
```

And you can use regular expressions to see whether something looks like what you expect:

```
like(time, qr/^\d+$/, "Time really ought to be a positive integer");
```

Another useful feature is cmp_ok. It performs explicit numeric, string, or boolean comparisons so you don't have to rely on DWIM. This takes two values and a Perl comparison function, allowing you to specify your tests like this:

```
cmp_ok(MyModule::foo( ), ">", 12, "foo greater than 12");
```

One advantage of is, isnt, like, and cmp_ok over ok is that they provide more detailed results when a test fails. These can be helpful in debugging a failure:

```
not ok 1 - Checking whether test_function returns 1234
#     Failed test (more.t at line 5)
#          got: '4321'
#     expected: '1234'
not ok 2 - foo greater than 12
#     Failed test (more.t at line 9)
#     '12'
#          >
#     '12'
```

The final set of comparison tests deal with comparing structures, something that traditionally has been pretty tedious to do with the ordinary Test and Test::Simple styles of testing. The is_deeply subroutine compares one structure with another and reports if they're the same and, if not, at what point they vary:

```
$got = some_function( ); # Let's say it returned
```

---

* Well, other than laziness, impatience, or hubris.

```
                         # [ 1, { a => "foo", b => [ "bar" ] } ]

        $expected =  [1, { a => "foo", b => "bar" }];

        is_deeply($got, $expected);
```

This example's output is:

```
    not ok 1
    #     Failed test (t.pl at line 123)
    #     Structures begin differing at:
    #          $got->[1]{b} = 'ARRAY(0x6590)'
    #          $expected->[1]{b} = 'bar'
    # Looks like you failed 1 tests of 1.
```

showing us that we found an array where we expected a bar scalar.

Skips and Todos

In some cases, you won't want all of your tests to run. There are two major reasons
why: first, because the end user's system may not actually have some capability you
wish to test; second, you may have written tests for something your code doesn't
actually do quite yet. Test::More has the ability to handle both of these cases, which
it calls *skips* and *todos,* respectively.

Let's take an example. You've written a web services module, and you'd like to test it
by connecting to some Internet server and making a query. Unfortunately, not all the
world has always-on Internet access yet, so it's polite not to depend on the fact that
your tests can make network connections. We'll use the libnet bundle's Net::Config
settings to determine whether or not we should make Internet connections during
tests:

```
    use Net::Config qw(%NetConfig);

    my $may_make_connections = $NetConfig{test_hosts};
```

and if we can't talk to the network, we skip our network-related tests:

```
    SKIP: {
        skip "No network connection", 2 unless $may_make_connections;

        ok($client->connect("myhost.foonly.com"));

        is($client->request("2+2"),
            4,
            "Foonly calculator didn't make 2+2 equal 4"
        );
    }
```

The SKIP: label on the block is mandatory, as it allows Test::More to find the end of
the block. The parameters to skip are a string giving the reason why these tests are
skipped, and the number of tests to skip. These tests are marked as OK but contain

the keyword "skip" in the output so that test harnesses—the frameworks that check the output of test suites—will know that they haven't actually run.

```
ok 1 # skip No network connection
ok 2 # skip No network connection
```

The syntax for todo tests is similar, but the outcome is different. Skipped tests output ok and are marked with a skip; todo tests output not ok, but test harnesses will not fail the test suite because they will know that these are todos.

You mark a TODO block by setting the $TODO variable:

```
TODO: {
    local $TODO = "Insufficient funds";
    ok(eval { $man->put_on_mars });
    ok(eval { $man->colonize_planet });
}
```

When run outside of a testing harness, this will report:

```
not ok 2 # TODO Insufficient funds
#       Failed (TODO) test (t.pl at line 6)
not ok 3 # TODO Insufficient funds
#       Failed (TODO) test (t.pl at line 7)
```

but inside a harness:

```
t....ok
All tests successful.
Files=1, Tests=3,  0 wallclock secs ( 0.19 cusr +  0.01 csys =  0.20 CPU)
```

The advantage of this is that as you implement the missing functionality, the tests will gradually begin to pass and the test harness will report them as unexpected successes. Once all the tests pass normally, you can remove the TODO designation.

Automated Tests

As we saw when discussing is_deeply above, Test::More attempts to make it easy to do more complex tests. It also provides a few other features to help automate the testing process.

First, eq_set performs an order-agnostic array comparison. For instance, if you know your function is going to return a list from 1 to 10, but you don't know the order, you can make sure you get a full set of results as follows:

```
ok(eq_set([myfunc()], [1..10]), "We got a list from 1 to 10");
```

If you're testing object-oriented modules, Test::More has a few useful additions for you. The isa_ok function checks to see if an object belongs to a particular class; this is typically used to check a constructor:

```
my $s = IO::Socket->new;
isa_ok($s, "IO::Socket");
```

Finally, there's can_ok, for testing a variety of methods on an object. Strictly speaking, can_ok merely tests the interface to an object, ensuring that it can respond to the methods specified. It calls the can method on the class of the object. If you don't define your own custom version, the universal default can searches the object's inheritance tree for the named method:

```
can_ok($s, "accept", "timeout", "connected",
            "close"); # Inherited from IO::Handle
```

Using these methods together, a great deal of the pain of testing classes can be taken away. Later in the chapter, we'll see how these techniques can be combined with class-based testing to make the creation of such test suites even easier.

Test::Harness

When you've installed CPAN modules, you might have noticed two different styles of test output. In the first instance, you run something like perl -Mblib t/1.t and you see a list of results:

```
1..25
ok 1 - Loaded module
ok 2 - Can create a new object
ok 3 -  ... of the correct class
...
```

And in the second case, you run make test on a MakeMaker-generated install process or prove t/*.t, and you see something like this:

```
t/1..............ok
t/2..............ok
t/3..............FAILED tests 2, 5
        Failed 2/6 tests, 66.67% okay

...
Failed Test Stat Wstat Total Fail  Failed  List of Failed
-------------------------------------------------------------------------
t/3.t                    6     2 33.33%  2 5
Failed 1/20 test scripts, 95.00% okay. 2/349 subtests failed, 99.43% okay.
```

So, what's the difference? The difference is that, in the second case, something is running each test file in the *t/* directory—whether it's one file or many files—and collating the results. The thing that's doing the collating is Test::Harness. Its job is to gather up the test results and make sure everything went OK before the module gets installed.

So, if you're planning on writing tests that don't use the standard Test::Simple or Test::More modules (or indeed any of the other test modules out there), or you want to write your own test module, then you need to know how to produce test output that Test::Harness is going to be happy with. Otherwise, it will think your module is failing its tests. This standard output format is known as TAP—the Test Anything Protocol—and credit for the name goes to Joe McMahon and Andy Lester.

The interface to Test::Harness is the runtests function. You give runtests a list of filenames, it runs each one in turn and produces the summary you just saw. That's all. The interesting question is what Test::Harness expects from a test suite.

The first thing it expects to see from a test suite is a plan. A plan is a line of text, of the form 1..N, and it must appear as either the first or the last thing seen on standard output. This ensures that Test::Harness can determine whether your test ended when it was supposed to or died in the middle. If you don't know how many tests you're going to have until you've run them, you can put out a plan right at the end. But you must have one, and only one, either at the very start or the very end.

Each test must output the word ok, or the words not ok, and they must say this at the beginning of a line. They don't have to say what number they are, but it's useful.

Test output can contain comments. Like a comment in Perl, these begin with a hash character. After the ok (or the not ok) and the test number, you can have a description that says what your test is called. Usually these are introduced by a dash, but anything between the test number and either a # character or the end of the line is treated as the description. Here are some valid test results:

```
ok
not ok 2
ok 3 - Array in correct order
```

And here are some things that are not valid test results:

```
OK
Checking to see if we can parse the XML again... ok
4 not ok
```

Test::Harness treats certain test comments specially. These are called directives. If a comment starting with skip immediately follows the test number, then the harness notes that this test has been skipped. Similarly, as we saw when looking at Test::More, the harness marks a test with a TODO directive as non-fatal.

There are other things your test script might produce that Test::Harness knows how to deal with. You can specify that you want to skip the entire test file, by writing out:

```
1..0
```

Or you can abort the current test by outputting the magic words Bail out!. Most other things in your test output will be ignored by the version of Test::Harness current at the time of writing, although that may change. For more details on this format, read Test::Harness::TAP.

Test::Builder

But to be honest, who would want to write a test module from scratch anyway? Isn't there some module we could use to help us with that? Well, rather unsurprisingly, there is. Written by chromatic and maintained by Michael Schwern, the Test::Builder module provides you with useful functionality for, well, building a test module.

Test::Builder is an object-oriented module that implements the concept of a *test object*. This object performs some useful housekeeping work for us, such as keeping score of what test number we're at, how many tests have passed and failed, and so on, allowing us to concentrate on deciding whether or not a test should pass.

The test object also provides methods similar to the Test::More tests: ok, is, like, and so on. In fact, Test::Simple and Test::More are mostly just thin wrappers around Test::Builder methods.

Just like Apache->request, Test::Builder->new is a singleton object; future calls to new return the same object. This means you can use test routines from multiple different classes based on Test::Builder and they'll work together seamlessly maintaining a consistent count of passed and failed tests, along with the current test.

The usual incantation to begin using Test::Builder looks like this:

```
use Test::Builder;
my $Test = Test::Builder->new;
```

This creates a lexically scoped name for the singleton test object so you can refer to it directly within your test module. If you look into the code for Test::Simple, you'll find that's pretty much all there is to it: creating the Test::Builder object, an import subroutine, and an ok subroutine that simply calls the test object's ok method.

```
sub ok ($;$) {
    $Test->ok(@_);
}
```

The real magic is in the import routine. There are various different ways to set it up, depending on how important it is to be compatible with Perl 5.004 and earlier versions. One good example is in Test::Exception by Adrian Howard.

```
sub import {
    my $self = shift;
    if (@_) {
        my $package = caller;
        $Test->exported_to($package);
        $Test->plan(@_);
    };
    $self->export_to_level(1, $self, $_) foreach @EXPORT;
}
```

The critical bits of code here are the calls to the test object's exported_to and plan methods, which tell the test object where the test routines are exported to and set up the test plan. These two calls are wrapped in an `if` so that you can either use `Test::Exception` alone and have it set up its own test plan:

```
use Test::Exception tests => 5;
```

or use it together with `Test::More`:

```
use Test::More tests => 5;
use Test::Exception;
```

Suppose you wanted to support fuzzy matching. We'll start with the standard steps to create a `Test::Builder` object and export our custom test routine. We'll use `String::Approx` to perform the fuzzy matching between the tested value and the expected value.

```
package Test::Fuzzy;

use Test::Builder;
use String::Approx qw( amatch );

use base qw( Exporter );
our @EXPORT = qw( is_fuzzy );

my $Test = Test::Builder->new;
```

Finally, we write `is_fuzzy`. Just like `is`, we'll take two strings as arguments and an optional test description:

```
sub is_fuzzy ($$;$) {
    my ($got, $expected, $desc) = @_;
    my $result = amatch($expected, $got);
    $Test->ok($result, $desc);
}
```

We don't even have to define an `import` subroutine if we leave `Test::More` to handle the test plan. To use our custom testing module, we use `Test::More` and `Test::Fuzzy`, then call our custom `is_fuzzy` test routine:

```
use Test::More tests => 2;
use Test::Fuzzy;

is_fuzzy('one', 'none', "one is like none");
is_fuzzy('blue', 'green', "blue is like green");
```

These two tests produce the following output:

```
ok 1 - one is like none
not ok 2 - blue is like green
#     Failed test (fuzzy.t at line 7)
```

And that's it!

Test::Builder::Tester

If you have a particularly perverse mind, you may now be thinking, "So what do the tests for Test::Builder look like?" Well, even more perverse minds have got there first, and Test::Builder has its own test suite creation module, rather predictably called Test::Builder::Tester. (And here it bottoms out, as Test::Builder::Tester contains enough functionality to test itself.)

The basic premise of Test::Builder::Tester is this: you first declare what output you expect to see from your Test::Builder module for a particular test; then you run the test in a controlled manner, producing the output for real; then your *actual* test compares the expected output with the real output. This may seem a little meta until you see an example, so let's look at one now.

We're writing a test script for our new Test::Fuzzy module; we begin by using Test::Fuzzy and also Test::Builder::Tester to provide the meta-testing functions and to state our test plan.

```
use Test::Fuzzy;
use Test::Builder::Tester tests => 1;
```

We're going to run two tests that should pass, so we declare that we expect to see two successful results:

```
test_out("ok 1");
test_out("ok 2");
```

This tells Test::Builder::Tester what to expect on its standard output.

Now we actually run the two tests that should pass:

```
is_fuzzy("motches", "matches");
is_fuzzy("fuzy",    "fuzzy");
```

All being well, this should output:

```
ok 1
ok 2
```

since they do match approximately. But in this case, the actual output is not written to the screen but stashed away by Test::Builder::Tester so that it can be compared against our predictions.

The final stage is to see whether or not the test output that's been stashed away really did meet our prediction:

```
test_test("Two trivial tests passed OK");
```

If it did indeed output the right thing, then Test::Builder::Tester finally *does* output something to the screen, like so:

```
ok 1 - Two trivial tests passed OK
```

There are extensions to `Test::Builder::Tester`, such as `Test::Builder::Tester::Color`, which allows it to disambiguate between, for instance, expected and unexpected failures by means of color-coding, but if you're going that deeply into metatesting, you'd probably be best learning the ropes for yourself.

Keeping Tests and Code Together

Putting your tests in a separate file is the usual and traditional way to write a test suite. However, as with documentation, it's easier to keep your tests updated if they're right there alongside your code. The `Test::Inline` and `Pod::Tests` modules help you do this.

The weird thing about `Test::Inline` is that it doesn't actually do anything. It contains no code, only documentation on how to write inline tests. Inline tests are written as ordinary Pod, Perl's plain old documentation format, designed to go alongside the Pod for the subroutines you're implementing.

`Test::Inline` explains how you can add testing blocks to the documentation of your modules, like so:

```
=head2 keywords

    my @keywords = keywords($text);

This is a very simple algorithm which removes stopwords from a
summarized version of a text and then counts up what it considers to
be the most important "keywords". The C<keywords> subroutine returns a
list of five keywords in order of relevance.

=begin testing

my @keywords = keywords(scalar `perldoc -t perlxs`);
# reasonable sample document

is_deeply(\@keywords, [qw(perl xsub keyword code timep)],
          "Correct keywords returned from perlxs");

=end testing

sub keywords {
    ...
```

With this layout, the documentation section makes it clear what the subroutine should do and then the testing section contains code to test it; keeping the documentation and tests together makes it clearer what *ought* to be tested. It also means that changes to the functionality can be made in the three important places at the same time: in the code, in the documentation, and in the tests.

This is all well and good, but once we've got these embedded tests, what do we do with them? The `Pod::Tests` module contains a driver for extracting tests, *pod2test*:

```
% pod2test lib/Keywords.pm t/Keywords-embedded.t
% make test
...
```

The `Test::Inline::Tutorial` documentation provides some information about how to automate the extraction process, as well as tricks to make sure the example code that you give in your Pod works properly.

Unit Tests

As we mentioned in the introduction, the rise of movements like Extreme Programming[*] has led to both a revolution and a resurgence of interest in testing methodologies.

One particular feature of the XP approach is unit testing, an old practice recently brought back to the limelight; the idea that one should test individual components of a program or module in isolation, proving the functional correctness of each part as well as the program as a whole.

Needless to say, Perl programming devotees of XP have produced a wealth of modules to facilitate and encourage unit testing. There are two major XP testing suites, `PerlUnit` and `Test::Class`. `PerlUnit` is a thorough implementation of the standard xUnit suite, and will contain many concepts immediately familiar to XP devotees. However, it's also insanely complete, containing nearly 30 subclasses and related modules. We'll look here at `Test::Class`, which can be thought of as unit testing in the Perl idiom. We'll also be examining modules to help with the nuts and bolts of unit testing in areas where it may seem difficult.

Test::Class

The `Test::Class` module can be viewed in two ways—first, as a module for testing class-based modules and, second, as a base class for classes whose methods are tests.

Suppose we have the following very simple class, and we want to write a test plan for it:

```
package Person;
sub new {
    my $self = shift;
    my $name = shift;
    return undef unless $name;
    return bless {
        name => $name
    }, $self;
}

sub name {
    my $self = shift;
```

---

[*] *Extreme Programming Explained*, by Kent Beck (Addison-Wesley), is the canonical work on the subject.

```
        $self->{name} = shift if @_;
        return $self->{name};
    }
```

We'll start by writing a test class, which we'll call Person::Test. This inherits from Test::Class like so:

```
package Person::Test;
use base 'Test::Class';

use Test::More tests => 1;
use Person;
```

Tests inside our test class are, predictably, specified in the form of methods. With one slight special feature—test methods are given the :Test attribute. So, for instance, we could test the new method:

```
sub constructor :Test {
    my $self = shift;
    my $test_person = Person->new("Larry Wall");
    isa_ok($test_person, "Person");
}
```

Notice that the job of emitting the usual Perl ok and not ok messages has not gone away—to do this, we use the Test::More module and make use of its functions inside of our test methods.

Although it may seem initially attractive to name your test methods the same as the methods you're testing, you'll find that you may well want to carry out several tests using and abusing each method. There are two ways to do this. First, you can specify that a particular method contains a number of tests by passing a parameter to the :Test attribute:

```
sub name :Test(2) {
    my $self = shift;
    my $test_person = Person->new("Larry Wall");
    my $test_name = $test_person->name();
    is($test_name, "Larry Wall");

    my $test_name2 = $test_person->name("Llaw Yrral");
    is($test_name2, "Llaw Yrral");
}
```

Or you could split each test into a separate method—in our Person example, we could have name_with_args and name_no_args or get_name and set_name. In most cases, you'll want to use a mixture of these two approaches.

Never name a test method new. Because your test class inherits from Test::Class, this will override Test::Class's new method causing it to run only one test.

It's fine to define your own test class constructor named new, but make sure it includes the necessary behavior from Test::Class's new or calls SUPER::new.

Once you define all the tests that you want to run, you can then tell Perl to run the tests, using the runtests method inherited from Test::Class:

```
__PACKAGE__->runtests;
```

With that line in Person::Test, you can run the tests within a test file with just use Person::Test, or on the command line by running perl Person/Test.pm. A more common strategy is to provide a test script that runs all the class tests for a project:

```
use Test::Class;
my @classes;
Test::Class->runtests(@classes);
BEGIN {
  my @found = code_to_find_all_classes();
  foreach my $class (@found) {
    eval {require $class};
    push @classes if $class->isa('Test::Class');
  }
}
```

That's how we define test methods and un the test, but how does Test::Class know which test methods are defined, and in what order does it run the tests?

Well, the truth is quite simple—the Test::Class module goes through the methods defined in the test class, looking for methods marked with the :Test attribute, and it calls them in alphabetical order. (Although, depending on the ordering is generally thought to be a bad thing.)

The problem with this is that sometimes you want an object available all through your testing so you can poke at it using a variety of methods. Our test class, Person::Test, is a real class, and the test methods all get called with a real Person::Test object that can store information just like any other module. We want a fresh Person object in each test to avoid side effects as other test methods alter and test the object repeatedly.

To facilitate this, Test::Class provides another designation for test methods—certain methods can be set to run before each test starts and after each test finishes, to set up and tear down test-specific data. These special methods have special parameters to the :Test attribute—those marked as :Test(setup) run before each test, and those marked as :Test(teardown) run after each test. For instance, we could set up our Person:

```
sub setup_person :Test(setup) {
    my $self = shift;
    $self->{person} = Person->new("Larry Wall");
}
```

and now we can use this object in our test methods:

```
sub get_name :Test {
    my $self = shift;
    is ($self->{person}->name, "Larry Wall");
}
```

```
sub set_name :Test {
    my $self = shift;
    $self->{person}->name("Jon Orwant"); # What a transformation!
    is ($self->{person}->name, "Jon Orwant");

    $self->{person}->name("Larry Wall"); # Better put Larry back.
}
```

In other cases, setup may be an expensive process you only want to run once, or side
effects may not be an issue because the object is an unchanging resource. Test::Class
provides alternatives to setup and teardown—methods marked as :Test(startup) run
before the first test method and those marked as :Test(shutdown) run after all the tests
have finished. For instance, if our testing requires a database connection, we could set
that up in our test object, too:

```
sub setup_database :Test(startup) {
    my $self = shift;
    require DBI;
    $self->{dbh} = DBI->connect("dbi:mysql:dbname=test", $user, $pass);
    die "Couldn't make a database connection!" unless $self->{dbh};
}

sub destroy_database :Test(shutdown) {
    my $self = shift;
    $self->{dbh}->disconnect;

}
```

One useful feature of Test::Class is that it will do its utmost to run the startup and
finalization methods, despite what may happen during the tests; if something dies
during testing, this will be reported as a failure, and the program will move on to the
next test, to assure that the test suite survives until finalization. For this reason, other
suggested uses of startup and shutdown methods include creating and destroying tem-
porary files, adding test data into a database (and then removing it or rolling it back
again), and so on.

Test::MockObject

One idea behind unit testing is that you want to minimize the amount of code
involved in a given test. For instance, let's suppose we're writing some HTML and
web handling code that uses an LWP::UserAgent in its machinations. We want to test
one subroutine of our program, but to do so would pull in a heap of code from LWP
and may even require a call out to a web site and a dependency on particular information there. LWP has its own tests, and we know that it's relatively well behaved. We
just want to make sure that our subroutine is well behaved. We also want to avoid
unnecessary and unpredictable network access where we can.

Wouldn't it be nice, then, if we could get hold of something that looked, walked,
and quacked like an LWP::UserAgent, but was actually completely under our control?

This is what `Test::MockObject` provides: objects that can conform to an external interface, but allow the test developer to control the methods.

Let's first create a new mock object:

```
use Test::MockObject;

my $mock_ua = Test::MockObject->new( );
```

This will eventually become the mock `LWP::UserAgent` that our subroutine uses. In order to be like an `LWP::UserAgent`, it needs to respond to some methods. We add methods with the mock method:

```
$mock_ua->mock('clone',  sub { return $mock_ua    });
```

`Test::MockObject` offers a series of alternatives to mock—such as `set_true` and `set_false`—that are shortcuts for common cases. For example, `set_always` creates a mock method that always returns a constant value:

```
$mock_ua->set_always('_agent', 'libwww/perl-5.65');
```

After we've built up a set of methods and established what we'd like them to do, we have a mock user agent that can be passed into our subroutine and produce known output to known stimuli.

 Be careful that the mock object's interface matches the real object's interface. You could end up with passing tests but failing code if, for example, a mocked method expects an array-reference where the real method expects an array. Integration tests are a good way to protect against this.

This is all very well if we are passing in the object to our routine, but what about the more common case where the routine has to instantiate a new `LWP::UserAgent` for itself? `Test::MockObject` can get around this—in addition to faking an individual object, we can use it to fake an entire class.

First, we lie to Perl and tell it that we've already loaded the `LWP::UserAgent` module—this stops the interpreter loading the real one and stomping all over our fakery:

```
$mock_ua->fake_module("LWP::UserAgent");
```

Note that this must be done during a `BEGIN` block or in some other manner before anything else calls use `LWP::UserAgent`, or else the real module will be loaded.

Now we can use our mock object to create a constructor for the fake `LWP::UserAgent` class:

```
$mock_ua->fake_new("LWP::UserAgent");
```

After this, any call to `LWP::UserAgent->new` returns the mock object.

In this way, we can isolate the effects of our tests to a much better-defined area of code and greatly reduce the complexity of what's being tested.

Testing Apache, DBI, and Other Complex Environments

There are many opportunities for us to avoid writing tests, and the more lazy of us tend to take any such opportunity we can find. Unfortunately, most of these opportunities are not justified—absolutely any code can be tested in some meaningful way.

For instance, we've seen how we can remove the dependency on a remote web server by using a mock user agent object; but what if we want to test a mod_perl application that uses a *local* web server? Of course, we could set up a special test Apache instance, something the HTML::Mason test suite does. This is a bit of a pain, however.

Thankfully, there's a much easier solution: we can mock up the interface between our application and Apache, pretending there's a real, live Apache server on the other end of our Apache::Request object. This is a bit more complex than the standard Test::MockObject trick and is certainly not something you'd want to set up in every test you write. The Apache::FakeRequest module gives you access to an object that looks and acts like an Apache::Request, but doesn't require a web server.

In the majority of cases, you can just call your application's handler routine with the fake request object:

```
use Apache::FakeRequest;

my $r = Apache::FakeRequest->new( );

myhandler($r);
```

However, given that the ordinary Apache request is a singleton object—subsequent calls to Apache->request return the same object—you may find that lazier programmers do not pass the $r object around, but instead pick it up themselves. To allow testing in the face of this kind of opposition, you will have to override the Apache->request and Apache::Request->new methods, like so:

```
use Apache::FakeRequest;

my $r = Apache::FakeRequest->new( );
*Apache::request = sub { $r };
*Apache::Request::new = sub { $r };

myhandler($r);
```

This way, no matter what shenanigans your handler attempts to get a request object, it should always get your fake request.

In some cases, however, you've just got to bite the bullet; if you want to test a database-backed application, you're going to have to set up a database and populate it. How you do this depends on your situation. If you're developing an in-house product, it makes sense to use your real development database and have something like Test::Class's startup and shutdown routines insert and delete the data you need.

If, on the other hand, you're writing a CPAN module and want remote users to be able to test the module, things become more tricky. You can, of course, have them set up a test database and provide your test suite with details of how to access it, but it's difficult to do this while keeping the suite non-interactive: developers using the CPANPLUS module to automatically install modules and their dependencies won't appreciate having to stop and set up a database before going on; neither do software packagers such as those involved in the Debian project need the hassle of setting up a database just for your tests.

In these cases, one decent solution is to use the DBD::CSV or DBD::AnyData modules—simply put your test data into a set of colon-separated files and have your test suite work from that instead of a real RDBMS. If your module requires slightly heavier database access than that, a reasonable solution is DBD::SQLite, a lightweight database server embedded in a C library. This allows you to ship a couple of data files with your tests, giving you pretty much everything you need from a relational database.

Conclusion

I'd like to end on a philosophical note, to try to persuade you to read through the chapter again, read Test::Tutorial, visit *http://qa.perl.org*, or otherwise expand your knowledge of testing with the many resources available.

I used to be extremely hubristic about testing. My attitude was "if it didn't work, I wouldn't have released it!" and I provided only the most minimal of tests with my modules. I've since become a reformed character. Over the past few years, I've become personally more and more convinced of the merit of writing comprehensive test suites for the modules and code that I produce.

Even if you're not a devotee of test-driven development—writing your tests first and then writing code until they pass—a full test suite makes sure that any future changes you make don't cause problems with old functionality; I've found it beneficial to add every bug report I've been sent as a test case, to aid regression testing. If nothing else, adding tests to a module gives the end user confidence that your code is thorough and robust. And, finally, even the most basic of tests can, to mix metaphors, nip glaring bugs in the bud.

In short, tests are a good thing. And, thankfully, with modules like Test::More and Test::Simple, they need not be a pain to write. I may have joked earlier that nothing bar laziness and hubris could stop one from writing tests, but even that doesn't stand up to examination—not writing tests is false laziness. The certainty that resolved bugs are not going to recur is ample payoff for the time spent writing tests.

Get into the discipline of testing. It will save you time, and it will spare you blushes.

## CHAPTER 9

Inline Extensions

Although Perl is a very powerful language, there are still some things that it cannot do by itself: it can't communicate directly with hardware or take advantage of complex mathematical libraries. Other things it can do, but not very quickly: you can ask Perl to rotate an image by reading in and parsing the image file format, doing all the transformations on a really big array, and writing it out again, but that takes a lot of time and effort. It's far better to ask a C library to do this for you, and the way to do this is to write an extension to allow Perl to talk to the C library. In fact, many graphical interfaces to Perl are merely extensions talking to the relevant C libraries.

The usual way to write an extension to bridge Perl and C is to use a complex and awkward intermediary language called XS (extension subroutines). If you want to do things the complex and awkward way, I suggest reading *perlxstut* in the Perl documentation, or my *Extending and Embedding Perl* (Manning). However, since one of the cardinal virtues of a Perl programmer is laziness, there has to be a less complex and awkward way to do it, right?

Thankfully, there is; Brian Ingerson got fed up with writing XS and ended up writing a very clever Perl module called Inline to do it for him. As we'll see later in the chapter, Inline has become generalized to handle languages other than C, so the module we'll look at for now is called Inline::C.

Simple Inline::C

The idea behind Inline::C is pretty straightforward: you write a C function as part of your Perl program, and the Inline library goes away and does the work required to make that function available from Perl. So, here's the simplest C function we could possibly wrap:

```
use Inline C => q[

void print_hi( ) {
    puts("Hi, world!");
```

```
    }

];

print_hi( );
```

The first time this program is run, it takes a little time; Inline::C has to parse the C code, determine what wrappings are needed to bridge the gap between C and Perl (almost nothing in this case), write the wrapping, fire up a C compiler, create a shared library that can be loaded by Perl, and load it up. Only then is the print_hi subroutine available to Perl.

If we had to go through this rigmarole every time we executed the program, Inline wouldn't actually buy us very much. But if we run our program again, we should find that it's considerably faster. All Inline needs to do in this case is make sure that the C code we're compiling hasn't changed, and then load up the shared library it created last time.

Taking and Giving

Of course, real functions are a little more complicated than that; they take arguments, they return a value. With Inline, interfacing with these real functions isn't that much more complicated at all.

Let's take a relatively noncontrived example. You want to display some information to the user, such as:

```
You have 2 lives left; score 1500, with 15 gold pieces.
```

However, you also want the user to be able to customize this information, if they prefer seeing:

```
[Lives: 2 XP: 1500 GP:15]
```

So what you do is set up the output format as a pattern for printf, and have something like this:

```
my $pattern = $user_pattern ||
              "You have %i lives left; score %04i, with %2i gold pieces";
printf $pattern, $lives, $xp, $gp;
```

But then you hear that allowing users to supply their own format string caused Korea to be knocked off the Net last week, which didn't seem too much of a big deal to you, but then someone starts telling you scary stories about the %p format, and you start wondering how you can sanitize the format string you were passed.

And then you remember that you're developing on a BSD Unix, which has the very handy fmtcheck function in the C library just for this purpose.* So you write a quick C function that selects the right format, like so:

```
char* score_format(char* pref_format, char* user_format) {
    return fmtcheck(user_format, pref_format);
}
```

And once you put that in your Inline section, you can call it just like a normal Perl subroutine. This time, use a slightly different formulation of Inline; instead of passing in a string, put your C code into the DATA section at the end of the program. To tell Inline what to look at, add the __C__ marker after the __DATA__ marker.

```
use Inline C;

my $pref_format = "You have %i lives left; score %04i, with %2i gold pieces";
my ($lives, $score, $gp) = (3, 2500, 50);

my $user_format = "[Lives: %i, XP: %i, GP: %i]";

printf(score_format($pref_format, $user_format), $lives, $score, $gp);

__END__
__C__
#include <stdio.h>

char* score_format(char* pref_format, char* user_format) {
    return fmtcheck(user_format, pref_format);
}
```

This determines that the user's format it safe and uses that instead of your format. Inline::C automatically knows how to deal with int, long, double, char*, and many other types as specified in the default Perl typemap (found in the *ExtUtils* subdirectory of your @INC path). Later on in the chapter, we'll see how to use more complex structures with Inline.

C is not Always a Win

But first a cautionary tale: there are any number of people who will complain that Perl is too slow, and if you're doing anything serious, you should rewrite it in C for speed. OK, then. This time, we're going to write a function to find the number of alphabetic characters in a string. We could use Perl's tr operator, but perhaps calling out to C will be faster. Here is the C function we're going to use:

```
int count_alpha(char* foo) {
    int i = 0;
    do {
      if (isalpha(*foo)) i++;
```

---

* OK, we said it was relatively noncontrived. So we lied.

```
    } while (*foo++);
    return i;
}

use Inline C;

use Benchmark;
$test = "a b cd e fg" x 10000;

timethese(10000,
    {
        Perl => sub { $test =~ tr/[a-zA-Z]//; },
        C    => sub { count_alpha ($test) }
    }
)

__DATA__
__C__

int count_alpha(char* foo) {
    int i = 0;
    do {
     if (isalpha(*foo)) i++;
    } while (*foo++);
    return i;
}
```

This produces output similar to:

```
Benchmark: timing 10000 iterations of C, Perl...
        C: 24 wallclock secs (20.80 usr +  0.15 sys = 20.95 CPU) @ 477.33/s
(n=10000)
        Perl: 10 wallclock secs ( 8.05 usr +  0.04 sys =  8.09 CPU) @ 1236.09/s
(n=10000)
```

Unfortunately, we find that when we run this, the Perl built-in version is around
twice as fast; this is a good reminder that it's not always beneficial to recode things in
C for speed.* However, we've found that it *is* easy enough to wrap simple C functions in Perl, receiving and passing values between the two languages without worrying about the usual XS glue.

---

* With considerable hand-optimization and tuning of the Inline options, we can produce a C function that
  competes reasonably well with the Perl built-in. However, the time spent shunting around between Perl and
  C means that the built-in will win every time.

More Complex Tasks with Inline::C

On the other hand, there are times when we want to mess about with the XS glue, and Inline allows us to do this, too. In this section, we'll look at some advanced uses of the Inline::C module.

Dealing with Perl's Internal Values

Anyone who's familiar with XS at all knows that Perl doesn't use simple types like ints, char *s, and so on internally; it uses its own special types, SV*s for scalars, AV*s for arrays, and HV*s for arrays.

If we know the functions for manipulating these types,* then we can gain a little flexibility by using them directly in our Inline::C programs.

Here's an example; there's no (clean) way of telling directly from Perl if a reference is an object or just an ordinary reference. But this simple piece of XS uses the sv_isobject API function to determine whether an SV* is an object or not.

```
use IO::File;
use Inline C => <<'EOT';
int blessed (SV* sv) {
    if (SvMAGICAL(sv))
        mg_get(sv);      /* Call FETCH, etc. if we're tied */

    return sv_isobject(sv);
}
EOT

my $a = \123;
my $b = IO::File->new;

print "\$a is a blessed reference\n" if blessed($a);
print "\$b is a blessed reference\n" if blessed($b);
```

This prints out:

```
$b is a blessed reference
```

What else can we know about a scalar? Well, there are various subtypes of scalar: integers, numbers, and strings. The Perl guys call these IV, NV, and PV types, respectively. Let's first look at converting between these types and accessing information about the value of our scalar.

First, there's SvTYPE, which tells us what sort of SV we're dealing with. It returns a member of an enum, shown in Table 9-1.

---

* You can find a handy guide in the *perlapi* documentation, or the Perl API chapter of *Extending and Embedding Perl.*

Table 9-1. Valid svtypes

SVt_NULL	Undefined value (undef)
SVt_IV	Integer
SVt_NV	Floating-point number
SVt_PV	String
SVt_PVAV	Array
SVt_PVHV	Hash
SVt_PVFM	Format
SVt_RV	Reference
SVt_PVCV	Code
SVt_PVGV	Typeglob
SBt_PVIO	I/O type (file handle)
SVt_PVIV	Like SVt_PV, but also holds an integer value: a stringified integer or a string used as an integer
SVt_PVNV	Like SVt_PV, but also holds a floating-point value and an integer value: a stringified floating-point number, a string or integer used as a floating-point number, or a floating-point number used as an integer
SVt_PVLV	Various types with LValue behavior
SVt_PVMG	Blessed or magical scalar
SVt_PVBM	Like SVt_PVMG, but does a fast lookup of its string value using the Boyer-Moore algorithm

Note from this that arrays and 3hashes are just advanced types of SVs—although we refer specifically to these two types as AV and HV later on in our XS programming, it's worth remembering that these are just specialized names for something that's an SV underneath.

We can ask the scalar to transmogrify itself into an IV, NV, or SV, and read its value using the suitably named SvIV, SvNV, and SvPV functions. We mustn't forget that in C, strings have two properties: where they start and how long they are. SvPV returns the start of the string but also sets its second argument to be the length of the string:

```
void dump_values(SV* sv) {
    STRLEN len;

    printf("As a float: %f\n", SvNV(sv));
    printf("As an integer: %i\n", SvIV(sv));
    printf("As a string: %s\n", SvPV(sv, len));
}
```

Notice that the type STRLEN is defined to be an appropriate type for storing string lengths. If we don't really care about the length, as in this example, we can use the SvPV_nolen macro instead.

We can also get at these properties of a string directly using macros: the SvCUR macro tells us the length of the string. Why is it SvCUR and not SvLEN? Because, predictably, SvLEN is used for something else—there is a distinction between the current length of the Perl string, and the amount of space allocated for it. Keeping track of this separately allows the Perl interpreter to extend a Perl string in place, without having to call out to memory allocation regions. SvLEN gives us the length of this allocated region. But how do they differ?

Suppose the following series of operations:

```
my $a = "abc";
for (1..10) {
    $a .= "d";
    chop $a;
}
```

Everyone knows that this produces the string abc at the end. However, how this is done is slightly complex. Because in C you need to take close care of the memory you allocate and release, Perl needs to track the length of the string. So we start with a C string four characters long—a, b, c, and the end-of-string null terminator. But now we need to add another character to the end, and we have only allocated four characters—we need to stop and allocate some more. Now our C string is five characters long, and our Perl string is four characters long.

Now, allocating memory during Perl's runtime is computationally expensive, relatively speaking, and so it's something we want to avoid doing. So when we chop the string, what Perl *doesn't* do is shrink the string back to four characters. This would be particularly silly in this case, since the very next thing we do is go around the loop again and add another character to it, requiring another reallocation. Instead, it keeps track of the fact that it's *allocated* five characters, even though, after the chop, it's only presently using four of them. Hence, as the Perl string can expand and contract at will, the allocated memory never shrinks; it only expands. SvCUR tells you the *current* length of the Perl string, and SvLEN tells you the total length allocated. (Incidentally, since these macros are just accessors into a structure, we can efficiently chop a scalar with something like SvCUR(sv)--;).

Of course, just accessing the data is not always enough; sometimes we need to modify it as well, and this is where the sv_set... series of functions come in. We can set a scalar's integer, number, and string values with sv_setiv, sv_setnv and sv_setpv, respectively. We can also find out what values the scalar currently thinks are valid by using the SvIOK, SvNOK, and SvPOK macros. For instance, given:

```
$a = "5";
```

the value held in $a will only have been used as a string, and hence it will be POK. If we now say:

```
$b = $a + 10;
```

then although $a's value has not changed, Perl will need to look at its numeric value in order to add 10 to it. This means it will now be both POK and IOK (or NOK before 5.8.0). If we now do something like:

```
$a .= "abc";
```

then we will *denature* its integer value, and only the string value will be current—it will now only be POK. We'll see more examples of these macros later in the chapter.

Other interesting things to do with scalars include looking at and fiddling with their internal state—as one might imagine, this is not something to do carelessly. For instance, the macro SvTAINTED tells if a scalar contains tainted data; corresponding macros SvTAINTED_on and SvTAINTED_off alter the state of that flag:

```
void dodgify(SV* sv) {
    SvTAINTED_on(sv);
}

void blow_away_all_the_security_in_my_program(SV* sv) {
    SvTAINTED_off(sv);
}
```

A scalar's reference count tells you how many copies of a scalar are knocking around. For instance, we know that if we have an object like so:

```
{
    my $f = IO::Handle->new;
}
```

then the object will be destroyed once $f goes out of scope. However, if we store a copy of it somewhere else:

```
{
    my $f = IO::Handle->new;
    $My::Copy = $f;
}
```

then the reference count is two; it drops back to one once $f goes away and no longer holds a copy of it, but will remain at one until $My::Copy stops referring to it. The object will only be destroyed when the reference count drops to zero—when $My::Copy stores something else, or at the end of the program. We can fiddle the reference count with SvREFCNT_inc and SvREFCNT_dec:

```
int immortalize(SV* sv) {
    SvREFCNT_inc(sv);
    return SvREFCNT(sv);
}
```

This fools the scalar into thinking that something else is holding a copy of it, and it won't go away until the end of the program. It tells Perl that you also have a reference to the scalar, and not to destroy it when all the references that Perl knows about go away. Once you remove your private reference to it, you need to decrease the reference count with SvREFCNT_dec, otherwise Perl goes on thinking that someone, somewhere is referring to it, and hence doesn't correctly tidy it away. Decreasing the reference count avoids a leak. Unless, of course, someone fiddles with it again, like this:

```
void kill_kill_kill(SV* sv) {
    SvREFCNT(sv) = 1;
```

```
    SvREFCNT_dec(sv);
}
```

This forces the scalar to be destroyed (calling the DESTROY method if it's an object), but woe betide any variables that still believe they refer to it.

Certain special scalars are accessible from C: PL_sv_yes and PL_sv_no refer to true and false values, respectively; as these are intended to be singleton SVs, they are always referred to by pointers. Hence you should use &PL_sv_yes and &PL_sv_no in your code:

```
SV* tainted(SV* sv) {
    if (SvTAINTED(sv))
        return &PL_sv_yes;
    else
        return &PL_sv_no;
}
```

There's also &PL_sv_undef for undef.

What if you want to get hold of a normal global variable from Perl-space inside your C function? The get_sv function returns an SV given a name; this is the usual way to get at options from your extension code:

```
if (SvTRUE(get_sv("MyModule::DEBUG", TRUE)))
    printf("XXX Passing control to library function\n");
```

While there are a large number of other functions for dealing with SVs, these are by far the most common you will use. Let's now move on to looking at a situation where you need to use SVs: varying numbers of arguments.

Handling the Stack

Anyone who has some XS experience may expect that we could quite easily retrieve variable arguments using an AV* in the function's prototype. Unfortunately, this doesn't quite work; Inline::C by default only handles a fixed number of arguments to a function. If you want to handle arrays and varying numbers of parameters, you'll need to handle the stack yourself. Inline::C provides several macros to help you do this: Inline_Stack_Vars sets up the variables used by the other stack handling macros, Inline_Stack_Items tells you the number of arguments to your function, and Inline_Stack_Item retrieves an item from the stack.

```
    use Inline C => q{

    void print_array(SV* arg1, ... ) {
        Inline_Stack_Vars;
        int i;

        for (i=0 ; i < Inline_Stack_Items ; i++) {
            printf("The %ith argument is %s\n", i,
                    SvPV_nolen(Inline_Stack_Item(i)));
        }
```

```
    }

};

    print_array("Hello", 123, "fish", 0.12);
```

Note that although we declared an explicit argument, arg1, it remains on the stack as Inline_Stack_Item(0).

So we can read multiple arguments from a stack and return zero or one values. If we want to return multiple values, then we also need to manipulate the stack.

It's well known that the Perl special variable $!, the error variable, is a bit, well, special; it holds both an integer (error code) and a string (error description):

```
% perl -le '$!=3; print $!; print $!+0'

No such process
3
```

We can create such values with the Scalar::Utils function dualvar. Here's a generic routine to return both values from this type of dual-valued scalar:

```
use Inline C => q{

void bothvars (SV* var) {
    Inline_Stack_Vars;
    Inline_Stack_Reset;
    if (SvPOK(var) && SvIOK(var)) { /* dual-valued */
        Inline_Stack_Push(sv_2mortal(newSViv(SvIV(var)))); /* Push integer part */
    }
    Inline_Stack_Push(var); /* Push string part */
    Inline_Stack_Done;
}

};

use Scalar::Util qw(dualvar);

my $var = dualvar(10, "Hello");
print "$_\n" for bothvars($var);
```

We use Inline_Stack_Vars as before, since we're manipulating the stack. Inline_Stack_Reset says that we're done taking the arguments off the stack (Inline has already done that for us, putting the value into var) and we're ready to start pushing return values back.

Now if it's a dual-valued scalar—it's OK to use both the string and the integer parts at the moment—then we create a new SV* holding the integer part, and use Inline_Stack_Push to place that onto the stack. We use Inline_Stack_Push again on the original value, as this will give us the string part.

Now we're done, and we tell `Inline` there are no more values to come, with `Inline_Stack_Done`.

If you want to have multiple arguments and multiple return values, you can just combine the two techniques.

Handling More Complex Perl Types

Of course, there's a far more natural way to deal with arrays in Perl subroutines—pass them around as references. But first we need to know how to get hold of references in XS and what to do with them when we've got them.

References

If we arrange our XS function to receive a reference, there are two things we need to do with it once we've got it—first, work out what sort of reference it is and, second, dereference it. As it happens, in XS, these two things are strongly related. We already know how to work out what type an SV is, using the `SvTYPE` macro and the `SVt_...` enumeration. The only other trick is to dereference the RV, and we do this with the `SvRV` macro.

For instance, we find the following code inside `Data::Dumper`:

```
if (SvROK(sv) && (SvTYPE(SvRV(sv)) == SVt_PVAV))
    keys = (AV*)SvREFCNT_inc(SvRV(sv));
```

This is saying that if `sv` is a reference, and the type of the referenced SV is an AV—as we noted when looking at `SvTYPE`, arrays are just specialized SVs—then we dereference it, increase its reference count (because we're about to hold a reference to it somewhere in a way that's not managed by Perl) and store it in `keys`.

Arrays

OK, so we've now got an array. What can we do with that? Naturally, all the Perl operations on arrays have equivalents in C space. We'll only look here at the most common three operations—finding the length of the array, getting an element, and storing an element.

The C equivalent to `$#array` is the `av_len` macro; like `$#array` it returns the highest index, or -1 if the array is empty. Hence we can imagine an array iterator would look something like this:

```
for (i = 0; i <= av_len(array); i++) {
    SV* elem;
    ...
}
```

Now we come to extracting the individual SVs. We have two ways to proceed: the official way uses the `av_fetch` function. This takes three parameters: an AV, an index, and a boolean determining whether or not the element should be created if it does not already exist.

```
for (i = 0; i <= av_len(array); i++) {
    SV** elem_p = av_fetch(array, i, 0);
    SV* elem;
    if (elem_p)
        elem = *elem_p;
    ...
}
```

As you can see, this returns a pointer, which tells us whether there's a valid SV in that array element. (Naturally, if we'd passed in a true value for the third parameter to av_fetch, then we'd always get valid SVs and wouldn't need to check elem_p.) If we say something like this from Perl:

```
my @array;
$array[3] = "Hi there!";
```

then elements 0, 1, and 2 will not have a valid SV, and so av_fetch can't return anything.

The less official, but faster, way to retrieve elements takes notice of the fact that AVs are implemented as real C arrays underneath. The macro AvARRAY gives us a pointer to the base of the array:

```
SV** base = AvARRAY(array);
for (i = 0; i <= av_len(array); i++) {
    SV* elem = base[i];
    if (elem)
        printf("Element %i is %s\n", i, SvPV_nolen(elem));
}
```

Finally, storing SVs in an array uses the predictably named av_store function. This also takes three parameters—the array, the element, and the index to store. Naturally, as the array stores pointers to the underlying SV structures, you only need to call this when you're putting a completely new SV into an element; if you're just modifying the existing SVs, there's no need to call av_store afterward, because av_fetch( ) gave you a pointer to the SV in the array, and the array is still pointing to that same SV:

```
for (i = 0; i <= av_len(array); i++) {
    SV** elem_p = av_fetch(array, i, 0);
    if (elem_p) {
        SV* elem = elem_p;
        sv_setiv(elem, SvIV(elem) + 1); /* add 1 to each element */
    }
}
```

Hashes

And what about hashes, then? These also have two functions for getting and setting values, hv_fetch and hv_store. The hash key is passed to each function as a string and an integer representing the string's length. The hv_fetch function, like av_fetch, returns a pointer to an SV*, not an SV* itself. For instance, `DB_File` reads some configuration values for a DBM file from a Perl hash:

```
svp = hv_fetch(action, "ffactor", 7, FALSE);
info->db_HA_ffactor = svp ? SvIV(*svp) : 0;

svp = hv_fetch(action, "nelem", 5, FALSE);
info->db_HA_nelem = svp ? SvIV(*svp) : 0;

svp = hv_fetch(action, "bsize", 5, FALSE);
info->db_HA_bsize = svp ? SvIV(*svp) : 0;
```

Again, like `av_fetch`, the final parameter determines whether or not we should create an SV at this point if there isn't one already there. In fact, given that Perl will happily create SVs for us, we can pretty much do without `hv_store`:

```
SV** new_sv = hv_fetch(hash, "message", 7, TRUE);
if (!new_sv)
    croak("So what happened there, then?");
sv_setpv(*new_sv, "Hi there!");
```

(`croak` is the C interface to Perl's `die` and takes a format string à la `printf`.)

However, if you prefer doing without the surreality of using a function called "fetch" to store things, `hv_store` works just fine:

```
SV* message = newSVpv("Hi there!", 9);
hv_store(hash, "message", message, 0);
```

This creates a new SV, gives it a nine-character-long string value, and then stores that SV as the `message` key into the hash. The `0` at the end of `hv_store` tells Perl that we didn't pre-compute the hash value for this key, so we'd like Perl to do it for us. Precomputing hash keys is unlikely to be worth your while, so you almost always want to supply `0` here.

As usual, for more hash manipulation functions, look at *perlapi*.

Wrapping C Libraries

A common use of extending Perl is to allow access to functions in existing C libraries; it's no fun making up your own C code all the time. Let's first look at an example of linking in a C library to our ordinary `Inline` functions.

We'll use Philip Hazel's *pcre* library[*] as an alternative regular expression engine. Here's a wrapper function around the library that sets up a regular expression structure and tries to match against a string.

```
use Inline C => q{

#define OVECCOUNT 30
```

---

[*] Perl Compatible Regular Expressions (*http://www.pcre.org/*).

```
#include <pcre.h>

int pcregrep( char* regex, char* string ) {
   pcre *re;
   const char *error;
   int rc, i, erroffset;
   int ovector[OVECCOUNT];

   re = pcre_compile( regex, 0, &error, &erroffset, NULL );
   if (re == NULL)
     croak("PCRE compilation failed at offset %d: %s\n", erroffset,
error);

   rc = pcre_exec( re, NULL, string, (int)strlen(string), 0, 0,
               ovector, OVECCOUNT );

   if (rc < 0) {
     /* Matching failed: handle error cases */
     if (rc == PCRE_ERROR_NOMATCH)
        return 0;

     croak("Matching error %d\n", rc);
   }

   return 1;
}

};
```

Of course, this won't work out of the box—we need to tell Inline where to get the pcre_compile and pcre_exec functions. We do this by specifying additional configuration options to Inline C:

```
use Inline C => Config => LIBS => '-L/sw/lib -lpcre' => INC => '-I/sw/include';
```

The special option Config tells Inline that what follows are options to Inline::C; the LIBS option tells the compiler to link in *libpcre*, while the INC option says that the *pcre.h* header file we refer to lives in */sw/include*.[*] By adding the preceding line before our wrapper function, we set up the compiler's environment correctly. Now everything works fine:

```
use Inline C => Config => LIBS => '-L/sw/lib -lpcre' => INC => '-I/sw/include';
use Inline C => q{

#define OVECCOUNT 30
#include <pcre.h>
/* The big long function we saw before. */
};
```

---

[*] Usually the header file and library would live in */usr/local/include* and */usr/local/lib*, but on this machine, they're in */sw/*.

```
if (pcregrep("f.o", "foobar")) {
    print "It matched!\n";
} else {
    print "No match!\n";
}
```

And this does indeed print It matched!.

But we don't always want to write wrapper functions around C functions in a library; sometimes we want to call the functions directly. In this case, we use the Inline::C configuration option AUTOWRAP, which tells the module to parse function prototypes it finds in our code; now we only need to provide a prototype for the functions we are interested in:

```
use Inline C => Config => LIBS => '-L/sw/lib -lpcre' =>
                          INC => '-I/sw/include' =>
                          ENABLE => AUTOWRAP;
use Inline C => "char* pcre_version( );";

print "We have pcre version ", pcre_version( ), "\n";
# We have pcre version 3.9 02-Jan-2002
```

(Notice that we *don't* specify an argument type of void; this confuses the Inline::C parser.)

If we have a suitably written header file, we can merely include that and automatically wrap all our library functions. This is a quick and easy way of getting access to a C library, but it's not terribly flexible. However, for many quick hacks, it's good enough.

Debugging Inline Extensions

The reason I point out that we shouldn't specify void in prototypes is, well, bitter experience, to be honest. I initially had this code:

```
use Inline C => "char* pcre_version(void)";
```

and had no idea why it was not working. Running the program gave me a torrent of errors:

```
pcreversion_c1dc.c: In function `pcre_version':
pcreversion_c1dc.c:20: parse error before '{' token
pcreversion_c1dc.c:21: parameter `sp' is initialized
pcreversion_c1dc.c:21: parameter `mark' is initialized
...

A problem was encountered while attempting to compile and install your
Inline C code. The command that failed was:
  make > out.make 2>&1

The build directory was:
/Users/simon/_Inline/build/pcreversion_c1dc
```

```
To debug the problem, cd to the build directory, and inspect the
output files.
```

When a compilation fails, Inline keeps all the files around that it used to build the
shared library, and tells us where to find them. If I look at */Users/simon/_Inline/build/*
pcreversion_c1dc/pcreversion_c1dc.c, I can quite quickly spot the problem:

```
...
#include "INLINE.h"
char* pcre_version(void)
#line 16 "pcreversion_c1dc.c"
#ifdef __cplusplus
extern "C"
#endif
XS(boot_pcreversion_c1dc)
...
```

Oops! I forgot the semicolon at the end of my prototype, so the compiler's seeing
char* pcre_version(void) XS(boot_pcreversion_c1dc), which is horribly nonsensical.

But things didn't immediately improve when I added the stray semicolon:

```
Can't locate auto/main/pcre_versio.al in @INC (@INC contains:
/Users/simon/_Inline/lib /System/Library/Perl/darwin
/System/Library/Perl /Library/Perl/darwin /Library/Perl /Library/Perl
/Network/Library/Perl/darwin /Network/Library/Perl
/Network/Library/Perl .) at pcreversion line 6
```

Now everything has compiled just fine—which means Inline has cleaned up the
build directory and we don't have the source any more—but the function in question doesn't seem to have been defined properly.

In this case, what we need to do is force Inline to keep the build directory around so
we can have a poke at it. We do this by passing the option noclean to Inline; the easiest way to do this is on the command line:

```
% perl -MInline=noclean pcreversion
```

As Inline options accumulate, this doesn't replace any of the options we gave in our
script itself.

Now we can go digging around in *~/_Inline/build/* and look at the generated code. In
this case, however, it's not majorly informative—everything looks OK. So, another
couple of handy options we can add are info, which produces informative messages
about the progress of the Inline process, and force, which forces a recompile even if
the C source code has not changed. These options are case-insensitive, so we end up
with a command line like the following:

```
% perl -MInline=Force,NoClean,Info ~/pcreversion
```

```
Information about the processing of your Inline C code:

Your source code needs to be compiled. I'll use this build directory:
```

```
/Users/simon/_Inline/build/pcreversion_5819
```

and I'll install the executable as:
```
/Users/simon/_Inline/lib/auto/pcreversion_5819/pcreversion_5819.bundle
```

```
No C functions have been successfully bound to Perl.
```

Ah, OK. Now we have a hint about the problem—Inline::C scanned our C code but didn't find any functions that it recognized and, hence, didn't bind anything to Perl. This tells us that there's something wrong with our prototype, and, lo and behold, getting rid of the void clears everything up.

Packaging Inline Modules

In the past I'd always seen Inline::C as useful for prototyping, or a simple glue layer between C and Perl for quick hacks, and would discourage people from using it for the "serious" business of creating CPAN modules.

However, Brian "Ingy" Ingerson has worked hard on these issues and there are now two equally suitable ways to write fully functional Perl modules in Inline, without bothering with XS.

The first way is a bit of a hack and is still my preferred method: first, create a skeleton XS module with h2xs:

```
% h2xs -n My::Thingy

Writing My/Thingy/Thingy.pm
Writing My/Thingy/Thingy.xs
Writing My/Thingy/Makefile.PL
Writing My/Thingy/test.pl
Writing My/Thingy/Changes
Writing My/Thingy/MANIFEST
```

You can see the dreaded XS file in there, but don't worry about that for now.

Next, leave that alone and develop your Inline::C-based program. Run it with the -MInline=NoClean option to leave the build directory around, and then simply grab the auto-generated XS code from the end of the *.xs* file from there and add it to the end of *Thingy.xs* into your module directory.

The advantages of this are that you end up with a pure XS module that can be used completely independently of Inline and doesn't require the end user to drag down another CPAN module; the disadvantage is that you end up grubbing around in XS code, something you set out to avoid.

The second way, which Ingy recommends, is much simpler but ends up with a module that does depend on Inline being installed. (As Inline is finding its way into the Perl core, and so will be installed with every instance of Perl, this should soon cease to be a consideration.) With this, you start writing your module as though it were pure-Perl:

```
% h2xs -XAn My::Thingy
Writing My/Thingy/Thingy.pm
Writing My/Thingy/Makefile.PL
Writing My/Thingy/test.pl
Writing My/Thingy/Changes
Writing My/Thingy/MANIFEST
```

You then need to set @EXPORT and the other Exporter variables in the usual way,[*] and pass the NAME and VERSION options to Inline in your *Thingy.pm*:

```
our $VERSION="1.01";

use Inline VERSION => '1.01',
           NAME => 'My::Thingy';
```

Finally, open up the *Makefile.PL* and change ExtUtils::MakeMaker to Inline:: MakeMaker. This ensures that the C part of the module is compiled only once, when the end user runs make, and then the C shared library is installed along with the rest of the module in the usual way during make install.

Inline:: Everything Else

Originally, Inline was just for wrapping C code; however, pretty soon developers[†] saw the potential to extend the concept to other languages. Brian rewrote the original Inline.pm to support a greater degree of pluggability, and now CPAN contains a whole host of Inline:: modules.

To round off the chapter, we'll take a look at some other languages you can use in the Inline style.

Inline::Python

Perhaps the most advanced of the non-C Inline modules is Neil Watkiss's Inline:: Python; together with his PyPerl, one can mix Python and Perl code in a near-seamless way.

The first and most obvious thing we can do with Inline::Python is the same sort of thing we've been doing with Inline::C—wrap Python routines and use them from Perl:

```
use Inline Python => q{
import os
def orig_path():
    return os.defpath.split(os.pathsep)
```

---

[*] See the *perlnewmod* documentation if you're not sure what the "usual way" of creating Perl modules is.
[†] Particularly Neil Watkiss, at the time Brian's coworker at ActiveState.

```
};

    print "$_\n" for orig_path();
```

Python's os.defpath method returns a built-in search path for executables (unmodified by the value of the $PATH environment variable); we then split this on the separator character for paths (generally ":" on Unix systems) and return it as a Python array.

Inline::Python takes care of turning that Python array into an array that we can use in Perl.

Again, just like Inline::C, we can import library functions without specifying code for them:

```
use Inline Python => q{
from quopri import encodestring
};

    print encodestring("quoted=printable"); # quoted=3Dprintable
```

However, we can also import entire classes, allowing access to Python classes and their methods. Let's use the RobotFileParser class contained in the Python *robotparser* library, used for reading and querying *robots.txt* files on remote web sites:

```
use Inline Python => q{
from robotparser import RobotFileParser
};

    my $parser= RobotFileParser->new();
    $parser->set_url('http://www.musi-cal.com/robots.txt');
    $parser->read();
    # ...
```

Once we've imported a class, all of its methods are available from Perl as though we were using the class from Python—all arguments to the methods and any return values come through the Inline::Python bridge, appearing to Perl like Perl values and appearing to Python like Python values. This allows for a pretty seamless integration of Python libraries into Perl.

But what if we want to mix the two languages even more? When Inline::Python starts up, it loads a special Python library called *perl*. We can use this to grab subroutines from the Perl environment.

```
use Inline Python => q{

def callperl():
    print "This is Python speaking..."
    perl.hi_world()
};

    sub hi_world { print "Hello! I'm in Perl!\n" }

    callperl();
```

Our Perl main package appears as the perl class inside the Python interpreter. Using the same magic that wraps Python methods into Perl subroutines, Inline::Python also turns Perl subroutines into Python methods. *That*'s seamless integration.

Inline::Python also provides a few other functions that make for a smooth transition in and out of Python; perl.eval inside Python and py_eval inside Perl can evaluate strings in the appropriate foreign language, and there are facilities for controlling the binding of Perl and Python routines.

Inline::Python works well for applications where the mother tongue is Perl; Neil's PyPerl is a first-language Python equivalent. Neil has worked hard to produce an extremely robust framework for fluid movement between Perl and Python, and the Inline::Python module is a huge bonus for anyone who wants or needs to use Python classes in their Perl code.

Inline::Ruby

Ruby (*http://www.ruby-lang.org*) is an interesting, modern, object-oriented scripting language created by Yukihiro Matsumoto (Matz). As you might be able to guess, Inline::Ruby allows you to call Ruby methods and access Ruby classes from Perl. It works precisely the same way as Inline::Python, but doesn't support the same sort of two-way communication. However, you can define methods in Ruby and import Ruby libraries and have them callable from Perl.

An interesting, but slightly complex, feature of Inline::Ruby is the ability to pass Perl subroutines to iterators. Ruby distinguishes between two types of usage for what Perl calls anonymous subroutines: the first type is called a Proc object in Ruby, and it is what most uses of Perl anonymous subs turn into; with the second type, all Ruby methods can take an optional block as an argument following the ordinary formal parameters. This acts as a callback, and the Ruby method can yield control to the callback with the yield keyword.

When a method iteratively calls yield over the contents of a data structure, it's referred to as an *iterator*. Here's an example of iterating over an array:

```
array = ["Hello", "there", "Ruby!"]
array.each { |x| puts x }
```

The each iterator method is a little like Perl's for loop: it calls the attached code block on each element of the array in turn.

You might asssume that we could happily say something like this in Inline::Ruby:

```
$object->each(sub { print $_[0] });
```

However, as we've mentioned, the code block isn't passed to the iterator as an ordinary argument—it's attached separately. To get the same effect in Inline::Ruby, we need to associate the code block like so:

```
$object->iter(sub { print $_[0] })->each;
```

This first prepares the object for calling the iterator with the right code block, and then calls it with no ordinary arguments; this does what we mean.

If you haven't taken much of a look at Ruby thus far, I'd encourage you to do so; maybe start by looking at my rubyisms Perl module, which brings some of the more interesting features from Ruby into Perl.

Inline::CPR

We've seen how Inline::C can create Perl extensions to C libraries; the usual topic that goes along with extensions is *embedding*. This is the process of creating a C program that contains a Perl interpreter and can call Perl subroutines.

Unfortunately, embedding is tricky—possibly trickier than XS. Ingy's solution is the curious Inline::CPR module. It works a little like this: you write a C program in the usual way that contains a main() function. Here's a simple one:

```
void main(void) {
    printf("Hello, C!\n");
}
```

Now you do something a bit funny with it; you add a shebang (#!) line to make the C program run under the CPR interpreter, like so:

```
#!/usr/bin/cpr

void main(void) {
    print("Hello, C!\n");
}
```

At this point, we have a C program that is a CPR script.

The CPR interpreter is a little program that starts a Perl interpreter and passes your C program wholesale to Inline::C. This compiles your C functions and binds them to Perl subroutines. Once the Perl interpreter has finished doing the usual Inline::C thing, it calls the main subroutine. Conceptually, you've written a Perl program like this:

```
#!/usr/bin/perl

use Inline C => q{

void main(void) {
    printf("Hello, C!\n");
}

};

main()
```

Once this is done, your C program is up and running inside the context of a Perl interpreter.

The neat part is that because you have a C program running inside Perl, you can use all the `Inline::C` tricks you've learned about already in this chapter.

`Inline::CPR` is still in the development stages, and you can't really do anything too clever with it, but it's an interesting framework for solving the embedding problem.

Inline::Struct

You may be thinking that `Inline::C` is all very well for interfacing to relatively simple C libraries, but in the real world, libraries use more complicated variable types than just the strings, integers, and floating-point types we've seen so far. Most libraries define their own structures and expect us to pass and recieve these structures. How can we do this with `Inline`?

The answer is to use Neil Watkiss's `Inline::Struct`. This gives us an object-oriented approach to C structures. To enable this, we simply add the following to our `Inline::C` programs:

```
use Inline C => Config => ENABLE => STRUCTS;
```

And then, theoretically, any structures defined in your C code will be wrapped into Perl classes.

Miscellaneous Other Inlines

There are now more Inline-style modules on the CPAN than it's sensible to describe, so we'll end this chapter by throwing out a few pointers to other modules worth looking at.

For many years, the only way to plug Java and Perl together was the O'Reilly JPL (Java Perl Lingo) project. This used the JNI (Java Native Interface) C library to embed a Java interpreter inside a Perl interpreter. It was slow, complex and not entirely well documented. Now we have `Inline::Java`, a Perl-Java bridge that can use either JNI or a socket connection to a standalone Java server process.

`Inline::ASM` is an obvious extension of the `Inline::C` concept which lets you write assembly code inline; this is turned into a little library that is wrapped with `Inline::C` in the usual way.

`Inline::Basic` is an interesting language extension because it doesn't actually call out to a separate interpreter; it uses a Basic interpreter written in Perl (the `Language::Basic` module) to interpret your `Inline` code. Finally, `Inline::Files` is not actually an *Inline.pm* module at all, but uses a similar technique to allow you to put multiple virtual files into a `__DATA__` section of a Perl program, instead of just the one.

Conclusion

The `Inline` modules are an easy-to-use interface for incorporating code and libraries from other languages in your Perl code. You won't use them every day, but they are a valuable addition to any Perl programmer's toolbox.

## CHAPTER 10

Fun with Perl

Perl programming isn't all work and no play. Unlike many other languages, it's in the essence of Perl culture not to take itself too seriously—thanks in part to Larry himself. After all, it's hard to be too serious about anything whose mascot is a camel.

So Perl programmers have invented many and varied ways of amusing themselves in their time off, and understanding these things will get you a step closer to understanding Perl culture. What's particularly interesting about having fun with Perl, though, is that it can teach you a great deal. When people are trying to squeeze every last character out of a Perl golf entry, they'll come up with some interesting tricks in the language that you may not have thought of; part of the appeal of JAPHs is that they do obvious things in completely unexpected ways; and some of the Acme:: modules use extremely advanced or clever techniques in order to do something totally frivolous.

Some people say that you've really mastered a language when you can tell jokes in it; by the end of this chapter, your sense of Perl humor will be honed a little further—and, hopefully, your mastery of the language will be furthered, as well.

Obfuscation

Detractors of Perl will invariably say something about it looking like line noise; they point to wonderfully obvious, but not necessarily friendly, constructions like @{$_[0]||[ ]} as examples of how ugly Perl can turn out. (However, put the same detractors in front of a COBOL program and they'll complain about it being too verbose—you can't please some people.) At any rate, the reputation Perl has achieved for being incomprehensible is largely due to the recreational activities of the Obfuscated Perl Contest[*] and Perl Golf competitions. (Thanks, guys!)

---

[*] The Obfuscated Perl Contest was run by *The Perl Journal* from 1996 until 2000 and took its inspiration from the International Obfuscated C Contest (*http://www.iocc.org/*), although for some reason most people don't think of C as looking like line noise.

But obfuscation is not only about producing code that looks like line noise. Obfuscations are really an outlet for creative impulses that—as professional programmers—we can't always use in our day jobs. Working on an obfuscation, we exchange the various operational constraints of work for another set of constraints: aestethics, cleverness, shortness, etc. The fact that the program prints "Just another Perl hacker" or does whatever the rules for the golf hole said is only a side effect.

As an example, we're going to take on a challenge posed on the Belfast Perl Mongers mailing list: write a program to solve the game of Boggle™* as quickly as possible. I wrote a pretty quick algorithm but decided to obfuscate it before entering. Here's the idea I had: first, give the dice coordinates from (1,1) to (4,4). Now we construct a matrix of each die's neighbor:

```perl
my @neighbors=
(undef,[undef,[[1,2],[2,1],[2,2]],[[1,1],[1,3],[2,1],[2,2],[2,3]],[[1,
2],[1,4],[2,2],[2,3],[2,4]],[[1,3],[2,3],[2,4]]],[undef,[[1,1],[1,2],[
2,2],[3,1],[3,2]],[[1,1],[1,2],[1,3],[2,1],[2,3],[3,1],[3,2],[3,3]],[[
1,2],[1,3],[1,4],[2,2],[2,4],[3,2],[3,3],[3,4]],[[1,3],[1,4],[2,3],[3,
3],[3,4]]],[undef,[[2,1],[2,2],[3,2],[4,1],[4,2]],[[2,1],[2,2],[2,3],[
3,1],[3,3],[4,1],[4,2],[4,3]],[[2,2],[2,3],[2,4],[3,2],[3,4],[4,2],[4,
3],[4,4]],[[2,3],[2,4],[3,3],[4,3],[4,4]]],[undef,[[3,1],[3,2],[4,2]],
[[3,1],[3,2],[3,3],[4,1],[4,3]],[[3,2],[3,3],[3,4],[4,2],[4,4]],[[3,3]
```

This tells us that, for instance, the top left die (1,1) has neighbors (1,2), (2,1), and (2,2). Naturally, I used a small Perl program to pre-compute this for speed.

Next, we need to read the board from standard input and also keep two pieces of information about it—first, we want to know what letters we have on the board in total, and also we want to have a hash that looks up dice by the letter on them. That's to say, given the following board:

```
iane
nvpo
oire
ewlg
```

we can look up "e" and get (1,4), (3,4), and (4.1).

```perl
for my $line (1..4) {
  chop(my $row = <>);
  my @row = split //, $row;
  $has.=$row;
  push @{$where{ $row[$_] }}, [$line, $_] for 1..4;
}
```

---

* Boggle™ is a word game that uses a grid of lettered dice; you have to find find words by tracing paths through adjacent letters, without using the same die twice. So in the grid on this page, you can start at p and trace out peril, but you can't have piper because that would require going over the p twice.

(We used one-based arrays to simplify the generation of the @neighbors variable—detecting that $neighbors[0] is undef is easier than having to check that we don't accidentally get an inaccurate answer by looking at $neighbors[-1].)

Next, we read in a word list and determine whether we can find the word in the Boggle grid. You might think it would be better to look through the Boggle grid and see what words you can make, as a human would, but this turns out to involve nearly half a million possibilities, whereas we can get any word list down smaller than that.

The key to this is in noting that we're only interested in words made up of letters that can actually be found on our grid; that's the $has variable:

```
while (<>) {
    chomp;
    next unless /^[$has]{3,9}$/o;
    my @stuff = split //, (my $word=$_);
```

We then locate the first letter of the word in our %where hash, giving us all possible starting points. The path subroutine takes a position, a hash of the positions already visited (so we don't go over the same letter twice) and the letters left to find, and returns a true value if there's a path that traces out the letters:

```
for (@{$where{shift @stuff}}) {
    print $word
        if path($_, { $_->[0] . $_->[1] => 1 }, @stuff);
}
```

As you might be able to guess, path is a recursive subroutine; it looks at the available positions of the next letter to be found, checks that they're neighbors of the current position and that they're not in the history, and then does the same for the next letter to find.

```
sub path {
    my ($pos, $history, @left) = @_;
    my @neigh = @{ $neighbors[ $pos->[0] ][ $pos->[1] ] };
    for my $newpos (@{ $where{ shift @left } }) {
        next if (!scalar grep { $newpos->[0] == $_->[0] &&
                                $newpos->[1] == $_->[1] } @neigh)
            || $history->{ $newpos->[0] . $newpos->[1] }++;
        return !@left || path($newpos, $history, @left);
    }
}
```

OK, we've spent a long time explaining the algorithm. Let's go around obfuscating it. First, we look at variable and subroutine names. You'll get no points for having descriptive naming, and brevity is a strong element of obfuscation. Let's replace @neighbors with @n, $history with $h, $nextpos with $n (note the useful distinction between @n and $n), and so on. We also get rid of obvious extraneous whitespace to give us:

```
#!/usr/bin/perl -l
my@n=
(undef,[undef,[[1,2],[2,1],[2,2]],[[1,1],[1,3],[2,1],[2,2],[2,3]],[[1,
```

```
2],[1,4],[2,2],[2,3],[2,4]],[[1,3],[2,3],[2,4]]],[undef,[[1,1],[1,2],[
2,2],[3,1],[3,2]],[[1,1],[1,2],[1,3],[2,1],[2,3],[3,1],[3,2],[3,3]],[[
1,2],[1,3],[1,4],[2,2],[2,4],[3,2],[3,3],[3,4]],[[1,3],[1,4],[2,3],[3,
3],[3,4]]],[undef,[[2,1],[2,2],[3,2],[4,1],[4,2]],[[2,1],[2,2],[2,3],[
3,1],[3,3],[4,1],[4,2],[4,3]],[[2,2],[2,3],[2,4],[3,2],[3,4],[4,2],[4,
3],[4,4]],[[2,3],[2,4],[3,3],[4,3],[4,4]]],[undef,[[3,1],[3,2],[4,2]],
[[3,1],[3,2],[3,3],[4,1],[4,3]],[[3,2],[3,3],[3,4],[4,2],[4,4]],[[3,3]
,[3,4],[4,3]]]]);
for my $l(1..4){chop(my $r = <>); my @r = split //, $r; $h.=$r;
push @{$w{$r[$_] }}, [$l, $_] for 1..4;}
while (<>) {chomp; next unless /^[$h]{3,9}$/o; my @s = split //, (my
$w=$_);p($_,{$_->[0].$_->[1] => 1},@s) and print $w for @{$w{shift @s}};}
sub p { my ($p, $h, @l) = @_; my @n2 = @{$n[$p->[0]][$p->[1]]};for my
$n (@{$w{shift @l}}) {
    next if (!scalar grep {$n->[0]==$_->[0]&&$n->[1]==$_->[1]} @n2)
||$h->{$n->[0].$n->[1]}++; return !@l||p($n,$h,@l);}}
```

Well, this is still just about comprehensible, so we need to add a few more touches. For starters, Perl is amazingly tolerant of whitespace. Not only can we get rid of more whitespace where it's not needed (such as, for instance, all the whitespace in my @r = split //, $r) but we can add whitespace where it might not be expected—for instance, a pleasing addition is a newline between the $ and r of a variable. We can also trim the code by replacing those undefs with zeros, and swapping a few control structures around—X&&next instead of next if X, for instance. And, of course, no obfuscated program is complete without being formed into a nice regular shape:

```
my@n=(0,[0,[[2,2],[2,1],[1,2]],[[2,3],[2,2],[2,1],[1,3]
,[1,1]],[[2,4],[2,3],[2,2],[1,4],[1,2]],[[2,4],[2,3],[1
,3]]],[0,[[3,2],[3,1],[2,2],[1,2],[1,1],[1,2]],[[3,3],[
3,2],[3,1],[2,3],[2,1],[1,3],[1,2],[1,3]],[[3,4],[3,3],
[3,2],[2,4],[2,2],[1,4],[1,3],[1,2]],[[3,4],[3,3],[2,3]
,[1,4]]],[0,[[4,2],[4,1],[3,2],[2,2],[2,1],[2,2]],[[4,3
],[4,2],[4,1],[3,3],[3,1],[2,3],[2,2],[2,3]],[[4,4],[4,
3],[4,2],[3,4],[3,2],[2,4],[2,3],[2,4]],[[4,4],[4,3],[3
,3],[2,4]]],[0,[[4,2],[3,2],[3,1],[3,2]],[[4,3],[4,1],[
3,3],[3,2],[3,3]],[[4,4],[4,2],[3,4],[3,3],[3,4]],[[4,3
],[3,4]]]);my@b=[ ];my($h,%w);for my $l(0,1,2,3){chop(my
$r=<>);my@r=split//,$r;push@b,[0,@r];push@{$w{$r[$_]}},
[$l,$_]for 1..4;$h.=$r}while (<>){/^[$h]{3,9}$/o||next;
chomp;my@s=split//,(my$w=$_);p($_,{$_->[0].$_->[1]=>1},
@s)&&print$w."\n"for@{$w{shift@s}}}sub p{my($p,$h,@l)=@
_;my@z=@{$n[$p->[0]][$p->[1]]};for my$n(@{$w{shift@l}})
{next if(!scalar grep{$n->[0]==$_->[0]&&$n->[1]==$_->[1
]}@z)||$h->{$n->[0].$n->[1]}++;return!@l||p($n,$h,@l)}}
```

It was at this point that we tripped over a Perl 5.6.0 parser buffer overflow:

```
syntax error at boggle.pl.old line 14, near "5{"
Unrecognized character \x02 at boggle.pl.old line 14.
```

which suggested that this was obfuscated enough.

But I am but an amateur at the obfuscation game; for instance, it's possible to determine what my algorithm does by inspection—it doesn't do anything interesting like rewrite itself on the fly or redefine subroutines at runtime. I don't make use of the interesting properties of Perl's special variables, such as the wonderful discovery that $} (and hence @}, %}, and *}) is a legal variable name that happens to be unused by the system.

For a piece of code that uses all these tricks and more, check out Damian Conway's SelfGOL. This program, if we can call it such, is just more than 1,000 bytes of pure, unadulterated evil. Instead of entering a different program for each category of the Obfuscated Perl Contest, Damian entered "SelfGOL" to all four.

SelfGOL can reproduce itself; it can turn other programs into a quine; it can display a scrolling banner; it plays the Game of Life; and it contains no (ordinary) loops, goto statements, or if statements. Control flow is done, well, interestingly. We reproduce it here in its entirety without comment, as it takes Damian three to seven hours to explain it:

```
#!/usr/bin/perl -s
$;=$/;seek+DATA,undef$/,!$s;$_=<DATA>;$s&&print||(*{q;::\;
;}=sub{$d=$d-1?$d:$0;s;';'\t#$d#;,$_})&&$g&&do{$y=($x||=20)*($y||8);sub
i{sleep&f}sub'p{print$;x$=,join$;,$b=~/.{$x}/g,$;}sub'f{pop||1}sub'n{substr($b,
&f%$y,3)=~tr,0,0,}sub'g{@_[~~@_]=@_;--($f=&f);$m=substr($b,&f,1);($w,$w,$m,0)
[n($f-$x)+n($x+$f)-(${m}eq+0=>)+n$f]||$w}$w="\40";$b=join'',@ARGV?<>:$_,$w
x$y;$b=~s).)$&=~/\w/?0:$w)gse;substr($b,$y)=q++;$g='$i=0;$i?$b:$c=$b;
substr+$c,$i,1,g$i;$g=~s?\d+?($&+1)%$y?e;$i-$y+1?eval$g:do{$b=$c;p;i}';
sub'e{eval$g;&e};e}||eval||die+No.$;
__DATA__
$d&&do{{$^W=$|;*_=sub{$=+s=#([A-z])(.*)#=#$+$1#=g}}
@s=(q[$_=sprintf+pop@s,@s],";\n"->($_=q[
$d&&do{{$^W=$|;*_=sub{$=+s=#([A-z])(.*)#=#$+$1#=g}}'
@s=(q[%s],q[%s])x2;%s;print"\n"x&_,$_;i;eval};
])x2;$_=sprintf+pop@s,@s;print"\n"x&_,$_;i;eval};$/=$y;$"="=",";print
q<#!/usr/bin/perl -sw
!$s?{do{>.($_=<>).q<}:do{@s=(q[printf+pop@s,@s],q[#!/usr/bin/perl -sw
!$s?{do{>.(s$%$%%$g,y=[====y=]==||&d,$_).q<}:do{@s=(q[%s],q[%s])x2;%s}
])x2;printf+pop@s,@s}
>
```

These are its command-line switches:

```
% selfgol -g          # play the Game of Life
% selfgol -s          # reproduce
% selfgol -d          # display banner
% selfgol -f script.pl # convert script.pl into a quine
```

We cannot leave the topic of obfuscation without mentioning B::Deparse. More than a few people have come up with the bright idea of writing auto-obfuscation programs in order to safeguard their code against prying eyes for commercial reasons; still others produce horrifyingly obfuscated code that you would prefer to understand before running. Deparse helps with both of these. For instance, Mark-Jason Dominus's entry in the 5th Obfuscated Perl Contest looks like this:

```
@P=split//,".URRUU\c8R";@d=split//,"\nrekcah xinU / lreP rehtona tsuJ";sub p{
@p{"r$p","u$p"}=(P,P);pipe"r$p","u$p";++$p;($q*=2)+=$f=!fork;map{$P=$P[$f|ord
```

```
($p{$_})&6];$p{$_}=/ ^$P/ix?$P:close$_}keys%p}p;p;p;p;p;map{$p{$_}=~/^[P.]/&&
close$_}%p;wait until$?;map{/^r/&&<$_>}%p;$_=$d[$q];sleep rand(2)if/\S/;print
```

If you want to deconstruct this, you could do worse than starting with the following:

```
% perl -MO=Deparse mjd-japh
```

```
@P = split(??, '.URRUUxR', 0);
@d = split(??, "\nrekcah xinU / lreP rehtona tsuJ", 0);
sub p {
    @p{"r$p", "u$p"} = ('P', 'P');
    pipe *{"r$p"}, *{"u$p"};
    ++$p;
    ($q *= 2) += $f = !fork;
    map {$P = $P[$f | ord $p{$_} & 6];
    $p{$_} = / ^$P/xi ? $P : close *$_;} keys %p;
}
p ;
p ;
p ;
p ;
p ;
map {close *$_ if $p{$_} =~ /^[P.]/;} %p;
wait until $?;
map {<$_> if /^r/;} %p;
$_ = $d[$q];
sleep rand 2 if /\S/;
print $_;
```

B::Deparse is a module designed to work with the Perl compiler, *O.pm*. If we tell O to use the Deparse backend, (use O 'Deparse', or perl -MO=Deparse as it's more commonly spelled) instead of spitting out C or Perl bytecode, it spits out Perl as parsed by the Perl parser and then unparsed again.

If you need another hint, the -p option to Deparse can be used to add additional parentheses:

```
% perl -MO=Deparse,-p mjd-japh
...

    (($q *= 2) += ($f = (!fork)));
    map({(($P = $P[($f | (ord($p{$_}) & 6))])});

..
```

Just Another Perl Hacker

A long time ago, in a Usenet newsgroup far, far away, Perl hacker Randal Schwartz (coauthor of *Learning Perl* and the early *Programming Perl* books) signed off a Usenet post with the famous words:

```
Just another Perl hacker,
```

Of course, since Randal was talking about Perl and demonstrating techniques in Perl, this signature very soon mutated into the very obvious Perl code:

```
print "Just another Perl hacker,\n";
```

and at this point, the *JAPH* was born. As Randal and others demonstrated a Perl programming technique in their Usenet articles, the point would be highlighted by a valedictory JAPH. For instance, when demonstrating the fact that sort sorts lexicographically with uppercase characters first, one might sign off:

```
print join" ", (sort(qw(another Just Perl hacker,)))[0,2,1,3];
```

Since then, it has become a Perl tradition to produce programs that output the words "Just another Perl hacker" in cute, educational, or unexpected ways. The undisputed king—or perhaps, queen—of JAPHdom is the Dutch hacker Abigail, who has contributed some of the most surprising JAPHs to the Perl community. The JAPH culture is so established that some of Abigail's JAPHs have been included in recent versions of Perl as regression tests, since they expose some of the strangest edge cases of the *perl* interpreter's behavior.

Abigail's JAPHs use many of the tricks involved in obfuscated Perl but always end up surprising many readers. For instance, here's one of the more famous ones:

```
* * * * * * * * * * * * * * * * * * * * * * * * * * * * *
/ / / / / / / / / / / / / / / / / / / / / / / / / / / / /
% % % % % % % % % % % % % % % % % % % % % % % % % % % % %;
BEGIN {% % = ($ _ = " " => print "Just another Perl Hacker\n")}
```

The fact that this prints out a JAPH should be no surprise, since this is given entirely in the last line; the surprise should be in the fact that the whole thing parses as valid Perl code. But if you remember that // is a valid pattern match, %% is a perfectly good name for a hash, and ** is a perfectly good glob, then all should become relatively clear.

There's a varying degree of complexity involved in JAPHs. The most basic JAPH somehow encodes the JAPH string, and then decodes it. This is pretty boring:

```
$_ = q ;4a75737420616e6f74686572205065726c204861636b65720as;;
    for (s;s;s;s;s;s;s;s;s;s;s;s;s)
        {s;(..)s?;qq qprint chr 0x$1 and \161 ssq;excess;}
```

Then there are the kind of JAPHs that obviously contain the JAPH string, but it's not at all obvious how it reaches standard output:

```
eval {die [[qq [Just another Perl Hacker]]]};; print
${${${@}}[$#{@{${@}}}]}[$#{${@{${@}}}[$#{@{${@}}}]}]
```

And then there are those JAPHs that look like they might contain something like the JAPH string, but the rest is unclear:

```
BEGIN {$^H {q} = sub {$_ [1] =~ y/S-ZA-IK-O/q-tc-fe-m/d; $_ [1]}; $^H= 0x28100}
print "Just another PYTHON hacker\n";
```

This particular JAPH relies upon a little-known feature of the overload pragma—explained in Chapter 1—combined with a little-known feature of its implementation—the fact that it relies on placing specific values in the magic variables $^H and %^H.

A similar effect, it turns out, can be obtained by tying special variables:

```
tie $" => A; $, = " "; $\ = "\n"; @a = ("") x 2; print map {"@a"} 1 .. 4;
sub A::TIESCALAR {bless \my $A => A} #  Yet Another silly JAPH by Abigail
sub A::FETCH     {@q = qw /Just Another Perl Hacker/ unless @q; shift @q}
```

Here, the $" variable, which is used to join array elements when they are interpolated in double-quoted strings, is tied; hence, when we interpolate the (empty) array @a, the tied variable pulls out another word from the JAPH string stored in @q.

Special variables also play an interesting part in this Abigail creation, but in a very different way:

```
map{${+chr}=chr}map{$_=>$_^ord$"}$=+$]..3*$=/2;
print "$J$u$s$t $a$n$o$t$h$e$r $P$e$r$l $H$a$c$k$e$r\n";
```

This takes advantage of the very fortuitous coincidences that the value of $= (the default number of lines on a format page) plus $] (the Perl version, generally just over 5 for now) is 65, the ASCII code for "A," and three-over-two times $= is 90, the ASCII code for "Z." Combined with the fact that the ASCII character set is arranged so that you can flip between lower- and uppercase letters by flipping the 5th bit (32, the value of a space character, as stored in $"), the first line of this JAPH sets $a to a, $b to b, and so on through to $Z; once this is accomplished, the second line follows naturally.

$A++

This discipline was invented by the Paris Perl Mongers, who also host a list of results at *http://paris.mongueurs.net/aplusplus.html*. The challenge is to increment the value of $A by one. There are currently 288 entries, ranging from the simple:

```
$A++;
```

to the mind-blowing:

```
y ccccd x s vvchr oct oct ord uc ave x s vvucve le
s vvuc ave x s vvchr oct oct oct ord uc bve x eval
```

Perl Golf

The golfers are another example of the funny side of Perl; these are players of the game invented by Uri Guttman and played out on the *golf@perl.org* (Perl Golfers) mailing list and far too many other places, such as in front of those asking for help with relatively trivial problems on comp.lang.perl.misc. The goal of this particular sport is to solve a programming problem in as few characters as possible.

For instance, consider generating the Fibonnacci series (1, 1, 2, 3, 5, 8, etc.). One might start with the following uninspired program:

```
perl -e '$a=$b=1; while (1) {$c= $a+$b; print $c,"\n"; $a=$b; $b=$c; }'
```

This weighs in at an abysmal 61 characters, or *strokes*. We can immediately improve on this by removing extraneous whitespace and making use of the -l option to print newlines after every print statement:

```
perl -le '$a=$b=1;while(1){$c=$a+$b;print$c;$a=$b;$b=$c;}'
```

This gives us a slightly more respectable 48 (the -l counts as a stroke), but that's still way over par. Let's notice that the second "1" constant isn't doing anything, the assignment followed by print will always yield a true value, so we can use that instead:

```
perl -le '$a=$b=1;while(print$c=$a+$b){$a=$b;$b=$c;}'
```

We're now down to 43, and we can get rid of the initial $a= and the last semicolon for another three strokes. Maybe you feel we would be better off without an intermediate variable:

```
perl -le '$b=1;while(print$a+$b){($a,$b)=($b,$a+$b)}'
```

but this again yields 43 strokes. A new train of thought is required.

So far we've been computing the *n*'th term and printing it, then shuffling our variables around so we stored the *n*'th and *n*-1'th. But what we can do is carry about the *n*'th and *n*-1'th terms and increment each by the other: *f(n)* + *f(n-1)* yields *f(n+1)*, and *f(n+1)* + *f(n)* yields *f(n+2)*. This time we generate two terms inside our loop:

```
perl -le '$b=1;while(1){$a+=$b;print$a;$b+=$a;print$b}'
```

We're now back up to 45 strokes, but this formulation leads naturally to:

```
perl -le '$b=1;while(1){print$a+=$b;print$b+=$a}'
```

and thence to the beautifully symmetric:

```
perl -le '$b=1;print$a+=$b while print$b+=$a'
```

This is 35 strokes, not bad; I dare say it can be improved upon, but aesthetics forces me to stop here. Ooh, no, one more thing:

```
perl -le 'print$a+=$b while print$b+=$a||1'
```

33 strokes in all. Oh, and we can shave a character by using a special variable instead of $b, because then we won't need the space after while:

```
perl -le 'print$a+=$}while print$}+=$a||1'
```

32 strokes. Beat that if you can!

All right, I admit it; it's addictive.

Perl Poetry

Programming Perl mentions the arcane art of Perl Poetry—writing valid Perl programs that, shall we say, have greater literary than pragmatic value.

The trend for writing Perl Poetry began, of course, with Larry and the first Perl haiku:

```
print STDOUT q
Just another Perl hacker,
unless $spring
```

However, Perl haiku have problems—they require the reader to agree on certain syllabic conventions. In this case, STDOUT must be read as "standard out" instead of the more usual "studout," and the $ in $spring must be pronounced.

To avoid these kinds of confusion, Perl poems have gravitated toward the abstract, generally without a rhyme or syllabic structure. The first example of this, and the most widely known example of Perl poetry, is attributed to Larry: the Black Perl poem that can be found in *Programming Perl*.

As noted there, the undisputed master of Perl poetry is Sharon Hopkins, whose *listen*, *reverse*, *rush*, and *shopping* poems have received widespread critical acclaim and publication in major periodicals.

The practice of Perl poetry has passed its azimuth and is now in decline, save for the occasional Perl poetry contest and entries on the Poetry page of *perlmonks.org*. This is partially due to lack of interest and partially due to a concerted effort by Larry to ensure that Black Perl does not run on modern versions of Perl. That said, I wish to humbly offer a personal example, inspired by the great masterwork of Proust, *À la Récherche du Temps Perdu*:

```
for(long => time) {$early && $self->went($bed);}
rand time && do {
```

```
    while ($candle--) {
        (time => $eyes->shut()) < (time => print "Falling asleep!")
    }
};
```

Acme::*

With all this crazy hackery going on, an outlet was needed on CPAN for less serious module contributions to the Perl world. The Acme namespace was set aside for wacky, explosive, or Heath-Robinsonian modules, and has very quickly become one of the more densely populated namespaces on CPAN. Most, if not all, of Acme:: is, in some way, London.pm's fault.

It all started with the Bleach module, a neat toy by Damian Conway that spawned a host of less amusing and sadly uninspired imitators. Because of the host of imitators that followed, clogging up the root of the CPAN namespace, it was decided that silliness should not be discouraged, but moved to Acme::, and Bleach became Acme:: Bleach. Bleach is really clever; it takes an ordinary program, like so:

```
use Bleach;
for my $i (1..10) {
    print "Hello! $i\n";
}
```

The first time this program runs, it appears to do nothing at all. However, when you come to look at the code again, it now looks like:

```
use Bleach;
```


The really clever part is that it still runs, and it now prints out the message 10 times. This is astonishing until you know the trick. How does Bleach work, then? Everyone assumed this was done with source filters, but the business end of Bleach is a mere 11 lines long:

```
my $tie = " \t"x8;
sub whiten { local $_ = unpack "b*", pop; tr/01/\t/; s/(.{9})/$1\n/g; $tie.$_ }
sub brighten { local $_ = pop; s/^$tie|[^ \t]//g; tr/ \t/01/; pack "b*", $_ }
sub dirty { $_[0] =~ /\S/ }
sub dress { $_[0] =~ /^$tie/ }
open 0 or print "Can't rebleach'$0'\n" and exit;
(my $shirt = join "", <0>) =~ s/.*^\s*use\s+Acme::Bleach\s*;\n//sm;
local $SIG{__WARN__} = \&dirty;
do {eval brighten $shirt; exit} unless dirty $shirt && not dress $shirt;
open 0, ">$0" or print "Cannot bleach '$0'\n" and exit;
print {0} "use Acme::Bleach;\n", whiten $shirt and exit;
```

It all becomes pretty obvious when you look at what the subroutines do. The `whiten` sub-routine takes a string, turns it into its binary representation, and turns the zeros and ones into different types of whitespace. The `brighten` subroutine does the opposite, after first removing the signature `$tie`. The `dirty` subroutine checks to see if there's anything in a string that isn't whitespace, and `dress` checks to see if the signature is present.

So the module loads up your code by using a slightly nifty Perl trick, found in the documentation of open:

> If EXPR is omitted, the scalar variable of the same name as the FILEHANDLE contains the filename.

That is, by opening a filehandle called 0, we take the filename from $0, the location of our program. Then we lop off everything before use `Acme::Bleach`, and turn off warnings by setting the warn handler to an irrelevant subroutine. Now the code we've read in could be already bleached, in which case it's not `dirty` and will be `dressed`; if this is the case, we `brighten` it and execute it. If not, we `whiten` it and write it back.

Very simple, once you've seen the trick. Other modules based on the same principle include `Acme::Buffy`, `Acme::Pony`, and many other London.pm in-jokes.

There are, of course, some `Acme::` modules that do other things. They range from the amusing but simple and uninspired (`Acme::Handwave`—you tell it what data you expect, and it returns it), through amusing, simple, and inspired (`Acme::Don't`—like a do block, but not quite) right up to the spectacular.

`Acme::Eyedrops`, for instance, deserves an honorable mention. This takes an ordinary Perl program—and let's use a classic:

```
print "hello world\n";
```

and automatically obfuscates it:

```
perl -MAcme::EyeDrops=sightly -e 'print sightly("helloworld.pl")'

eval eval
'""'.('['['^'+').('['['^')').('`'`'|')').('`'`'|'.').('['['^'/').('{'{'^'[').'\\'.'""'.
('`'`'|'(').('`'`'|'%').('`'`'|',').('`'`'|',').('`'`'|'/').('{'{'^'[').('['['^',').('`'`'
|'/').('['['^')').('`'`'|',').('`'`'|'$').'\\'.'\\'.('`'`'|'.').'\\'.'""'.';'.('!'^
'+').'""'
```

(We've reformatted the actual output slightly for, um, readability.)

Now you can probably see what it's done here—it's encoded the ASCII values of each character in the program: the first character is `'[' ^ '+'`, which is p, and so on. But that's not all it can do; it can pour that mess of punctuation into pretty shapes. For instance, if you pass the `shape => "simon"` option, you get a rather unflattering portrait[*] of your humble author:

---

[*] Based on a very flattering portrait.

```
eval eval '""'.
                        ('['^'+').("\["^
                     ')').("\`"| ')').('`'
                    |'.').('['^'/' ).('{'^'[')
                  .'\\'.'"'.("\`"| '(').((`'`')|
                 '%').('`'|('`')).( '`'|',').('`'
                |'/').('{'^'['`).('['^ ',').('`'|'/'
               ).('['^')').('`'|',').(  '`'|'$').'\\'
              .'\\'.('`'|'.').'\\'.'"'  .';'.('!'^'+')
             .'"';$:='.'^'~';$~='@'|'(' ;$^='')'^'[';$/
            ='`'|'.';$_='('^'}';$,='`'| '!';$\='')'^'}';
           $:-'.'^'~';$~=('@')|     '(' ;$^          =')'^'['
          ;$/='`'|'.';$_='('                          ^'}';$,
         ='`'|'!';$\=(')')^                           '}';$:=
        '.'^'~';$~='@'|'('                            ;($^)=
       ')'^'[';$/='`'|'.';                            $_='('
      ^'}';$,='`'|'!';$\=                             "\)"^
     '}';$:='.'^"\~";$~= (                            '@')
    |'(';$^=')'^'[';$/ =                              '`'
   |'.';$_='('^'}';$,  =                             ((
  '`')|'!';$\="\)"^    (                             ((
 '}'))));$:='.'^'~'; (    ( ( (         (  (  (
$~))))))))='@'|"\("; (     (        (         (        (
$^)))))=')'^'[';$/   ='`'|          '.'  ;      (
(  $_))='('^'}';$,    ='`'|'!'          ;($\) =    (
( ')'))')'')^'}';$:               =     (
  '.')^"\~";                (          $~)
   =  '@'                   |           (
    (                       (           (
    (                       (           (
   (  (                                 (
  ( ( (               (     (  (         (
    (                 (     (  (         (
    (                 (     (  (
    (                                    (
   (  (
  (    (              '('))))))   )
  )     )             )))))))))))))
  )     )              )))))))))  ;
  (         (              $^))=')'^'[';
  #       ;         #                  ;
  #         ;     #                      ;
    #         ;                        #
      ;           #  ;  #            ;
  #             ;
      #                           ;
        #                       ;
    #   ;                            #
      ;                            #
```

Some modules are perhaps better left unwritten.

On the other hand, there are some Acme:: modules that are interesting ideas in other ways—Acme::Your, for instance, works like our, but you get to use unqualified package variables *from a different package*. This is an inventive (and possibly even useful) use of source filters, which allow you to wrap a filtering layer around Perl's parser, affecting the program code it sees.

Source Filters

Source filters were invented by Paul Marquess and provide a way of intercepting Perl source code before it reaches Perl's parser. Using the functions in `Filter::Util::Call` to talk to the Perl internals, you can install Perl subroutines into the way of the *input stream*, the way Perl reads a program.

The easiest way to do this is with the `Filter::Simple` module, which abstracts away a lot of the business of registering filters, reading from the input stream, putting things back into the input stream, and so on. Instead of the original, clumsy source filter mechanism, you can now say:

```
package Filter::Rot13;

use Filter::Simple;
FILTER { tr[a-z][n-za-m]; }
```

When some code now use's `Filter::Rot13`, all code after the use statement will be passed through the `FILTER` block, here rotating the alphabet 13 places.

Many `Acme` modules derive their usefulness from `Filter::Simple`, whereas `Switch`, which provides an implementation of a switch-case statement for Perl, is possibly the most comprehensive use of source filters.

A final Acme curiosity, and one of my favourites, is `Acme::Chef`, an implementation of David Morgan-Mar's Chef programming language. In Chef, programs are expressed in the form of recipes:

```
Hello World Souffle.

This recipe prints the immortal words "Hello world!", in a basically
brute force way. It also makes a lot of food for one person.

Ingredients.
72 g haricot beans
101 eggs
108 g lard
111 cups oil
32 zucchinis
119 ml water
114 g red salmon
100 g dijon mustard
33 potatoes

Method.
```

```
Put potatoes into the mixing bowl. Put dijon mustard into the mixing
bowl. Put lard into the mixing bowl. Put red salmon into the mixing
bowl. Put oil into the mixing bowl. Put water into the mixing
bowl. Put zucchinis into the mixing bowl. Put oil into the mixing
bowl. Put lard into the mixing bowl. Put lard into the mixing
bowl. Put eggs into the mixing bowl. Put haricot beans into the mixing
bowl. Liquify contents of the mixing bowl. Pour contents of the mixing
bowl into the baking dish.

Serves 1.
```

Acme::Chef comes with a Chef interpreter and a compiler to turn Chef programs into
Perl programs. I can't help wondering how much programmer time gets spent on this
sort of thing.

Conclusion

In this chapter, we've looked at some of the things that Perl hackers do to let their
hair down: obfuscation, poetry, JAPHs, and plain, all-out silliness.

If these things sound like your idea of fun, I have three pieces of advice for you:

- Subscribe to the *fwp@perl.org* Fun With Perl mailing list.
- Visit the appropriate sections on *perlmonks.org*.
- Seek professional guidance.

Index

We'd like to hear your suggestions for improving our indexes. Send email to *index@oreilly.com*.

B

B module, for inspecting bytecode tree, 17–19
back-references, object, 133
Balanced, Text::Balanced, 46
Bayes's theorem, 160
B::Deparse, 260–261
BEGIN blocks, 34–35
Belfast Perl Mongers, 257–258
Berkeley DB, 118
binary serialization, 123
blocks (see code blocks)
boggle, 259
bottom-up parsers
    overview of, 43
    yacc, 68
Bowden, Tony, 137, 142
braces (see {})
BROKEN subroutine, Text::Template, 88–89
built-in functions
    recoding in C vs. Perl built-in function, 12–14
    replacing with CORE and CORE::GLOBAL, 12–14
Burke, Sean, 75, 150
byte mode, data handling, 179
bytecode, inspecting, 16–19

C

C libraries
    DBMs and, 118
    fmtcheck function, 235
    Perl and, 233
    recoding in C vs. Perl built-in function, 235–236
    SQLite and, 135
    wrapping, 245–247
C++ overloading, 26
calculators, parsing applications, 72
caller function, HOOK::LexWrap, 14–15
can method, UNIVERSAL class, 20
CDBI (see Class::DBI)
Ceglowski, Maciej, 166
CGI::Application, 147
character code, in Unicode, 173
character encoding, in Unicode, 173
character mode, data handling, 179
character repertoire, in Unicode, 173
character set, ASCII, 172

characters, in Unicode, 173
CHECK blocks, 35–38
Chen, Francine, 164
chr, 178
class subroutine, 19
Class::Accessor::Assert module, 119
Class::DBI
    combining with Template Toolkit, 142–144
    extensions, 141
    Maypole and, 144–147
    object relational mapping with, 135, 137–141
    relationships, 139–140
    schema and classes, 119
    setting up, 137–138
    updates, 138
classes
    Test::Class, 226–229
    UNIVERSAL, 20–23
Class::PINT, 141
closures, 9–10
COBOL, 256
code
    keeping tests and code together, 225
    testing (see testing)
code blocks
    actions and, 50
    matiching portions of data stream, 47
    parsing, 60
codepoint, in Unicode, 173
<commit> directive, Parse::RecDescent, 53–54
comp method, HTML::Mason, 104
components, HTML::Mason, 96–97
components, POE
    high-level, 212–213
    medium-level, 208–210
    overview of, 207–208
components, Template Toolkit, 112–113
concatenation operator, 33
conditional statements, parsing, 54–55
conditions, HTML::Template, 90–92
Config::Auto, 78
configuration files, parsing, 77
context sensitivity, 51
Conway, Damian, 23, 36, 44, 150, 260
CORE, 12–14
CORE::GLOBAL, 12–13
CPANPLUS module, 124

About the Author

Simon Cozens is an open source programmer and author. He has released over 100 Perl modules, including Email::Simple, Mail::Audit, Maypole, Plucene, and B::Generate. He's the coauthor of *Beginning Perl* (Wrox) and *Extending and Embedding Perl* (Manning) and was the managing editor of Perl.com from 2001 to 2004. A graduate of Oxford University with a degree in Japanese, he now lives in Wales and enjoys Japanese and Greek food, bizarre music, and fine typography.

Colophon

Our look is the result of reader comments, our own experimentation, and feedback from distribution channels. Distinctive covers complement our distinctive approach to technical topics, breathing personality and life into potentially dry subjects.

The animal on the cover of *Advanced Perl Programming*, Second Edition is a black leopard. Most leopards are easily recognized by the rosette-patterned spots on their coat. Black leopards, often called "black panthers," also have these spots, but they are difficult to see because of the darkness of the fur. Black leopards are born into the same litters as the more common yellowish leopards. They occur most frequently in the wet, forested areas of India and southeast Asia, where the dark color aids in camouflage and hunting.

Leopards are among the most widely distributed wild cats. Their range extends throughout most of Africa and India and into much of Asia, the Middle East, and the East Indies. Highly adaptable, leopards are able to hunt almost any animal, and can live in both very wet and arid conditions. Because they almost always share their range with bigger cats, such as lions or tigers, leopards are very cautious. After catching its prey, the leopard will carry it high up into a tree to devour it. The incredible strength of the leopard enables it to climb while carrying animals up to three times its own body weight.

Darren Kelly was the production editor, Cindy Gierhart was the copyeditor, and Kaesmene Harrison Banks was the proofreader for *Advanced Perl Programming*, Second Edition. Marlowe Shaeffer and Claire Cloutier provided quality control. nSight, Inc. provided production services. Jack Lewis wrote the index.

Edie Freedman designed the cover of this book, using a 19th-century engraving from the Dover Pictorial Archive. Karen Montgomery produced the cover layout with Adobe InDesign CS using Adobe's ITC Garamond font.

David Futato designed the interior layout. This book was converted by Joe Wizda to FrameMaker 5.5.6 with a format conversion tool created by Erik Ray, Jason McIntosh, Neil Walls, and Mike Sierra that uses Perl and XML technologies. The text font is Linotype Birka; the heading font is Adobe Myriad Condensed; and the code font is

LucasFont's TheSans Mono Condensed. The illustrations that appear in the book were produced by Robert Romano, Jessamyn Read, and Lesley Borash using Macromedia FreeHand MX and Adobe Photoshop CS. The tip and warning icons were drawn by Christopher Bing. This colophon was written by Clairemarie Fisher O'Leary.

Related Titles Available from O'Reilly

Perl

Advanced Perl Programming

CGI Programming with Perl, *2nd Edition*

Computer Science & Perl Programming: The Best of the Perl Journal

Embedding Perl in HTML with Mason

Games, Diversions, & Perl Culture: The Best of the Perl Journal

Learning Perl, *3rd Edition*

Learning Perl Objects, References and Modules

Mastering Algorithms with Perl

Mastering Perl/Tk

Mastering Regular Expressions, *2nd Edition*

Perl & LWP

Perl & XML

Perl 6 and Parrot Essentials, *2nd Edition*

Perl CD Bookshelf, *Version 4.0*

Perl Cookbook, *2nd Edition*

Perl Debugger Pocket Reference

Perl for System Administration

Perl Graphics Programming

Perl in a Nutshell, *2nd Edition*

Perl Pocket Reference, *4th Edition*

Perl Template Toolkit

Practical mod_perl

Programming the Perl DBI

Programming Perl, *3rd Edition*

Programming Web Services with Perl

Regular Expression Pocket Guide

Web, Graphics & Perl/Tk: The Best of the Perl Journal

O'REILLY®

Our books are available at most retail and online bookstores.
To order direct: 1-800-998-9938 • *order@oreilly.com* • *www.oreilly.com*
Online editions of most O'Reilly titles are available by subscription at *safari.oreilly.com*

Keep in touch with O'Reilly

1. Download examples from our books

To find example files for a book, go to:

www.oreilly.com/catalog

select the book, and follow the "Examples" link.

2. Register your O'Reilly books

Register your book at *register.oreilly.com*

Why register your books?
Once you've registered your O'Reilly books you can:

*   Win O'Reilly books, T-shirts or discount coupons in our monthly drawing.
*   Get special offers available only to registered O'Reilly customers.
*   Get catalogs announcing new books (US and UK only).
*   Get email notification of new editions of the O'Reilly books you own.

3. Join our email lists

Sign up to get topic-specific email announcements of new books and conferences, special offers, and O'Reilly Network technology newsletters at:

elists.oreilly.com

It's easy to customize your free elists subscription so you'll get exactly the O'Reilly news you want.

4. Get the latest news, tips, and tools

www.oreilly.com

*   "Top 100 Sites on the Web"—PC Magazine
*   CIO Magazine's Web Business 50 Awards

Our web site contains a library of comprehensive product information (including book excerpts and tables of contents), downloadable software, background articles, interviews with technology leaders, links to relevant sites, book cover art, and more.

5. Work for O'Reilly

Check out our web site for current employment opportunities:

jobs.oreilly.com

6. Contact us

O'Reilly & Associates
1005 Gravenstein Hwy North
Sebastopol, CA 95472 USA

TEL: 707-827-7000 or 800-998-9938
(6am to 5pm PST)

FAX: 707-829-0104

order@oreilly.com
For answers to problems regarding your order or our products. To place a book order online, visit:

www.oreilly.com/order_new

catalog@oreilly.com
To request a copy of our latest catalog.

booktech@oreilly.com
For book content technical questions or corrections.

corporate@oreilly.com
For educational, library, government, and corporate sales.

proposals@oreilly.com
To submit new book proposals to our editors and product managers.

international@oreilly.com
For information about our international distributors or translation queries. For a list of our distributors outside of North America check out:

international.oreilly.com/distributors.html

adoption@oreilly.com
For information about academic use of O'Reilly books, visit:

academic.oreilly.com